WINTER OF FROZEN DREAMS

KARL HARTER

CB

CONTEMPORARY
BOOKS

CHICAGO

Library of Congress Cataloging-in-Publication Data

Harter, Karl.
    Winter of frozen dreams : a true story of passion, greed, and
murder / Karl Harter.
        p.   cm.
    ISBN 0-8092-4105-6 : $17.95
    1. Murder—Wisconsin—Madison—Case studies.   I. Title.
HV6534.M22H37   1990
364.1'523'0977583—dc20

90-40607
CIP

Published by Contemporary Books, Inc.
180 North Michigan Avenue, Chicago, Illinois 60601
Manufactured in the United States of America
International Standard Book Number: 0-8092-4105-6

To Christina, who hears the clanging
of the sentences each day and still
listens for the melody

Contents

Author's Note

This book is the result of extensive research and scores of interviews. The detectives who conducted the homicide investigations, the lawyers involved in the case, and residents of Madison who patronized or worked in the city's massage parlors were my primary sources of information. The *Wisconsin State Journal* and the *Capital Times*, Madison's two daily newspapers, gave the case wide coverage. *Isthmus* and *Madison Magazine*, both local publications, carried articles on the homicides and trial. A local cable station broadcast the trial proceedings in their entirety.

The Barbara Hoffman case touched all levels of the Madison community. It involved lawyers and farmers, professors and cabdrivers, schoolteachers and insurance salesmen. More than one hundred people, directly or indirectly involved in the case, were interviewed. The victims were loners. The few friends and acquaintances they had in Madison and Stoughton were kind enough to share their observations.

Many of the people who discussed their relationship with Barbara Hoffman and their knowledge of the sex business in Madison agreed to do so only under the promise of strictest confidentiality. Some of these sources feared physical reprisal should their names become public. Where it was requested and where I felt it appropriate, the name of a minor character has been changed. These changes do not affect the truth of the story or the facts of what was revealed.

In a few instances scenes are re-created and conversation is presented that cannot be corroborated word for word. The events depicted are true. Recollection of the events may vary depending on the perspective of the people involved. Scenes have been dramatically emphasized to more effectively portray the major characters in the story. In some instances a name has been changed to avoid unnecessary embarrassment to the individual. When conversations are portrayed, an effort was made to verify their accuracy through interviews with the participants.

Acknowledgments

Any project of this size is impossible without the cooperation of others, and many people contributed ideas, insights, and information about this sad, sordid story.

My thanks go to Bob Newton, who helped coordinate the initial phases of the research and who assisted with many of the background interviews. Hayward Allen's early encouragement was a boost.

Many of the lawyers involved in the case were especially helpful. Jim Doyle, John Burr, and Don Eisenberg were generous with their time and knowledge. Burr and Eisenberg sat through long hours of interviews, tolerated my nagging questions, and discussed their strategies and opinions of the trial. Whenever I called back, asking for more time and more answers, they were patient and accommodating. Don Eisenberg has portions of the trial on videocassette, which he kindly loaned to me for study. Anita Clark of the *Wisconsin State Journal* shared her cogent insights into the complexities of the story and the personalities involved. The Madison Police Department and Captain Jack Heibl deserve mention for their cooperation.

There were scores of people I interviewed—cops, masseuses, lawyers, bartenders—whose names shall not be mentioned but to whom I owe great thanks. Steve Herzberg, at the University of Wisconsin–Madison Law School, and Bill Marten, at the Wisconsin State Historical Society, read an early draft of this manuscript, and I am grateful for their encouragement.

I am indebted to Victoria Pryor, my agent, for her careful reading, her excellent suggestions, and her hard work. Her enthusiasm has been essential. I also want to thank Harvey Plotnick at Contemporary Books for his enthusiasm and editorial assistance.

PART I
Winter of
Frozen Dreams

— 1 —

Christmas morning, and it was too cold to snow. Even by Wisconsin standards the weather was severe. Overnight an arctic breeze had descended on Madison. The temperature plummeted to twenty-two degrees below zero, and wind ripped off Lake Monona, pear-shaped and choked with ice. The eight inches of December's accumulation lay undisturbed by the gusts, frozen where it had fallen or been shoveled or plowed. Snow gripped telephone poles and parking meters. In the wire weave of a newspaper box snow was wedged like a sugary webbing.

Jerry Davies didn't notice the cold. He didn't notice the sky as flat and gray as the state office buildings that bordered the lake like chilly sentinels. His Chevrolet wheeled around the block one more time, and he feverishly composed what he would tell the police, desperately searched for a coherent pattern. For all of his thirty-one years Jerry Davies had had trouble focusing on events, on comprehending the essence of things going on around him. Christmas morning was no exception. Concentration seemed impossible. Thoughts formed and dissolved like a vapor inside his head.

At 10:15 A.M., December 25, 1977, Davies had his choice of parking spots. The downtown streets were deserted. A mountain of snow rose behind the Bank of Madison. Straight ahead towered the Wisconsin State Capitol—a granite fortress, gray tiers of columns and arches vaulting to the heavens, capped with a golden crown. A couple of blocks east the dull chimneys of Madison Gas and Electric shoved black billows of coal smoke

3

into the sky, panting overtime to give the city a semblance of warmth.

Davies parked on Monona Avenue. Forgetting it was a holiday, he dutifully plugged the meter. The quarter bought him an hour, more time, he presumed, than his mission would require.

Madison Police Headquarters was situated in the basement of City-County Building, a seven-story cement rectangle a snowball's heave from the lake. The aluminum handle of the precinct station door stung Davies's fingers with cold as he grabbed to open it, and the moisture of his palm instantly froze to the metal. For a moment he feared his flesh would tear as he pried the palm away. Curiously, the pain connected him to the present, to Monona Avenue, to Christmas morning.

Davies trembled. He wanted to quit, to curl up on the concrete steps and sleep. He was so very tired.

Hand snapped free of the aluminum, Davies opened the door and felt the hot breath of a heating duct as he walked inside. Each step was counted, for he began to feel woozy and was afraid he might faint before he reached the cop at the duty desk. Fluorescent lights hummed. Dust balls collected on the tile floor.

Jerry Davies was staggering. The desk sergeant eyed the visitor in the green parka with imitation-fur collar. Davies had not shaved in a couple of days. He wore neither cap nor gloves. Wire-rimmed glasses tipped down the bony cartilage of nose, and he pushed the spectacles back with a pudgy index finger. This simple action demanded a tremendous effort, and the cop guessed he had a gentleman who was either seriously inebriated or seriously ill standing, no, wavering in front of him.

The cop's mustache tilted as he cussed silently. Such a sorry individual could only bring him extra paperwork.

"Last night I helped bury a body in a snowbank," Davies blurted.

Ordinarily the desk sergeant shrugged at a dramatic statement from an obviously disoriented person and suggested a cup of coffee before inquiring what was really on the man's mind. But not on Christmas Day. People do not pull pranks on Christmas. People get nostalgic and drunk and depressed, but they do not fabricate outrageous tales. The man in front of him was tremulous and ashen, earnest and disturbed.

The cop paused and jotted down the time.

"I don't know who it was, but last night I buried a man in a snowbank. I can take you to where the body is," said Davies. His voice cracked like an icicle knocked to the sidewalk by the wind.

Chuck Lulling stood in the kitchen of his Madison apartment, reciting to his wife how he intended to roast a goose and a turkey for their Christmas repast. Marian, in blue bathrobe and bedroom slippers, was preparing the stuffing. Lulling served his wife a refill from the Mr. Coffee and poured himself another cup. He drank from a porcelain mug that read MY FAVORITE COP IS GRANDPOP.

Lulling's favorite and only grandchild would arrive at 4:00 P.M. for dinner. Her presents, as well as gifts for Lulling's two children and their spouses, were neatly wrapped and decorated with a profusion of ribbons and bows and waited beneath the silver boughs of an artificial tree.

At 10:40 A.M. the phone rang.

Lulling picked up the receiver with no thought in his mind except to add sugar to his coffee and say hello. When Marian heard him asking questions, she grimaced. Her husband always supplied answers; he never asked questions—except on a murder case.

For twenty-eight years police work had dominated their lives. Just as Ted Williams can name the exact pitch and the unfortunate hurler who threw it for each of his 521 home runs, Lulling remembered minute details from homicide cases he had investigated decades ago. A private journal contained notes from almost every investigation, as Lulling thought it would aid his technique and add to his understanding of the criminal mind, if such a thing can be said to exist. He attempted hobbies—building model sailing ships, collecting antique firearms—but these were diversions and of incidental interest. Lulling was a cop, and detective work had infiltrated his blood.

Due to the length of the phone briefing Marian Lulling anticipated the worst. It was not Chuck's absence on Christmas Day that she resented; it was the feeble apology he'd offer for the intrusion of work. And it was knowing he'd rather conduct a homicide inquiry than eat rich food and play cards with his family.

As he replaced the receiver, Marian brushed a veined hand through her silver hair—a color similar to that of the artificial tree—and considered how she would prepare the goose and the turkey. She watched the detective scribble on a notepad. He winced after a taste of coffee; he'd forgotten the sugar.

Chuck Lulling sighed. "Seems that a fellow buried somebody in a snowbank out in Middleton. Lovely Christmas present, huh?"

Marian wiped her hands on a dish towel. "What's it mean?"

"Means that me and a few other cops are going to miss our dinners, maybe. In this friggin' cold they got to drive out there and dig out the corpse. I better go along." He glanced at the goose, freshly plucked and hunched on the cutting board. "Hope you have a great recipe. I love leftovers." He forced a smile.

In five minutes he'd changed into wool slacks and a flannel shirt over long johns, a wool sweater, and a fur cap with ear flaps. He came back into the kitchen.

"We'll go out New Year's Eve, just you and me, Marian. We'll go to dinner, then dancing."

Marian shrugged. Her husband kissed her on the lips, snatched his pipe and a pouch of tobacco, and chased his life's calling.

— 2 —

Tomahawk Ridge crested six miles west of Madison, the apex in a topography of hills and valleys snug with dairy farms, horse stables, and country homes. In August the territory would be verdant and pulsating with life. Fields would be crammed with corn. Cows would graze among thistles and blackberry brambles.

Winter cast a different light on the landscape, however, and on December 25th the tone was somber. If a sun inhabited the sky, it was shielded by clouds of milk-bucket gray. Snow dominated the area, layering hillsides and tree boughs, power lines and barn roofs.

Cold had immobilized the countryside. Corn planters and grain drills were rooted to the ground with ice. Horse trailers and hay wagons sat frozen for the season. Nothing stirred except weather vanes, which twirled madly in the wind, and plumes of chimney smoke. Not even the barbed wire of the field fences shivered. The cold had clasped the metal taut.

Across this frigid winterland two Dodge Coronets, unmarked cars used by the MPD, and a Dodge van cruised in slow procession up Blackhawk Road. At the top of the climb a Buick Regal idled. An iron bar blocked the drive to the Blackhawk Ski Jump, but it didn't matter. According to Jerry Davies there was no need to go any farther than the plowed lot at the entrance.

Lieutenant Chuck Lulling climbed out of his Buick as the vehicles approached. He strode to his compatriots and bit the stem of his pipe so that his teeth wouldn't chatter. Three uniformed cops, the county coroner, and an assistant DA had accompanied Jerry Davies to the scene. All seven men quaked in the cold as a diffident Davies pointed toward a snowbank near a grove of maple trees. The patrolmen got hand shovels from the trunk of their car. They stepped within a few yards of the trees, then hesitated. What had appeared to be the snapped branch of a

maple lodged in the snow was unmistakably an arm jut-
ting out at an angle.

The elbow was bent. The fingers were tensed, as if
clutching an object that had been removed. The skin was
not white but closer in color to the bark of the trees.
Lulling glanced at Davies, who was mesmerized by the
arm, at once relieved it was there as promised yet horrified
the entire escapade hadn't been a perverse dream.

An icy gust kicked the eerie spell. The cops attacked
the snowbank with shovels. The snow didn't dislodge in
clumps; rather it blew off in a light powder, like sawdust.
The meticulous coroner, Clyde Chamberlain, insisted they
halt frequently so that as each section of the body was
exposed Officer Jon Sippl could snap a photograph.

As Sippl clicked the shutter of his Nikon, the other
officers fought the bitter cold. The harsh chill ate through
fur-lined mittens and down vests. Toes tingled. To keep
warm, cops flapped their arms, patted their shoulders,
stamped their feet, as if performing a crazy pantomime.

Meanwhile Sippl clicked a photo of the head of a male
Caucasian who had incurred a severe beating about the
frontal lobe and brow. The skull showed multiple contusions. The face was a mask of black tissue and dried blood,
frozen and expressionless.

"It's forty-one below with the wind chill, Clyde. You
want to take his fucking pulse and make sure the stiff is a
stiff?" bitched one of the cops, irritated by the coroner's
insistence on more pictures. "I want to get out of here
before frostbite sets in. Can't you take photos at the
morgue?"

"Quit complaining," said Lulling. "I could be home
drinking eggnog too."

"Chuck, you're the only one who likes it out here,"
said one of the cops.

The assistant DA, Chris Spencer, did a set of jumping
jacks to pound the blood through his system. He had been
playing ice hockey when the call came to report downtown
immediately. Underneath his parka bulged the heavy pads
of a hockey uniform. Canvas sneakers covered his freez-

ing feet. Spencer sneezed and tugged his balaclava over his head.

"Okay," said the coroner, "let's get the rest of the body out."

After a minute of shoveling, everyone ceased his efforts to keep warm and stared in astonishment. The man in the snowbank was colder than any of them. A digital timepiece on the left wrist was all the clothing he sported. The bashing about the skull, which had been uncovered first, looked to be no more than bumps and scratches compared to what was next revealed. The genitals had been battered and were hideously swollen. The penis was huge—tumescent and bloodied—and the distended skin wore an ugly shade of purple. The testicles were bloated, like two shiny black tomatoes brimming to burst.

A camera shutter clicked. Wind kicked through the valley. Though it seemed impossible, the day got colder.

"Un-fucking-real," gasped a cop.

"A jury is going to love those glossies," someone muttered.

Lulling ignored the banter. He studied Jerry Davies, who was bent at the waist and vomiting into the pristine snow.

— 3 —

Coffee splashed out of the Styrofoam cup as Jerry Davies raised it to his mouth. His Adam's apple bobbed as he sipped. The courage summoned to enter police headquarters in the morning had collapsed when he'd viewed the body. It was a morbid Christmas present, naked and battered and stuck in the snow, the arm extended like a ghoulish ribbon.

Davies paced the room. He wondered how long he could endure his own recollections of December 23rd, and when he considered Barbara's reaction he shuddered. She had secured a promise that he speak to no one regarding their furtive errand. Now he had brought her unwarranted trouble, and that was not his intention. He simply wanted to be relieved of the memory.

While Detective Lulling probed the past two days, the frozen corpse pricked Davies's remembrance—a vivid Technicolor slide of the genitals flicked before his eyes, as lucid as if it had been beamed onto the wall, and abruptly Davies was hunched over a wastepaper basket. What tasted like dry, hard chips of wood spit out of his mouth and clattered against the metal.

Davies wiped the debris from his lips and forced down more coffee. In his work boots, leather and crepe-soled, he paced the room again. His clothes, which had not been changed in a day and a half, were as rumpled as his psyche. The khaki Haggar slacks and brown V-neck sweater were glued to his body by perspiration and fear. The wire-rimmed glasses slid down his nose, and instinctively he pushed them back.

According to his driver's license, Jerry Davies, age thirty-one, was 5'10", 160 pounds, yet he appeared bulkier. A loneliness nestled into the furrows of his face, a loneliness that had been collecting since early in life, a loneliness that had polished deep, sad scoops beneath his eyes. Fear and bewilderment had aged him a decade in two days. However, the eyes glassy with tears, the quiver in the voice as he tried to explain how things happened, the "sir" at the completion of every other statement indicated a naïveté, a boyishness. Jerry Davies was a man who had seen little of the world, yet that small glimpse had wearied him immensely.

"When can I go home?"

"That depends, Jerry. We'd like to know who it was you helped bury," said Lulling.

Davies gripped his stomach. His complexion blanched. "I need to go to the bathroom again, please."

"Officer Cloutier is right outside the door."

As Davies was escorted down the hall, Lulling stirred his vending machine coffee with a wooden stick. There was nothing more to wring out of Davies, not on Christ-

mas Day, Lulling thought. Though Davies claimed not to
know who the dead man was, the information already
extracted was plentiful; the lieutenant wished only it
hadn't been so agonizing to mine.

The interrogation was in its fourth hour. Davies had
answered inquiries concerning his personal history and
his relationship with a Barbara Hoffman tersely and with
reluctance. Examining his connection to the body in the
snowbank and its transportation from Hoffman's apartment to Tomahawk Ridge proved excruciating work. Davies had stammered, sobbed, hyperventilated as the recollection became too real. His fragility had alarmed Lulling,
who had Davies taken to a local hospital for an examination. The doctor declared him to be suffering from extreme emotional trauma and lack of sleep but with no
ostensible physical ailment.

Ordinarily Lulling would have been contemptuous of
such a performance. With Davies he felt pity. Lulling had
talked sports with the distraught Davies to calm his
nerves. Besides his fiancée, Barbara Hoffman, and his job,
cataloging and shipping educational films for the University of Wisconsin, Department of Audio-Visual Instruction, sports was the single subject Davies knew much
about. They had discussed the Packers' dismal season and
the U.W. Badgers' football campaign and jawed as though
farm boys on a lazy afternoon stroll. Of course the loath-
some topic always returned, and the detective would drag
his companion farther along the road, trying to keep his
panic in check.

Had Davies seen Barbara since the night of December
23rd? Who decided to drive to Tomahawk Ridge? Was
their relationship sexual? Barbara said she found the body
in her bathroom; did she say how it got there?

Davies would fold and refold his fingers, and he'd spit
an answer, never more than a few words, and they inched
ahead, Davies trembling as though he were standing outside in the twenty-below-zero afternoon.

When the witness returned from the bathroom—Davies had passed from suspect to witness in the detective's

judgment—Lulling informed him that he would be arraigned for harboring and abetting a felon. In the morning he'd have to submit to a polygraph test to corroborate his story.

Davies neither smiled nor frowned. It was as if the words struck straw. Barbara's scorn would be infinitely harder to bear than arrest and a night in the county jail.

Davies shrugged. He wanted sleep. He hadn't slept for a day and a half, and he wanted the terrifying dream of his waking hours to end. Things had not happened as he had imagined. Regardless of his emphasis to the contrary, he saw Lulling's suspicions gravitate toward Barbara.

Would she scuttle their wedding plans? For a second he feared he'd freeze numb. Then Jerry Davies did what had been the pattern of his life—he surrendered. He surrendered to the wheel of destiny set spinning, wobbling, careening when he'd met Barbara Hoffman at Jan's Health Spa in 1974.

Fingerprinted and booked, he was led to the building's seventh floor and locked alone in a cell in the county jail.

— 4 —

Feet propped on the desk, pipe drawing an easy fire, Chuck Lulling collected his thoughts on Jerry Davies and reviewed the bizarre tale that had interrupted his Christmas.

The data sheet said Gerald Davies had been born and reared in Spring Green, a rural community tucked into the prosaic Wisconsin River valley, forty-five miles west of Madison. He was the youngest of four children from the marriage of Leo and Ruth Davies, a union that had disintegrated when Jerry was still a kid. Davies had not seen or conversed with his father in sixteen years.

Ruth Davies raised the clan alone and in impoverished circumstances. She worked as a seamstress and took on odd jobs. As the children became of age they moved away.

One brother enlisted in the navy. His sister married. Jerry had followed his siblings' example, and upon graduation from high school he enrolled at the U.W.–Madison, more out of aimlessness than academic orientation. After three semesters he quit the university and got a job at a Goodyear Tire center in Madison. But he could not break away from the hold of his mother. Every weekend he returned to Spring Green to visit Ruth and attend the high school's football and basketball games.

In 1968 he was hired by the university's Department of Audio-Visual Instruction. The work suited him. He earned less than $10,000 a year. The most significant of Davies's dozen years in Madison was 1974, when he'd gathered the temerity to enter Jan's Health Spa.

Lulling knew Jan's. The establishment was the most notorious of the massage parlors in Madison. At Jan's a person could get massaged, engage in oral sex or intercourse, watch two women make love, get tied up in leather and whipped, score a lid of dope, or buy a small-caliber weapon. For Madison, Jan's was hard-core.

The sex business in Wisconsin's capital had burgeoned since the early seventies. What had been a small, clandestine network was thrust into public view during the era of progressive attitudes toward sexual behavior and city hall's liberal interpretation of the vice codes.

Massage parlors thrived within the shadow of the state capitol. An adult bookstore opened next to a dentist's office. A nude photography studio rented retail space adjacent to a whole-foods store. Escort services advertised in the yellow pages. The public presence of the skin trade in Madison—a place *Life* magazine had once characterized as the ideal city in America in which to live and raise a family—outraged conservative members of the community. Zoning ordinances and city council resolutions were used as weapons to curtail the spread of the prosperous blue businesses. Civil libertarians forged an uneasy alliance with massage parlor owners to battle these tactics.

Chuck Lulling wasn't concerned with political issues or with sexual mores. What he needed to understand was the relationship between a timid country kid and a woman who had persuaded him to bury a dead man in a snowbank.

Davies's initial visit to Jan's was profound in two respects: it took three days and a six-pack of Old Style beer for him to gather the courage to enter the premises, and it was the first time a woman had ever touched his penis. Otherwise his first couple of samplings of what the massage world offered were strictly routine. On his third visit he was introduced to Barbara Hoffman.

Barbara was different. She didn't linger about the lobby in peekaboo negligees and black lace panties. She didn't toss seductive glances, didn't paint her face to resemble a Kewpie doll. A natural beauty emanated from her. Brown hair fell past her shoulders and framed a delicate face. The skin was smooth and pale. Her eyes were flecked brown and held a gentleness he hadn't expected to see. Her lips were not splashed red and were tilted almost pensively. Davies was immediately entranced. Barbara didn't smile coyly; she looked straight into his eyes. When she unbuttoned her blouse, Barbara didn't fondle her breasts and feign an excitement she didn't feel. She acted as shy as he felt. She went slowly. She coaxed him into conversation. When his cock stiffened, she didn't yank it in a hurry to finish, but played with it, coddled the erection between her fingers as if it were something special.

In the beginning Davies visited Jan's approximately once a month, always requesting Barbara and often sitting for an hour before his turn because she was occupied with other customers. Soon the frequency of his visits increased. He became impatient for her, longed for her touch, desired her presence. It was not the sexual release but the physical and emotional contact that Davies yearned for. Some sessions he didn't even climax. Barbara rubbed his belly and talked or encouraged his talk, and though his penis lay limp, Davies was satisfied simply by her attention. The 35-minute sessions expired in what seemed a dozen heartbeats.

It was Barbara who suggested they extend the relationship beyond the confines of the massage parlor. Davies was surprised and elated. That they dated only irreg-
ularly was irrelevant. Barbara was the first woman Davies
had dated, the first woman he had ever kissed. Davies
confessed to a friend that he was in love.

In May 1976 Barbara Hoffman quit working in the
massage parlors. A clerical position at EDS Federal, a large
firm that processed medical insurance claims, was available, and Barbara took the job and returned to school
part-time.

Because Barbara didn't have a car, Davies volunteered
transportation to work. Every morning he arrived at her
State Street apartment and drove her out to Madison's
south side to work, then drove back to the U.W. campus
and his job at the audiovisual department.

It was not a normal relationship, Davies admitted to
Lulling, yet he had little reference for comparison. Their
moments together didn't match the real depth of his feeling. Barbara wouldn't allow him more than one or two
dates a week. Indeed Barbara had difficulty reciprocating
his love. Their sexual contact was limited, and they had
refrained altogether from intercourse. Barbara experienced grave problems expressing physical love, Davies
reported, and she attended a therapy group at the U.W.
Hospital & Clinics to help conquer her fear of intimacy.

The irony of this statement was not lost on Chuck
Lulling. Davies had met the woman in a massage parlor,
where she performed sexual favors for whoever might
amble through the door, but she refused to engage in
premarital sex because of a psychological block. And the
smitten lover accepted the arrangement. Barbara was
fragile, Davies said. He trusted her.

It was too absurd and too ludicrous not to be true,
Lulling decided. The interview with Davies had been
taped, and Lulling jabbed the rewind button and spliced
Davies's clipped, hesitant answers into a coherent statement.

— 5 —

For Jerry Davies December 23rd started inauspiciously.
The alarm clamored, and after a minute of resistance he
hauled his sleepy frame out of bed. Though he didn't have
to report to work until 8:30, Davies rose at 7:00 A.M. so he
could drive Barbara to her job. He scratched his belly and
pushed open the window for a breath of air. Despite his
years in Madison he still expected Spring Green and the
ripe smells of cow manure and chemical fertilizer and
fresh-cut alfalfa. What entered was a faint whiff of diesel
fuel and the hydraulic growl of a garbage truck as it emptied the trash bins behind K mart. Davies zippered his
green parka. He lumbered out of the apartment on South
Park Street, scraped the frost from the windshield of his
Chevy Caprice, and drove to the curbside at 638 State
Street.

The three-story edifice included Yost's Campus Store,
a women's apparel shop, on the ground floor. Sunprint
Gallery, a cozy café that featured cappuccino, linzertortes,
and the art of local photographers, shared the second floor
with a dentist's office. The space above had been converted into small apartments leased primarily by students,
as the U.W. campus lay half a block away. Barbara Hoffman waited in the stairwell for her morning ride, and
before Davies could tap the horn she was in the front seat,
awarding her boyfriend a perfunctory kiss.

They spoke little during the ride to EDS Federal.

"When are you going home for Christmas?" Davies
asked as he parked in front of the office complex.

"Tomorrow, on the late afternoon bus."

"Do you want a lift to the bus station?"

"Thanks, but I can take a taxi."

"So will I see you before you leave?" he ventured
timidly, his hand circling the steering wheel.

"I don't think so. There's lots to do, and I won't have
any time. Call me a couple days after Christmas, okay?"

"Okay."

Barbara hopped out of the car, forestalling further conversation, and disappeared behind a revolving door.

The terse exchange led to a hellish day at work for Davies, filing film canisters, stacking spools of microfilm, battling wicked ruminations about his beloved Barbara. Davies fretted he was losing her affections. A week ago he'd discovered two cigarette butts stubbed out in a saucer on the kitchen counter in Barbara's apartment. She didn't smoke, and the story she'd devised was lame. Also, their time together had diminished. What had been visits once or twice a week had been pared to once every two weeks or less, and even then Barbara appeared nervous and distracted. In the spring, when Barbara had postponed their wedding, she'd reassured Davies that it was a delay, not a cancellation, and that they would indeed get married, though she shied away from announcing a definite date. This procrastination had caused the first crack in Davies's devotion. Now, again, he feared something was amiss.

The major decision of that evening was whether to eat at Pizza Hut or slip a Swanson's Hungry Man dinner into the oven. He bought a six-pack of Leinenkugel beer and chose the TV dinner. A phone call interrupted his meal. It was Barbara. Was he free, and did he still wish to visit her tonight?

Like smart game-show contestants, both knew the answer before the question was completed. Sure, he said, he could stop by in about an hour.

Because Barbara didn't want to sit at home, they drove out Park Street to Jerry's apartment and listened to music. The tension of that morning had evaporated. Barbara was complimentary, and her teasing lacked the venom it often contained.

At around 10:30 P.M. the couple returned to State Street. They nestled on the sofa and drank orange juice spiked with vodka for a nightcap. A candle flame and the blue haze of the twelve-inch TV screen were the only illumination. Johnny Carson provided the entertainment. Barbara curled in Davies's arms, docile, devoted, her long chestnut hair forming a puddle in his lap, which his fingers stroked languorously.

Barbara dozed. Davies felt the rise and fall of her rib cage, felt her slender shoulders, felt the notches of her vertebrae against his thigh. The silly thoughts, the paranoia and pessimism of that morning, had vanished. Where had they gone? How was it such worrisome thoughts could be eradicated so swiftly, so thoroughly?

Davies didn't have answers, and he let the questions fade. He smiled at his fortune and wondered what he had done to deserve to feel this happy. Lying with Barbara, he experienced a bliss unlike anything else in his life. His meditations drifted to his older brother Bob, who had joined the navy. He remembered the stories Bob told him of exotic women in Pacific ports, and he thought of Bob lying next to an Oriental woman. He thought of Chuck Richardson, his only friend from boyhood, now married and with a daughter, lying next to his schoolteacher wife. Did they enjoy this sense of luck and happiness when they rested next to a woman? Was this serene satisfaction that Davies felt the core of things, the bond that held men and women together? Was it intimacy rather than lust, the yearning for closeness rather than sex, that compelled the genders to unite?

Davies wasn't adept at deciphering these tangled emotions, and he wasn't used to basking in such deep pleasure. It touched at something extraordinary. He didn't have the words to formulate what it was that stirred him so remarkably. All he could conclude was that a warm sensation permeated his bones and mellowed his head, and the jagged worries of the morning seemed a vague dream. His big toe poked the off button, and Johnny Carson dissolved.

— 6 —

"Jerry, wake up."

The candle's bright flickerings imbued Barbara's face

with a golden intensity. She hovered over Davies. Darkness swallowed everything else.

"Jerry, we have something serious to talk about. Wake up."

"What time is it?" he grumbled.

"Wake up, please." Barbara plied his neck with her fingers and repeated her plea.

"Okay, I'm awake," he sputtered.

"Jerry, listen carefully. A horrible thing has happened. When I came home from work yesterday, there was a body in my bathroom, a dead body. I got scared. I didn't know what to do. You've got to help me get rid of it." The pupils of her eyes were huge, like brown bottle caps shining in the candlelight.

Davies blinked uncomprehendingly. He glanced at his wristwatch. It was 2:30 A.M., Christmas Eve morning. "Why don't we call the police?"

"We can't do that. How can I explain how a dead body got in my bathroom? I had nothing to do with it, but the cops won't believe that, and they'll try to implicate me. Jerry, I think people from the massage parlor, from Jan's, are behind this. They want to get me in deep trouble." Barbara bit her lower lip. "We have to get rid of it tonight, before anyone knows." Her fingers threaded Davies's fingers.

"How? People will see us."

"Everyone's gone. It's Christmas vacation. Go to the parking ramp and get your car and pull around back. I'll meet you there."

"Barbara . . ." His voice quavered. The apartment was still. Minutes passed.

"Goddamn, Jerry, my life has been messed up for too long. I'm finally pulling the pieces together, and now this. It's unbelievable. I had nothing to do with it. I don't even know who it is, but whoever it is, Jerry, his life is over and mine isn't. I can't be connected with the body."

The candle flared. Perspiration dampened Davies's armpits. His throat was dry.

Barbara again pleaded for his help.

Jerry sat up. "I'll go get the car."

As instructed, Davies pulled the Chevy into the tiny lot behind 638 State Street and backed to a mound of snow near a green Dumpster. The single beam from a neighboring spotlight bathed the night in a bluish haze. Madison was cold, desolate, soundless at 4:00 A.M.

Barbara crouched over the mound, brushed away layers of snow until she struck the frozen bedsheets—white on white—that enshrouded the body.

The bundle was heavy. Barbara grunted as they tried to wedge the corpse into the trunk. A body, especially one buried in the snow for twenty-four hours, does not bend and fold like a lawn chair. After minutes of smacking around, they decided to cram the corpse into the car.

It didn't fit across the backseat, so they lowered the front passenger's seat and maneuvered the body in on a diagonal. Thus Barbara was forced to ride in back with the covered head in her lap. Davies drove. The corpse's toes protruded from under the sheet and nudged the dashboard clock, which didn't work.

The Chevy traversed the U.W.'s sprawling campus, which, as Barbara had predicted, was abandoned. The route weaved past the red sandstone Science Hall, up the steep slope of Bascom Hill with its elm and oak trees sketching barren silhouettes, and onto Observatory Drive, with its panoramic view of Lake Mendota—twenty-six miles in circumference, frozen, cratered with ice and snow, a nocturnal lunar landscape—then down, past the tennis courts, now rectangles of snow, and behind the dormitories.

A silence and a stillness pervaded the night. Barbara proposed dumping the body out on Picnic Point, a finger of land that poked into Lake Mendota on the far west end of the campus, but when they idled at the gate she decided against the idea and commanded Davies to drive farther.

They passed through Shorewood Hills, an affluent village bordering the campus where a couple of the university professors that Barbara used to masturbate for fifty bucks a come shot now slept with their wives. No one disturbed their journey.

The fear that oozed from Davies was palpable, yet Barbara remained unfazed by their mission. She calmly issued directions. They drove out Madison's west side, out University Avenue, to Mineral Point Road and beyond. The countryside was a blur of bleak fields, fences, trees. The Chevy cruised past horse stables, turned right, and then an alcove of maple trees appeared at a crest of a hill. Barbara told Davies to pull over and stop.

The hot air from the car heater had loosened the wrap of the linen. As the furtive pair dragged the corpse from the car, the crumpled bottom sheet lifted and slid off, exposing the dead man from the waist down.

Barbara observed a look of fear transmute into terror as Davies sighted the crotch. Without comment she deftly snatched the sheet and re-covered the body.

Because they were cold and frightened, they buried the body neither thoroughly nor deep. It was dropped into the snow and hastily covered by the labor of guilty hands. Barbara stuffed the bedsheets into a garbage bag. Davies drove the car back onto the road. Barbara obscured their tire tracks with a pine bough.

The ride back to Madison passed without conversation. They sat in their separate worlds, distracted by what had happened, by what might happen next. Davies felt queasy. His flesh itched; sweat trickled down his back. Barbara seemed absorbed in private thought.

As they neared State Street, Barbara told Davies to vacuum the car. He was to buy K2R cleaner and wipe down the backseat, the dashboard, the whole interior. Davies nodded.

"Go home and rest, Jerry. And remember, I'm your fiancée."

At 638 State Street Barbara got out and didn't look back. Davies drove home. Sleep eluded him. He did his best not to think. He cleaned the car as Barbara had insisted. In the evening he drove to Spring Green, for he'd planned to spend Christmas, as he had every year of his life, at home with his mother.

—— 7 ——

Ruth Davies immediately noticed her son's exhausted condition. Soup and tea were administered. Jerry warded off his mother's questions, admitting only to an upset stomach and dizziness.

The inside of the one-story shack was decorated with a wreath, assorted bows, a string of colored lights. There was no Christmas tree, and the only presents on the kitchen table were those Jerry had brought from Madison. Ruth read a letter she had received from her son Bob.

Jerry idolized his brother and never compared himself to Bob, for comparison was folly. Bob did what Jerry was incapable of doing. He'd been a member of River Valley High School's only undefeated football team, a bulwark in a defense that had never been scored on. Jerry had been a second-string defensive back on a squad that matched River Valley's usual record for mediocrity. Bob's horizons extended far from home, while Jerry could get no farther from Spring Green than Madison. Bob boasted of his randy escapades, and Jerry had little to brag about. Barbara was the only woman he had kissed.

Ruth read the missive, interjecting her own opinions and asides so freely that Jerry couldn't distinguish what Bob had actually written and what were his mother's digressions. Jerry faded in and out of listening. The hours became elastic, each one stretching, snapping, popping to the next. When Ruth retired for the night, it was early Christmas morning.

Jerry remained at the wobbly kitchen table. He crossed his arms, which formed a cradle for his head. All the years he'd been away from home, and what had changed? Not the burlap curtains made out of old feed bags, not the brass teakettle on the old Amana stove, not his mother's tortuous talking, not the stump leg of the table, not the cobwebs in the corner near the stovepipe. What had changed was the year printed on the Agway Feeds calendar. Nothing else.

Davies shut his eyes to seal out the past and the present, to welcome sleep. But what greeted him in the darkness was a sheet lifting off a body and genitals swollen the size and color of the number-seven ball on a pool table, but not nearly so perfectly round, rather chipped and veined, and then the enlarged and discolored penis . . .

Davies's stomach surged like a spasm of white water. His lungs burned. Perspiration beaded on his forehead in large droplets, as if he were sweating translucent kernels of corn. The vision flashed again before his open eyes— the gray, the cold, the waxen skin discolored, disfigured, the pubic hair like a thousand frozen questions marks— and Davies sobbed. His trembling body rocked the kitchen table.

His mother scrambled eggs for breakfast and peppered him with questions. Davies nibbled at the eggs and fasted from talk. The phone rang. Ruth's daughter was calling from Indiana to wish her a merry Christmas, and while Ruth chatted long-distance, Jerry kissed his mother, told her he had to drive to Madison on an errand, and assured her he'd be home for dinner.

— 8 —

By late afternoon on Christmas Day a search warrant was issued for apartment 306, 638 State Street. Unable to locate the landlord and obtain a key, a quartet of police officers removed the door from its hinges to gain entry.

Inside, 306 was hot, muggy, and resembled a botanical garden. Spider plants were suspended from hooks in the ceiling, and their umbrella shoots bobbed in the air like green starbursts. Corn plants, ferns, a persimmon tree, and an azalea bush crowded the room. Philodendron and ivy spilled out of clay pots, sending leafy runners across the floor. Hibiscus flowered vermilion and scarlet. Under fluorescent tubes a miniature hothouse of exotic flora bloomed in badges of deep color. Because the thermostat registered seventy-nine degrees, the officers, in their police parkas, quickly began to perspire, and on a holiday, when an off-duty cop sweats, he often reeks of booze. One cop flopped on the sofa, dizzy from the severe temperature change and the day's consumption of alcohol.

Two glasses of eggnog had opened his day. The oatmeal his wife prepared for breakfast was washed down by a six-pack of Old Style. A second six got him through the construction of a bicycle he'd bought his daughter for Christmas. More eggnog for lunch. If it hadn't been so cold, he could have taken the kids sledding or ice skating or had some excuse, any excuse, not to sit in and drink. The hurried cup of coffee when the call came to report to work—pronto—didn't hint at sobering him up.

Hanrahan, the detective who directed the search, told the cop to stay on the couch and not throw up on anything.

None of the crew was exactly sober. The other three hadn't started drinking as early as their compatriot. Their eyes weren't road maps of red and white yet; they could still read, write, conduct the rudiments of a search. One of them could also hear, for he hollered at the others to hush.

"What's the fucking roar?"

"I thought it was inside my head," called a cop from the kitchen.

Hanrahan laughed. The roar was the bathroom fan. They were all so tight the fan sounded like a turbojet, and each man thought it was his own head blasting from booze, the cold, and a homicide investigation that demanded work on Christmas Day.

The air conditioner fan was activated too, Hanrahan noted. Why would a person turn on the a-c fan, which sucked in cold air, and the bathroom fan, which sucked out air, and at the same time burn the boiler at seventy-nine degrees?

One thought was all his headache permitted. The incongruity was jotted down, then forgotten.

The apartment was dusted for latent prints and

checked for signs of blood, with no success. Due to the parameters of the search warrant, the most curious items uncovered in 306 were not confiscated. But they were fun.

In the second drawer of the bedroom dresser, tucked under two plaid blouses, was a box containing flesh-colored rubber dildos of varying size, shape, and thickness, lace panties with a slit in the crotch, and an electric vibrator. A shoe box under the bed held photographs—snapshots of women making love with women—in beautiful Kodachrome. The acts and positions were explicit, and one woman—Barbara Hoffman—along with one or two or three different partners, appeared in every photo.

In the living room Detective Ken Couture knelt at a brick bookshelf half buried by houseplants and remarked that Hoffman's kinky tastes extended to her reading material. Interspersed with the textbooks on chemistry and microbiology were tomes on aberrant sexual practices and clinical studies on deviant psychosexual behavior, sexual taboos, and the sexual revolution of the sixties. There was one volume on poisons and toxic substances. There were also books on autopsies and forensic pathology. None of the books in this strange collection were corralled as evidence, because they weren't covered by the search warrant.

What was collected seemed a paltry haul: an address book, a bag of soiled laundry that could be tested for blood, a few latent prints. There was no indication of a struggle in the apartment—nothing broken, no glass shattered, no liquid soaked into a rug. The apartment was spotless.

Two cops trudged outside to the snowbank adjacent to the Dumpster and searched for traces of blood or hair. Immediately their sweat froze and the wind shivered their flesh. It was a tedious and frigid task. A layer of snow one inch deep was scraped, sifted, and discarded. In the twenty-below-zero afternoon thirty-five inches of snow were tediously removed before the shovel scraped blacktop. No hair, no blood—just snow and frozen fingers and icy curses.

The incinerator pipe on the roof was checked for hidden clothing or a weapon and was found to be nailed shut and undisturbed. The basement was checked. The gas furnace showed no signs of having been used to destroy clothing or any other evidence.

Finished, the cops woke their inebriated cohort, who had been snoring on the sofa, and sealed the premises. An ominous sign warned that the apartment was under police investigation and that anyone making unauthorized entry was subject to arrest and prosecution.

Hanrahan shrugged. They had found nothing of importance. At least none of them had deposited their Christmas joy on the bathroom tiles. Maybe the crime lab technicians would have better luck.

— 9 —

Lulling leaned back in his chair and puffed a cherrywood pipe. His hands were folded on the rise of his belly.

Ken Couture, the detective assigned to work with him on the case, summarized the search of Barbara Hoffman's apartment. No promising leads were discovered. The identity of the dead man remained unknown. The body had been too frozen to autopsy; thus cause of death was also unknown. It seemed there was little more they could accomplish that afternoon, and Couture was anxious to conclude for the day. Christmas Day might have been ruined, but Couture hoped to salvage the evening with his family. Lulling grumbled.

Couture had been a detective for all of three weeks, and he had been warned about Chuck Lulling. The department preferred to view criminal apprehension, arrest, and conviction as a team game, with the various elements of the law enforcement community operating in unison. Lieutenant Detective Lulling was feisty, obstinate, individualistic. According to those who worked with him, he rarely shared information. He seldom wrote police reports, and when he did he said as little as possible. Many believed that he didn't operate according to standard procedure; he'd been around before the book on standard procedure was written. He went on his way, conducting his own inquiries in his own manner. One didn't work with Lulling on a case; one worked for him, Couture had been cautioned.

"You eaten dinner yet?" Lulling asked.

"Not had a chance."

"We'll grab a bite on the way," said the older detective. "You and me are going to Park Ridge, Illinois, and visit Miss Hoffman for ourselves—see just what this lady is made of."

Couture was puzzled. To confront a murder suspect without knowing the identity of the victim, with no evidence, with no conception of what had happened, seemed unsound strategy. He voiced his concern. Lulling was unfazed.

"Maybe we should wait till she returns," Couture suggested, "watch her patterns, see if this is connected to anyone more than these two. Right now she doesn't know we've found the body. We can detain Davies. And what happens if she doesn't cooperate? She can fight arrest with extradition proceedings because she's in Illinois, and it would give her time to construct a defense. Going down tonight is risky."

"Hell, yes, it's risky. But Davies could barely sit in the chair to spill his guts, what guts he didn't spill in the wastebasket or the bathroom. How tough can she be? We go to Illinois and I squeeze that girl's balls, and I'll have a confession by midnight."

Lulling paused for a draw of tobacco.

"Nobody interrogates like me. We go to Illinois tonight, Ken, and you can celebrate Christmas tomorrow."

Since Couture had been a detective for twenty days, and Lulling for more than twenty years, the rookie didn't pursue his objections. From material found in the apartment he got Hoffman's parents' address. He phoned the Park Ridge police, enlisted their cooperation, and com-

pleted the appropriate paperwork. Faced with icy roads
and a three-hour ride, they decided to use Lulling's Buick
rather than one of the department Dodges. The sky had
faded gray to black when the Buick fishtailed out of the
basement garage and headed for the interstate south to
Chicago.

Park Ridge was an exit on Chicago's northwest corridor, a suburb of single-family homes replete with two-car
garages, sidewalks that were shoveled, front lawns with
lopsided snowmen, and blinking strings of Christmas
lights. There were shopping centers and drive-in banks.
The police station was cinder block and inconspicuous, the
type of one-story structure that could house a hardware
store or dental offices.

Good news greeted the Madison detectives at the
station sometime after 9:00 P.M. A message from the MPD
stated that the body dug out of the snowbank had a name.

On Lulling's suggestion, missing-person reports had
been checked. A woman had called earlier in the day and
said her brother had failed to attend Christmas dinner,
which was at noon, and his absence was highly unusual.
He was a bachelor with no other family and very few
friends. A drive to his residence indicated no one was at
home. Mail and the evening papers for the last two days
were uncollected on the porch, and the woman was worried.

The physical description—5'9" tall, 160 pounds, gray-
ing hair cropped short and balding, age fifty-two years—
matched the corpse. He wore no jewelry, no gold chains,
no rings, nothing except a quartz wristwatch the woman
and her husband had given him last Christmas. It was
requested that she or her husband drive to Madison immediately. The husband, Glen Hanson, viewed the body
and made a positive identification.

The dead man was Harry Berge. Berge was born in
the Koshkonong River valley on a farm outside Edgerton,
Wisconsin. He had moved to Stoughton, a small town
twenty miles south of Madison, a dozen years ago and

worked at the UniRoyal Tire Plant. Both parents were dead. His sister, with whom he'd enjoyed Christmas dinner for the past fifteen years, was the sole surviving relative. Berge was a loner and had very few friends, the brother-in-law confirmed.

Furthermore, Lulling learned that the coroner had an early prognosis. A cursory examination indicated Berge had been bludgeoned to death with a blunt instrument. A minimum of four blows were administered to the skull. The severe battering of the genitals probably anteceded the head contusions. An autopsy would be done in the morning.

Barbara Hoffman and her two sisters were in an upstairs bedroom at their parents' home, catching up on each other's lives. The youngest of three Hoffman children lived in and attended school in Chicago. The eldest was a social worker in Boston. They were gathered around a Scrabble board, but conversation and gossip held far more interest than the game. Downstairs in the den, their parents watched TV. It was after 9:30 when the doorbell rang. Robert Hoffman answered and was surprised to find two Park Ridge policemen.

They asked for Barbara. Giving the excuse of an accident concerning a friend in Madison, they asked if she'd accompany them to the station. Any information she had regarding the person would be helpful. Barbara declined her father's offer to drive her and accepted the police escort.

Lulling nudged Couture, sizing up his prey as Barbara Hoffman entered the station. It would be Couture's first questioning of a homicide suspect. For Lulling it would be the last.

— 10 —

Barbara Hoffman walked into the interrogation room and sat in a wooden chair. She glanced at the Madison detec-

tives from behind tortoiseshell glasses that obscured half
her face. Her thick lashes blinked once. Her eyes shined as
brightly as polished mahogany. Her skin gleamed smooth,
soft, unburdened by lines of worry. Her nose was small.
Her lips were thin etches of pink. She appeared lithe yet
not frail, slender yet not slight. A blue sweater with pearl
buttons covered small breasts and bony shoulders. Her
hands lay in the lap of her jeans.

Couture had expected someone painted and per-
fumed. The woman posed before him was cut from marble. She was natural and cold. Her features were delicate
but not fragile, and where one anticipated warmth—in the
skin, the eyes, the mouth—there was a clarity edged with
hardness.

Shifting the pipe to the corner of his mouth, Lulling
introduced himself and Couture. He paused to see if Barbara's curiosity or guilt would initiate the exchange. It
didn't.

"We met a friend of yours today, Miss Hoffman," said
Lulling, "and we had an intriguing chat. Jerry Davies told
us about the night of December 23rd and the early morning of the 24th."

Barbara Hoffman stared at him, as uninterested as if
he had recited what Santa Claus had brought him for
Christmas.

"We also met your friend, Mr. Berge," Lulling continued. "Harry didn't have much to say, except that you
bashed his skull and bashed his balls." Lulling smiled and
withdrew his pipe. The sweet scent of his tobacco filled
the room. "Would you care to tell us about it?"

"Fuck you."

Lulling flinched, as though she'd spit in his face.
"That kind of attitude isn't going to do you any good," the
detective warned.

"I want to talk to a lawyer."

"Detective Couture can take you to a phone, but Jerry
Davies talked for four hours this afternoon. We'd like to
have your statement about Berge's body, about how Mr.

Berge came to be bashed to death in your apartment."

"Am I under arrest?"

"No," Lulling said, "you're not under arrest."

"Then I'm going home."

"I'd advise you to show up in Madison tomorrow, with your lawyer and with a statement," Lulling said.

"Merry Christmas," Barbara Hoffman said, and she strode out, leaving behind an astounded Couture and an angry and defeated Chuck Lulling.

—— 11 ——

Al Mackey liked to drink. According to colleagues in the legal profession, he had a good heart and sincere intentions and both were subverted by a weakness for alcohol. When Mackey wanted shoptalk, he could pace from his law office in the Carley Building to the Pinckney Street Hideaway or the Inn on the Park, where lawyers and government bureaucrats imbibed. For a different flavor he might hustle over to the Fess Hotel, where young professionals sipped white wine, discussed pop psychology and adulterous relationships, and boasted of their rapidly ascending careers. For fun and nostalgia he could frequent the student end of State Street and the taprooms of his undergraduate days, where kids in painter's pants and flannel shirts slugged down the suds as easily as they ogled coeds.

But on Christmas night Mackey would probably be drinking alone. He had plenty of excuses to indulge. He was forty-six years old, and things were in shambles. His law practice was faltering. His domestic life was a mess. Although on respectful terms with his ex-wife, Al Mackey had not adapted well to divorce. Some men never adjust to life alone. And there was a daughter he missed and never enough time.

A phone call interrupted Al Mackey's Christmas night. It was Barbara Hoffman. The call was long-distance, and her voice held an urgency not normally present. Barbara was in trouble, and she needed him.

When Jan's Health Spa premiered in 1973, it was strictly a no-frills establishment. Enter with even mild expectations, and the first reaction was disappointment. At worst one anticipated a facade of civility. Instead the place reeked of sex. Jan's offered black walls, blue lights, and glassy-eyed girls in high heels and chintzy negligees who masturbated men with all the tenderness of fish market vendors. The lack of glamour and pretense, however, did not hurt business. On any given evening men milled about the lobby, drinking rum and Coke out of Styrofoam cups, telling dirty jokes, awaiting their turn. Most paid for a topless massage, negotiated for whatever extras the masseuse was willing to perform, and departed with a hint of satisfaction. It wasn't much, yet it was contact, regardless of the tawdry environs. Jan's proved so popular that on weekends the line of customers spilled out of the lobby and into the street.

Al Mackey was one of the hungry faces that visited the massage parlor. Perhaps he went because it was easier than hustling divorcées at the Ramada Inn. Maybe he appreciated the simplicity of the arrangement—$50 bought thirty-five minutes of attention. There were no commitments, no attachments, no apologies. On a sagging bed in a tiny room, in the dim glow of a blue light, and under a ceiling crisscrossed by water pipes and heating ducts, a nude woman washed you with soapy water, then plied your cock until you climaxed onto a towel. Somehow it was seedy and antiseptic at the same time. But, like many others, Al Mackey returned. It was on one of these visits that he met Barbara.

Barbara Hoffman was different. She was extraordinary. Her fragrance was sandalwood, not sweetshop. Her demeanor effected a pose of shy sensuality. Behind the broad-rimmed glasses were eyes flecked with mystery, imagination, innocence. It was a devastating combination, and Al Mackey was not the only man who succumbed.

Often a customer had to wait an hour or more for a session with her. Even on slow nights, when there might be two women idle, men lingered in the lobby, drinking cheap booze or instant coffee, waiting for their thirty-five minutes with Barbara.

"Queen of the massage parlors" someone had dubbed her. The moniker stuck. Jan's, the Rising Sun, Cheri's—in this naughty little world Barbara was royalty.

As she did with a few of her select customers, Barbara invited Al Mackey to see her outside of the depressing environment of the parlor. Like the others, Mackey probably felt flattered. And if Mackey was like the other men, not all their time together centered on sex. Barbara became a companion. Whether sailing on Lake Mendota, or attending a play at the University Theater, she was equally at ease. She could discuss mythology, classical music, or the sexual practices of primitive cultures. Barbara possessed more than a supple, experienced body. She had a facile, intelligent mind. And when she felt herself in a position of power, she rarely relinquished control.

Like coal from Santa Claus, Barbara had been delivered trouble on Christmas, and when she called from Park Ridge, Al Mackey chivalrously volunteered his services. If she needed legal advice and representation, he would provide it.

What was the difficulty? he inquired. As calmly as if it had been a motor vehicle violation, Barbara told him she expected to be charged with manslaughter or possibly second-degree murder.

They scheduled a meeting at her apartment for the next day.

Al Mackey walked to the bay window of his apartment, pushed aside the drapes, stared at Lake Monona. The vast surface was frozen and dusted with snow. Its edges were crusted with chunks of ice and blocks of shadow. The middle was gray and clear, illuminated by the moon, and he saw the squat shapes of ice fishermen with their bulging snowmobile suits and orange-flag fishing lines. He pondered their amazing endurance. If what Barbara had said was true, it was just such endurance that both he and she would need for the long days ahead.

While Hoffman and Mackey talked on the phone Christmas night, a second search warrant was issued for apartment 306. A couple of throw rugs and hand towels were confiscated from the bathroom. These would be forwarded to the state crime lab and tested for blood and hair samples. A more intriguing find was a manila envelope hidden in the closet. It contained a collection of personal effects belonging to a woman named Linda Millar.

Among the items were a receipt and a key for a post office box at the central postal station in Madison. There were also banking records and a passbook assigned to a Linda Millar, with a savings account totaling $22.80, along with a Madison Public Library card for the same woman. An envelope mailed to Linda Millar at Barbara Hoffman's address was also discovered. The envelope was empty.

Though the authorities were unaware of a Linda Millar, and what her connection to Barbara Hoffman might be, the materials were taken on the odd chance they might have a role in Harry Berge's homicide. The truth was, the investigators found so little of evidential value in the apartment that they grabbed at whatever seemed odd or unusual. It would give them something to chase, however thin.

— 12 —

It was December 26th. The mercury rose to fourteen degrees above zero. School kids on Christmas holiday tumbled over the outdoor skating rinks. Boys in turtlenecks and sweatshirts swatted hockey sticks at skidding pucks. The sun's rays streamed as golden as Land O'Lakes butter. Water pipes and gas lines thawed. The bitterness had departed and left only cold.

In his office District Attorney James Doyle, Jr., tugged the blinds and welcomed the sunshine. The rays cast an optimism that Doyle hoped would infect his mood.

Last night he had been briefed by Chris Spencer about the body in the snowbank, its identification, the arrest of Jerry Davies, and Chuck Lulling's risk and blunder in Park Ridge. When he arrived at work this morning, he was besieged by reporters on the granite steps of the City-County Building. A murder of ordinary proportion was front-page news in Wisconsin; a naked man buried in a snowbank, his genitals battered to a swollen pulp, was sensational. Lurid rumors swirled. There was conjecture that a suspect was in custody. The DA had waded through the crowd with an apologetic "no comment."

Jim Doyle was affable, ambitious, and he brewed his own coffee. That morning he prepared a pot of java extra-strong.

At thirty years of age Doyle was the youngest person elected to the DA's office in Dane County history. He was a hometown boy who had attended Stanford and the University of Wisconsin. He had married Jessica Laird—niece of Richard Nixon's secretary of defense, Melvin Laird—and for a honeymoon the couple had joined the Peace Corps. The couple were stationed at a rural village in Tunisia. An avid basketball player, Doyle took a ball with him to Africa. He fastened a hoop to a date palm tree and taught whomever he could interest how to dribble, float a jump shot, and run a pick and roll. After the Peace Corps Doyle was accepted at Harvard Law. Armed with a law degree and a strong sense of social commitment, the Doyles moved to Chinle, Arizona, and worked with local Indian groups on the Navajo reservation. Madison, with its liberal atmosphere and livable urban environs, beckoned, and they returned. Doyle played city-league basketball, became active in Democratic party politics, and soon won election as district attorney.

Some folks will be suspicious of any Irishman who prefers a hard game of basketball to a stiff shot of Jameson's whiskey, but even Doyle's harshest critics admitted that as a lawyer he played tough, honest, straight. He didn't renege on promises. If crossed, he could be rough, maybe vindictive, but never unfair. He considered himself more a populist than a liberal, in the tradition of "Fighting Bob" La Follette, Wisconsin's great progressive governor. Social concerns and discrimination cases were major targets of his administration. He vigorously enforced the city's affirmative action and equal opportunity statutes. Doyle harbored a quick wit and a keen intelligence. He was thorough, and sometimes his extreme competence assumed an edge of righteousness. He regarded the law with a profound respect and became indignant with lawyers whose ethics met less than the highest standard. Cheating had no place anywhere. Those who didn't play according to the rules were regarded with contempt. Deception belonged on the hardwood courts, not in a court of law.

An abbreviated transcription of Lulling's interview with Davies was forwarded to Doyle. The DA spoke with Hanrahan, who had conducted the search of Hoffman's apartment. At 10:00 A.M. he met Jerry Davies.

Doyle served coffee. Davies glanced about the room and noticed the walls decorated with an Indian rug, tribal masks from Africa, an autographed team photo of the 1971 New York Knicks. His immediate impression of the DA was favorable. He had expected an older man, someone gruff and patronizing. He realized he had mistaken Doyle for Doyle's father, a prominent lawyer and politician, who was now a federal court judge. In fact, Jim Doyle, Jr., and Jerry Davies were almost the same age, which bridged Davies's anxiety. More important was Doyle's relaxed manner. The smile was not forced. The words were not rehearsed.

They rehashed Davies's participation in the disposal of the body and delved into the depths of Davies's commitment to Barbara Hoffman. Davies confessed to Doyle that he and Barbara were engaged and that the wedding, scheduled for last spring, had been postponed.

His insecurities and doubts about the relationship were mentioned and then dismissed as Davies reiterated his love for Barbara and his implicit trust in her word. If she said there were no other men in her life, he believed her. If she said she had had nothing to do with the death of the man they buried in the snowbank, she was innocent.

How a dead body got into her bathroom was a mystery as unfathomable as the act of creation, and Davies wasted no energy contemplating it. What caused consternation was anticipating and recovering from her anger when she learned he had gone to the cops.

Would she end their engagement? he asked Doyle. The thought tossed Davies into a muddle. Desperation and loneliness oozed from his skin. That fleeting glimpse of the body as they had lugged it from the car to the snowbank had immersed Davies in a circumstance beyond his comprehension. The path in and the path out pivoted on Barbara Hoffman.

Their talk slowed. Doyle said that they would confer again soon. Davies stirred the granules of sugar substitute at the bottom of his coffee cup and nodded sullenly.

Doyle knotted his hands behind his head, revealing the black elbow patches on his herringbone jacket. He recited a Hopi Indian fable about simplicity and chaos, about the turbulence of a thunderstorm and the wonders that appear in its aftermath. Then Davies was taken downstairs to police headquarters and subjected to a polygraph test.

Doyle shuddered. According to the reports yesterday's search warrant had produced scant evidence to connect Barbara Hoffman to Harry Berge or his death, which meant Jerry Davies could well be the key witness to what had occurred on December 23rd, something that included Barbara Hoffman and Harry Berge and Davies and a homicide. Once Ms. Hoffman played with his mind, Davies would be unpredictable, and there was nothing Doyle could do to intervene. Thus it was essential to get as much from Davies on record as possible before he could recant, before his fragile memory could be tampered with and distorted.

— 13 —

If Harry Berge had ever visited Barbara Hoffman's apartment, the state crime lab technicians found no indication of it. The crew swabbed, scrubbed, dusted, vacuumed, and x-rayed. They scrutinized with the naked eye, examined with microscopes, irradiated the premises with ultraviolet light. Not a shred of Berge's physical presence was discovered.

And what about clothing? If Harry Berge had entered the apartment, presumably he wore more than a sari of white linen. The garbage Dumpster, which had not been emptied since the 21st, was checked, as was every other trash can and sand drum in the vicinity. The basement and furnace were checked. What Harry Berge wore his last night on earth, besides the bedsheet, would have to be conjecture.

The dearth of material evidence surprised the crime lab people and troubled the investigative team. No hair, no blood, no fingerprints, and no clothing threads implied that Barbara Hoffman had performed a meticulous and thorough cleaning job. To a jury it would imply serious doubt.

Especially no blood. Anyone whacked in the cranium a half dozen times with a blunt object—and with enough force to crinkle the forehead until it resembled a relief map of the Kickapoo River valley—bleeds and bleeds profusely. Pints of the stuff should have leaked out of the gashes and onto the linoleum of the kitchen floor, or the tiles of the bathroom, or the tongue-in-groove pine in the living room.

The crime lab experts blocked out the sunlight and dusted these areas with a special dye that would glow on contact with a foreign substance under a beam of ultraviolet light. Utilizing this technique, a smidgen of something was sighted in a crack in the bathroom's terrazzo tiles. Delicately, and with the nimble skill of a craftsman, Corrine Weiss attempted to resurrect the specimen. She was a veteran of numerous homicide investigations during her years of state work and was aware of the sample's potential importance. The stainless-steel picks she used might have been purloined from a dentist's office. Her diligent efforts recovered the minute specimen, which she transported to her lab and later identified as blood, not nail polish or iodine or a splat of toothpaste. However, the tiny flakes were too small a sample to survive the battery of tests required for a classification of type.

All that could be deduced with scientific certainty was that the specimen was blood, which was not an uncommon element to find on a bathroom floor. It could have dripped from Barbara when she shaved her legs. It could have been the last flake from what must have been the paint job Harry Berge's lacerated head did on the tiles. It could have belonged to anyone who had been in the apartment in the last several months.

There was no evidence that Harry Berge had ever been there.

— 14 —

When Barbara Hoffman found the entrance to her apartment sealed and padlocked by the Madison police, she raged. She stomped to Rennebohms, a drugstore–coffee shop at the end of the block, phoned Al Mackey, then plopped into a vinyl-upholstered booth and ordered hot tea with honey. A newspaper headline distracted her fury.

The discovery of Harry Berge's body, accompanied by

a fuzzy photograph of the snowbank at Tomahawk Ridge, was splashed across the front page of the *Wisconsin State Journal*. She dug a quarter out of her purse and bought a paper. Two articles reported the recovery of the body— battered about the head and genital areas—and a brief biographical sketch of the victim. A man had been detained for questioning, but no charges were imminent. Neither Barbara Hoffman nor Jerry Davies was named in print.

When Al Mackey arrived, he informed Barbara that he'd been on the phone with the DA. Her apartment would be unsealed in a few hours.

And what was she supposed to do until then? Barbara wanted to know. Her voice was more sanguine than the words indicated.

They needed to decide what to do next, Mackey said. The DA soft-pedaled the search. He'd be sending a copy of the search warrant to Mackey's office. The cops were told the body was originally found in Barbara's bathroom, so naturally they were going to conduct a thorough check. It was their job. Of course the DA would like to talk to Barbara. He said they currently had no suspects.

Mackey and Barbara discussed strategy and decided to comply. They reasoned it would look better if Barbara appeared voluntarily for questioning, with Mackey present as her lawyer. She would admit to coming home from work and finding a dead body in her bathroom but nothing more.

Since tax and probate statutes were Mackey's area of expertise, they solicited another opinion. Eric Schulenberg was an attorney who shared office space with Mackey, and he had experience in criminal law. On their way to the City-County Building, they consulted Schulenberg about their course of action.

He immediately nixed their plans. His advice was that Barbara should make no statement to the police and she should not cooperate with their investigation.

His counsel was heeded.

—— 15 ——

By midday of December 26th Harry Berge had thawed, and Dr. Billy Bauman, the county pathologist, conducted an autopsy. It confirmed what seemed obvious.

Multiple blunt-force injuries sustained by the head, face, and left side of the neck resulted in brain concussion, edema, and death. Furthermore, the head contusions were complicated by a severe pulmonary vascular congestion. Vomitus was present in the nose, mouth, and lungs. The eyes were blackened from hematoma. A superficial scrape four-and-a-half centimeters long was visible at the base of the neck, left side, consistent with what could have been caused by a fingernail's scratch, and was received prior to death. The abrasions and hemorrhage suffered by the genitalia occurred antemortem.

Berge was dead when placed in a cold environment, and exposure was not a factor in his death. The small bruises and contusions evident on his legs and torso were incurred after his expiration. Carcinoma of the right kidney was discovered, but the condition, though advanced, did not contribute to the victim's death. It was doubtful Berge was aware of the internal malignancy, and a check of his medical records did not show diagnosis or treatment. Bauman doubted Berge would have survived for a year if the cancer had continued untreated.

An examination of his gastric contents indicated that Harry Berge died within one to one-and-a-half hours after ingesting a large meal. A detailed analysis would show the food in his stomach was ham, cheese, beans from a three-bean salad, and coffee.

A biography of Harry Berge appeared as straightforward as the physiological causes of his death. He was the younger of two children born to a Norwegian Lutheran farm family in the Koshkonong River valley. The community was small and bound closely by a common heritage, a belief in hard work, and a strong connection to the land.

Berge's boyhood was an endless series of farm chores,

broken by trout fishing in the back streams, quail and rabbit hunting in the autumn brush. Books were of little interest, but he was good at tinkering with machines, repairing old radios or small engines, and patching together spare parts to keep the tractor and the pickup truck running. Upon graduation from high school in 1943, Berge opted to stay on the farm, harvesting hay and corn and soybeans and milking a small herd of guernsey cows. While other farmers in the valley did well, the Berges barely got by. Their property was neither large nor choice, and the family eked out a meager living from the marginal land. Frugality and thrift got them through hard times. Alma Berge's wizardry in the garden ensured sustenance but little else.

On Fridays the Berges ate lutefisk in the basement of the local church, where neighbors conversed in Norski, strummed guitars, wheezed accordions, strapped bells to their ankles and wrists, and strutted in the traditional dances as the smell of beer and fried fish wafted through the valley. The family attended the Rock County Fair each August, but rarely did they exhibit more than Alma's gooseberry or raspberry-rhubarb pies.

Family life was in Harry Berge's blood but not in his destiny. The mortgage and the tractor installments, the seed and feed and fertilizer bills axed the family's income by a wider notch each season, and finally the tree tumbled, their precarious financial balance tipped, and the Berges was forced to abandon their farm. On November 9, 1966, they sold the homestead and moved into Stoughton. Harry Berge was forty-one years old. It was the saddest day of his life.

The parents retired. Berge took a job as a forklift operator on the second shift at the local UniRoyal plant. The family settled into a white A-frame house, which, with one neighbor, was wedged between an A&W drive-in restaurant and a tractor and farm implements store. But the parents did not adapt to town living. Berge's father died of kidney failure a year after the move, and four years later his mother succumbed to a heart attack.

Harry Berge had never slept more than a week under a roof not shared by his mother. Suddenly, at age forty-six, he was alone. To his sister's recollection, Harry never dated, and his celibacy seemed perfectly natural. She had married and moved out at a young age, but it just seemed right that Harry stayed around home. If he harbored a complaint about anything except not being able to farm, Harry Berge never said it aloud.

Berge's entertainments were simple. He bowled one night a week, he drove to Madison to view a movie, and he converted the cellar and porch of the white A-frame house into miniature railroad yards, for Berge had developed a passion for model trains.

Hundreds of feet of track spanned the green felt-covered plywood tables in the basement where Lionel trains charged, locomotives pumping smoke. The red and yellow mail cars of the Santa Fe Express, the blue and silver sleepers of the Yankee Clipper, chugged through the landscapes he had constructed—prairie towns, farms, cities, mountains. Track twisted in loops, switchbacks, crisscrosses. Boxcars, dining cars, coal cars, cabooses were authentic in minute detail. Now and then Harry invited the neighbor's two boys down into his musty lair, where the hundred-watt bulbs beamed like toy suns in a brown sky of floorboard and two-by-six joists. He'd let the kids don his engineer's cap, flip the rail switches, turn the speed dials.

Otherwise Harry Berge lived a solitary existence. In the summer he grew tomatoes, wax beans, and rhubarb, the last of which he didn't know how to prepare. Without deviation he was a creature of routine. At 2:50 P.M. each afternoon his Oldsmobile backed out of his driveway as he went to work, and at 11:10 P.M. his headlights cut the dark, announcing his return. His wardrobe consisted almost exclusively of gray poplin work shirts, trousers, and a matching cap perched permanently atop his head. As the weather cooled, he added a sweater, then a red and black checked jacket in winter. Once a week his sister visited, cleaned the house, and did his ironing. On Sundays Harry

Berge toured the countryside, which often included a drive past the old farm and a visit to the Pierces in Cambridge.

Steve and Connie Pierce operated a dairy farm, and they adopted Berge into the family. Ten years their senior, Harry became a surrogate uncle, and the Pierce children called him Uncle Bud. Berge liked to roam the acreage, help Steve mend a fence or chop firewood, get cow shit in his nose again and burrs in his pants cuffs. Usually he'd stay for supper followed by a couple of games of cribbage, and by nine o'clock Harry mumbled good-bye.

In August 1977 Berge hinted he might have himself a girlfriend. His round face twitched in a sheepish grin; his large ears were red and blushing. He told the Pierces she was a younger woman, a student at the university in Madison. When quizzed for more details, Berge rolled his head, snorted and hawed, and said he'd have more to tell another time. The subject didn't come up again, and the Pierces didn't pry.

With fellows at work Berge was less taciturn. During lunch break one day in September the crew discussed the massage parlors in Madison, which two of the men had visited after their shift the night before. Berge, usually uninterested in the lunchtime chatter, tossed out a comment that intimated a familiarity with the city's sex dens.

The remark was surprising. His co-workers at Uni-Royal knew that Berge was not a religious man, but his conduct was reserved and unassuming. On the odd occasion when they coaxed him to the U-Name-It Tavern after work, he drank a Coca-Cola and hurried home, as if the barroom was an iniquitous place. Berge refrained from using tobacco, liquor, and cuss words. He'd be more apt to discuss train sets and the weather than women.

From that day on, however, Berge's behavior made it undeniable that he possessed an intimate and extensive knowledge of the massage parlor scene. He showed one fellow pictures he'd taken at a photographic studio, posed pictures of naked women. His compatriots were startled and agreed that Madison's blue world seemed a peculiar universe for the meek Berge's travels. What none suspected were the range and frequency of his journeys.

In the bedroom closet of the white A-frame house, in a shoe box hidden by a J. C. Penney catalog, were stuffed sixty-nine MasterCard receipts from various Madison parlors. The crinkled mass of paper covered December 1974 to July 1977 and totaled $1,630. A study of the receipts showed Berge liked his strokes on Sundays and holidays. On Easter, the Fourth of July, and Thanksgiving, for each of these years, Berge had been provided with $50 worth of pleasure. Harry Berge had been a massage parlor connoisseur.

— 16 —

It was evening, December 26th, when Barbara Hoffman was given permission to return to her apartment. First she would have tended her plants. The cops had treated them courteously and left no damaged tendrils or broken stems. Next she would have checked the kitchen cupboard and noted that the contents had not been disturbed. The china bowl of white crystals, which any visitor would have mistaken for granulated sugar or crystalline vitamin C, remained exactly where she had left it.

Barbara picked up the telephone, listened for the subtle click of a wiretap, and heard nothing but a dial tone. Not satisfied, she dialed a number connecting her to a clearing line in Capitol Heights, Maryland, that AT&T used to identify wiretaps or line tampering. If her phone was bugged, a loud buzzing would signal. Her call went through with no warning alarm, and she hung up before the recorded message informed her that she had reached an unassigned number.

Barbara picked up the phone, dialed a New York City area code and number, but got no answer. She didn't need to talk to Matt anyway. Matt had run scared when things were intense.

She had met Matt Bradley in Salt Lake City, where she was doing research on lipoproteins in a summer program at the University of Utah in 1974. He'd followed her to Madison. They lived together, briefly and almost happily. But Barbara was changing too quickly. Her massage parlor job seemed to consume her. They did a lot of drugs—marijuana, hashish, Quaaludes. When she booked him a motel room because she was bringing another man to their apartment, Matt despaired and fled to New York City. Nevertheless, they corresponded. Barbara could talk to him. Matt listened.

The refrigerator chilled a bottle of Chablis. Barbara popped a Quaalude, swished it down with wine. She turned on the TV, and the six o'clock news featured Harry Berge as the lead story.

How death can immortalize a trivial life, Barbara later confided to a friend. Discounting the work crew at Uni-Royal, approximately eight people were aware of the man's existence: his sister and brother-in-law, the Pierce family, his Christian Scientist neighbor, and Barbara. Now Harry Berge was a household name in Madison, a name forever associated with a mysterious Christmas tragedy.

Barbara curled up on the sofa and fell asleep.

The persistence of the telephone ringing woke her hours later. It was Jerry Davies. He asked for a rendezvous the next evening. She agreed to meet him at a local bar, the Kollege Klub.

She rolled herself a stick of marijuana. Marijuana did not affect her like Quaaludes. 'Ludes mellowed her head when it churned overtime, at high speed, mashing thought into thought, vision into vision, which it seemed to do often during her conscious hours. Barbara sometimes wished she could have a switch installed that would snap off the thoughts when they collided and overwhelmed her. In the absence of an internal device she opted for 'ludes and achieved the same effect. Quaaludes allowed moments of tranquillity and negotiation. Marijuana rendered perspicacity and light. When she drew the sweet smoke into her lungs, the storm that clashed in her brain took a focus.

She knew exactly what was real and what was not, or so she believed.

Barbara dialed the clearing-line phone number again. Then she called Liza, who had worked at Jan's with her, Liza who preferred grass to the Quaaludes Barbara favored, Liza who sucked and fucked tricks at the parlor but who refused to provide other amenities, no matter that Barbara explained it was the other amenities that paved the path to riches in their sordid business.

Barbara Hoffman's sad, rambling voice was too familiar. Liza lit a cigarette. The hour was late. Tomorrow was a working day that would arrive too soon. At least she wasn't masturbating farmers and lawyers and drunken carpenters for a living. That was behind her, Liza consoled herself; it was in the past. Instead she sat at a desk, in an office crammed with desks and file cabinets in a four-story building crammed with desks and file cabinets—Liza and dozens of other women, none of whom were like her, she decided—and for eight hours each day they rapped typewriter keys and squinted at computer terminals and pretended to ignore the boredom of their labor.

Liza thought of herself as a chicken in a roost. Each day another piece of her life slipped away, slipped into an irretrievable place. She regretted it and she resented it. But it was better than whacking the flaccid penis of a man for money.

Damn, Barbara, Liza cried into the phone; you're giving me nightmares. But Liza didn't hang up. She sucked on her cigarette. If Barbara had been the queen of the massage parlors, then she was the queen of nightmares too.

The rumor was that when Barbara quit the parlors and signed on for a straight job she had taken a couple of lucrative johns with her and discreetly set up shop at home. Liza had never confirmed the rumor, but it was apparent from her conversation that Barbara had not forsaken her commerce. Barbara liked the money, and in a weird way Barbara liked the power she wielded over men. She also experienced a paranoia concerning its repercussions, both physical and psychological. Barbara's dreams often expressed her fears, and it was a dream episode Barbara was relating now, over the phone.

Liza mumbled to reinforce her presence, although it didn't matter. Liza had known Barbara Hoffman for maybe two months in early 1975 when these calls had commenced. They came without regularity or pattern, except that Barbara always called late at night. Sometimes Barbara cried about her pains and confusions. Sometimes Liza cried with her.

When Barbara left the parlors, several of her steady customers drifted to Liza, who was one of the prettiest masseuses at Jan's. Prepped with the proper and discretionary amount of cosmetics, provided with seven consecutive hours of sleep, Liza radiated a natural beauty. A sprinkle of freckles dotted her cheeks. A bucket of blond hair bounced with her walk. She was wholesome, cheerful, with a dose of cynicism that kept her from being a caricature. What she lacked was the charisma that Barbara emanated and the instincts that Barbara had honed.

A wealthy real estate developer chose Liza as a substitute when Barbara retired. I want you to listen, he said, as Liza massaged sandalwood oil into his skin and listened as he talked. The man talked about nothing: a remark concerning his wife, a quip about business, a joke about sex. Liza worked on his cock, coaxed it to stiffen as he palavered. Gradually and gently she brought him to a sustained climax, which she cleaned with her mouth.

The man lay on the massage table insulted and unsatisfied. "You don't know how to listen," he reprimanded Liza. "You didn't hear a word I said."

Liza could have repeated his mundane monologue verbatim.

You didn't listen like Barbara, the man scolded her. He pulled a dog collar out of his jacket. He explained that he was going to fix the collar to her neck and take her for a stroll, on her hands and knees, of course. Liza ran out of the room.

Barbara had laughed when Liza recounted the story.

Barbara admitted that sometimes she played a game with the men who adored her. She listened and responded so intently, Barbara boasted, that she convinced some of the fools they had orgasmed when they hadn't. She would stroke their pricks and rub their minds with attention, then feign as if they had come sweetly, powerfully, into her hands or mouth or vagina. The tension drained from their bodies, the buttocks softened, the pulse eased. The irony, she had lectured Liza, was that the ones being used, the women, were the ones who held the power, who spun the magic.

Liza blew smoke toward the ceiling, imagining Barbara conjuring illusions to bedazzle the lonely. Who had been tricked? Liza wondered.

A bottle of Valium rested on the middle shelf in the bathroom medicine chest. One for now, to sleep; one for work in the morning, Liza decided.

Frost stained the bedroom window. A street lamp revealed the glittering patterns on the glass. Barbara was exhausted. She had smoked a stick of marijuana, and everything had become so clear. She had called Liza to tell her about the clarity, about how her life was.

She apologized to Liza if she had talked too much. The hour was late, and she needed sleep. She bid Liza good night.

— 17 —

The Kollege Klub is a basement bar where students assemble to drink and carouse. Michelob and Old Style are on tap. Two dozen imported and domestic beers are available by the bottle. Mixed drinks with monikers like "The Bucky Bash" can be ordered. Chablis and rosé are served. The requisite burger and fries, with house variations, can be grilled for the hungry, and for the health-conscious salads have been added to the menu. Whether dictated by a change in management or merely slumping beer sales, the interior is refurbished periodically. The KK has sported a woodsy, rustic ambience, passed through a glass and glitter phase, and currently could be called just another fun bar.

On Friday afternoons the KK is packed for happy hour, regardless of marketing fashion and collegiate trend. It is frequented by kids from the fraternity and sorority houses that litter Langdon Street, kids who jog every other day, who are in ROTC or business school, who go to Wisconsin football games but have to read the Sunday paper to discover the final score, who have smoked marijuana once, maybe twice, but prefer a six-pack of Budweiser, kids who chew Dexedrine like Chiclets during final exam week, kids from Ladysmith and Little Chute and Oconto and Wauwatosa who know their four years in Madison will be unlike any other time in their lives. A football jersey or a plaid button-down shirt, jeans, and a cap that reads SKOL or WISCONSIN or WAYNE FEEDS will make you one of the crowd if male. If female, apply makeup so lightly it seems you are wearing no makeup, pull on a crewneck sweater, lace up canvas Tretorns, and you will blend in fine.

Inside the KK the sixties never happened. Social awareness is ogling the incoming freshman girls. These kids think it's cleansing for the body to get so drunk once a month that you puke on the sidewalk. Yet they monitor their GPAs like they are the Dow Jones. Unlike their parents, they do not equate success with money but with happiness. Money is a variable in the equation, perhaps the largest single factor, but the kids from the KK will insist it doesn't have to be that way. None of them, however, will take the chance. They mouth platitudes that life is what one makes of it, and they agree that grades measure neither intelligence nor knowledge, but after happy hour on Friday they will sober up and spend Saturday in the library, drinking coffee and eating junk food from the vending machines, studying to ensure entry into an engineering school or an MBA program.

Jerry Davies fidgeted in a booth. The Kollege Klub was not his kind of hangout. College students irked him. No good reason why; they just weren't his kind of people. If Davies had a hangout, it would have been the Pizza Hut on South Park Street, near his apartment.

What upset him the evening of December 27th was not the KK, but the fact that Barbara Hoffman would stride down the cane-matted steps presently. The knot in his stomach felt the size of a gnarled mass of tree root. Beer slid over the tangle and filled his bladder. In an adjacent booth two plainclothes cops sipped Cokes.

The original plan was for Davies to be wired so that the conversation with Barbara Hoffman, along with any threats, recriminations, or admissions, could be recorded. But Lulling and Doyle had watched Davies tremble at the idea, and revised their strategy. His instructions were to keep talking, remain in the bar for as long as possible, and under no circumstances retire to Barbara's apartment. Both Lulling and Doyle had a real concern for Davies's safety, even if Davies himself thought the idea that Barbara might harm him preposterous and irrational. Besides, the surveillance would end once Davies entered apartment 306, and Lulling wanted to know what was said between them.

The foam of his beer was flat. Jerry Davies had expressed doubts about his role in this eavesdropping scenario. It entailed duplicity toward Barbara. Worse, her words, however innocent and unintentional, would be misconstrued and twisted to incriminate her. But his apprehension was overcome by Lulling. If Davies was anxious about Barbara, he was also intimidated by the gruff detective. A customer fed the jukebox. The crash of rock music resounded, and Davies was grateful for the distraction.

The noise caused Russ Kurth to grimace. Dressed in an argyle cardigan, with his black hair stylishly long, the tall, athletic detective could have been a graduate student in marketing and finance. Kurth sat with his back to the

empty seat opposite Davies, the seat Barbara was to occupy. If the blare of the music didn't drop several decibels,
he'd need to pull up a chair and join the conversation to
hear what was being said. He and his partner were debating slicing the cord or simply pulling the plug when Barbara appeared, looking like a bashful coed in her jeans,
blue turtleneck, and tortoiseshell glasses.

"Order me a glass of Chablis, please," she told Davies.
She sauntered to the jukebox, stuffed a dollar's worth of
quarters in the slot, and punched her selections.

"I'll bet they've got you wired to the fucking heavens," she said. Her brown eyes narrowed and were hard as
cloves.

Davies flinched. He uttered an apology.

Barbara retorted viciously. Davies stammered, his
right index finger readjusting his wire-rimmed glasses.
Barbara accused him of betrayal.

The police had jumped to conclusions, Davies said,
flustered. The beer and Barbara's acrimony played havoc
with Davies's head. He had insisted she was an innocent
victim of some awful circumstance.

Barbara scowled.

He didn't want this mess either, he said. He wanted
their lives to return to how they had been, or almost how
they had been.

Not a chance, Barbara said.

Davies dabbed at his runny nose with a napkin. The
flaccid muscles in his neck tightened. He hadn't snitched
on her; he had defended her.

Then Barbara mellowed. The accusation and acerbity
disappeared from her voice. Her words came in whispers.

The Rolling Stones shouted a rock & roll cover from
the jukebox. Snatches of their talk floated past Russ
Kurth, but he couldn't fit the pieces together. He strained
to listen. Barbara's subdued tone and the blast of the music
machine prevented his stealing their exchanges.

Kurth moved to the bar, where he could catch a
glimpse of the couple. What he observed was useless as
evidence, but it provided a fascinating lesson in human

relations. It was not the talk that held the gist of this meeting; it was the negotiation and manipulation of that silent space that separates two human beings, that area of intimation and gesture, the region between faces where contact is established or deflected. Barbara was an expert in that territory. With Davies she controlled that zone, ruled its interior with the same quiet skill that a grand master employs to control the center of a chessboard. She maneuvered emotion with gesture, not words. A tilt of her head, a petulant curl of her lip, the angle and intensity of her eyes; disappointment, pain, reassurance were conveyed in a murmur, an expression, a fingertip that lightly traced the back of his hand. They whispered intently, and the whispering made the booth their private sphere; it cut them off, sealed them away from whomever else was present. The hushed voices created distance.

For three days a panoply of forces had shoved Jerry Davies around: his conscience, the cops, his doubts, his commitment to Barbara. Davies needed a sanctuary where he could rest and clarify his allegiances. Barbara intuited this. She acted injured and forgiving. A tear skipped out of her eye. Davies brushed it away. She invited him to walk her home.

Kurth trailed them. He feigned a call from a street phone booth and observed the push and pull as Barbara attempted to persuade Davies to come up to her apartment for a cup of hot tea. Kurth expected to lose him.

The couple climbed the stairs as Kurth waited below. Barbara's litany was powerful. "If you love me, Jerry . . ." was her tack, and Davies wavered. He professed his love hastily, as if it were a cumbersome weight that he feared would crush him. His fervent clichés echoed in the stairwell. Barbara whispered, sweet and enticing, but Davies's better judgment and the strict lecture from Lulling held forth.

They did not kiss good night. Barbara stroked his cheek with her fingers, tenderly, and she vanished behind the door to apartment 306.

Davies stood there. It took him two full minutes to

pry his work boots from the terrazzo tiles and to descend the stairs. The night's cold, which had been biting at Kurth's toes, sobered Davies. He paced steadily to his car.

Whatever secrets Barbara had spoken during their moments together Davies refused to repeat to Kurth, who joined him on the Lake Street parking ramp. The confounded lover shrugged his shoulders to Kurth's questions, and the cop didn't push. His assignment was to trail and listen and to make certain Davies got home safely.

Before Davies drove away, he rolled down the car window and displayed a weak smile. He looked like a turtle, his neck craning out of the fur collar of his parka. "She said we have to stick together. Tell Mr. Doyle the engagement's still on—probably for the spring."

—— 18 ——

By December 28th police had executed four search warrants for Barbara Hoffman's apartment. They had gathered little evidence for their efforts. Jerry Davies had been subjected to a polygraph exam, which he passed. What he had told Lulling on Christmas and expanded for Doyle the next day seemed to be the extent of his involvement and knowledge concerning Harry Berge's homicide. Al Mackey had appeared at Doyle's office claiming to represent Ms. Hoffman. Her cooperation with police investigators was asked for, but Mackey denied her participation in Berge's death or the disposal of the body. She would make no statements and answer no questions unless subpoenaed.

It was mid-morning. Doyle completed administrative work. Nagging in the back of his mind was the material on Linda Millar. Who was she, and what were her papers doing in Barbara Hoffman's possession?

He took a phone call from Ken Buhrow, an attorney in nearby Cambridge. Buhrow had information on Berge's estate that he wanted to volunteer. Doyle jotted down notes.

Buhrow had handled the few legal chores the Berge

family had required, and when Alma Berge died he advised Harry to amend his will, as his mother was the sole beneficiary of his property and his life insurance. For five years Berge did not heed the counsel.

On October 6, 1977, Berge dropped in without an appointment. His mood was jocular and unharried. The acquaintances shared coffee, swapped stories, and moseyed around to business. Harry wanted his will changed.

The A-frame house on U.S. 51 and his life insurance policies were to be left to a woman named Linda Millar. Buhrow politely inquired about her relationship to Berge. Harry Berge said that she was his fiancée. He wanted things to be in proper order for her. Buhrow recommended that Berge wait until the marriage had taken place before instituting the changes. Harry shrugged. The marriage was close to happening. Besides, he wasn't seeking advice, Berge said, friendly but firm.

Buhrow had studied the man across the desk for indication of stress or pressure or anxiety. There was none. His impression was that Berge looked healthier than he had ever remembered him. Though the change requested was straightforward, Buhrow stalled and told Harry the paperwork would take a week to complete. Maybe the extra couple days would allow Harry to reconsider.

Harry Berge returned in one week, signed the documents that pronounced Linda Millar his sole heir, paid cash for the service, and disappeared back into his life.

Doyle thanked Buhrow for the information. But who was Linda Millar? Another massage parlor sweetheart? Maybe Harry Berge wasn't as lonely as his sister had imagined. Yet so far Linda Millar was a ghost.

There were two Linda Millars listed in the Madison phone book. Neither one knew Barbara Hoffman, nor did their social security numbers match the numbers found in Barbara's apartment. Prostitution and drug arrest records were checked for a clue to Millar's identity, with no results.

Doyle was frustrated. Harry Berge left everything of value that he owned to an imaginary creature? But Doyle didn't need a ghost; he needed something solid. He had a dead body in a snowbank and testimony from a fragile witness who helped put the body there and nothing else. Hoffman wasn't cooperating. He couldn't place the body in her apartment, except on Davies's word, which was hearsay. What was needed was hard evidence—something or someone to corroborate Davies's story, and a murder weapon, and another witness, and Berge's car and clothes. Then he'd have a case.

Every city-operated parking ramp, every public lot downtown, east and west at the malls had been scoured for Berge's vehicle, but no car had been spotted.

Doyle called homicide and reported Buhrow's call to one of the detectives on the case. Lulling, Doyle was told, was in Stoughton, requestioning workers at UniRoyal whom the police had talked with yesterday. Apparently the lieutenant did not regard the information as adequate and wanted to pose his own questions.

Typical of Lulling's style, said a detective. There was derision in his voice. Three days in, and Lulling had seeded the investigation with dissension, which also was typical of his style, thought Doyle.

Lulling may have been unorthodox, and he may have jeopardized the investigation by rushing off to Park Ridge to confront a woman whose poise and intelligence he'd vastly underestimated, and he may have alienated fellow cops because he didn't trust their detective abilities, yet he remained pertinacious. In the morning he laid out a map of the center city and assigned officers to knock on every door of the 500 and 600 blocks of State Street. When they finished, they were to shag their flat feet to Langdon Street, which ran one block closer to the lake and parallel to State, and repeat the procedure. The majority of the tenants would be students, and most would be gone for the holidays, but someone might have had a late exam or missed a travel connection. Foreign students would be around. It was doubtful anyone might have been roaming the streets at 2:00 or 3:00 A.M. in the winter, but students have queer habits, Lulling explained.

After a couple days of routine and boring police work and a rereading of the autopsy report and tedious calculation, Chuck Lulling was confident he had reconstructed December 22nd, the last day of Harry Berge's life. Until the final minutes the events were absolutely ordinary, which convinced the detective that his scenario was correct.

Because UniRoyal had intended to close for the long Christmas weekend, the second shift was given half a workday on December 22nd. Berge had left home for his job at 2:50 P.M.

"You could set your watch by him pulling out of his driveway," a neighbor had told Lulling.

Berge punched in at 2:59 and punched out at 7:00. The plant held its annual Christmas party, which the second shift joined in progress. A buffet was served. Foreman Tom Bemis remembered seeing Berge in the food line "around 7:30." Other co-workers confirmed Bemis's recollection.

Larry Aaberg encouraged Berge to attend the post-party festivities at the U-Name-It Tavern, but Berge declined with a sheepish smile. He had a date in Madison. After a hasty meal Berge departed.

No one recalled Berge's presence at the company fete after about 8:00, and no one saw him at the U-Name-It later. Lulling surmised that Berge drove straight home. When officers examined Berge's house on December 26th, they found his dirty work clothes on the bed. The evening newspaper was folded as the paperboy had tucked it and lay unread on the dining room table along with two pieces of mail, unopened, addressed to "Occupant." The watchful neighbor had attended a church function that evening, so when Berge left for Madison was unknown. But considering that the autopsy reports indicated Berge had died within one to one-and-a-half hours after ingesting a large meal, he could not have dallied at home for very long.

Lulling duplicated Berge's itinerary for that fatal night. The detective meticulously timed every stage of the journey. He walked from the time clock to the parking lot,

which took two minutes. The drive to Berge's home covered eight-tenths of a mile and took three minutes. Once
inside, he undressed, washed up, brushed his teeth, and
put on fresh clothes. At a leisurely pace this took no more
than fifteen minutes. The trek from Stoughton to Madison was eighteen and two-tenths miles, which Lulling
drove at the speed limit, and took thirty minutes, including parking in the Lake Street ramp. The entire procedure
took fifty minutes, which meant that Harry Berge was at
Hoffman's apartment by 9:00 easily. The timing coincided
with the autopsy findings.

These computations pleased Lulling immensely. The
time scheme, combined with the autopsy data, provided a
plausible framework for the murder.

For three days Chuck had worked at the case almost
every waking hour. Finally he had a theory as to what had
transpired.

Berge had arrived at Barbara Hoffman's apartment
before 9:00 P.M. He and Hoffman argued, maybe over
Jerry Davies, maybe over this mysterious Linda Millar.
The scratch on Berge's neck indicated that the hostility
flared into actual violence. Maybe Berge foisted himself on
her; maybe he threatened her. Barbara clawed to get away.

Undeterred, angry, and hurt, Berge stalked her. Berge
approached, and Barbara kicked him in the balls as hard as
she could. Berge doubled over, groaned, then groped for
her.

She was the only woman he'd ever dated, and he was
losing her. The adoration he felt for her turned quickly to
bitterness. Maybe he shouted. They were in the kitchen.
Barbara grabbed the frying pan from over the stove and
cracked his skull once, twice, a third time before she could
control her rage. Berge dropped unconscious.

Blood poured from Berge's head. Barbara rushed to
the bathroom, gathered towels, and administered first aid,
but to no avail. Berge was dead. In her panic and fear she'd
killed him.

Berge was nothing to her except a trick, a lonely old
man who bought her nice gifts. Moreover, Barbara

realized, Berge was nothing to anyone, trapped as he'd been in his solitary existence. She knew of his isolation. She counted on his disappearance going relatively unnoticed.

She stripped his clothes, cleaned her apartment of his blood, and waited until the deepest part of night to dispose of his body. She wrapped the body in a bedsheet and dragged it down three flights of stairs—which accounted for the abrasions on the hips, legs, and lower back, which the pathologist said were postmortem inflictions.

Once outside she buried the body next to the Dumpster, against the fence where the snow had been plowed. Then she returned momentarily with Berge's car. But rigor mortis had set in, and Berge's body was awkward. She couldn't wedge it into the trunk. Barbara needed help.

The following day she enlisted Davies's aid. Aware of his sensibilities, she was also aware of his malleability. If anything went awry, she could control Davies, or so she had guessed. Once Berge was buried on a secluded country lane, chances were slim that he'd be discovered before the spring thaw.

The speculations needed refinement, but the outline was feasible and fit what the police had learned. It sounded horrid and too true: a misplaced love, an argument, desperation, a woman's fury.

Yet as Lulling listened to his own conjecture, serious doubts that Berge's death was a crime of passion, a spontaneous and angry flash of violence, needled him. Something more lay under the surface, something they had scratched yet not uncovered. The terse interview with Hoffman in Park Ridge had convinced him of her supreme self-control. The woman was cold, tough, and Lulling wondered what seethed beneath that hard exterior.

What could a fifty-two-year-old forklift operator from Stoughton have said to rile her so? Now it was Lulling's guess that the whole scene was premeditated and arranged. Berge was not beaten in self-defense. He was battered repeatedly after it had been clear that he wasn't going to move, that he wasn't going to threaten. But if it was premeditated, why choose a third-floor apartment on a street in the center of Madison? There had to have been more convenient places to commit murder.

Chuck Lulling was puzzled. What they needed was more police work as well as a little hard evidence to hang a theory on.

—— 19 ——

The dashboard lights of the Oldsmobile Cutlass illumined a melancholy face whose ruddy complexion seemed to glow in the semidarkness of the car. Al Mackey concentrated on his driving.

A black arrow shone on a yellow background, warning of a sharp turn in the road. The Olds slowed. The headlights beamed on a narrow ribbon of blacktop winding between banks of snow and telephone poles sleeted with ice, past dairy farms and frozen cornfields. Two hours of driving and the scenery hadn't changed. Al Mackey was as fatuous as when he'd started the trip, as when he'd consented to it, which could be traced back to an evening at Jan's Health Spa when he first met Barbara Hoffman, which was precipitated by . . .

Why replay the past? It never changed.

The Oldsmobile Al Mackey drove had been owned by Harry Berge. He was smuggling a dead man's car across the Wisconsin countryside in the quiet of the night, returning it to the city of the alleged crime, driving the back roads and county trunks to avoid detection, for if he was stopped by a state trooper, or if he skidded on ice and buried the Olds in a ditch of snow, it would mean grave trouble. Accessory after the fact was not an immodest charge. He would be suspended or disbarred from practicing law. He would be arrested and put in jail.

It was preposterous, yet this was all he could do to help Barbara. Certainly he was incapable of properly defending her in a court of law. If manslaughter or second-degree murder were the charges, she would need the best, and he had a recommendation. Then, when she was settled with a new lawyer, he'd depart on a vacation, visit family in California, and ponder the possibility of permanently escaping the cold, the walls of snow that bordered the roadside, the icy bridges, the frosty winds.

Al Mackey was being used, and he submitted to it willingly. He wasn't complaining. But he needed to get away. Perhaps the climate in California would sober him. Perhaps he didn't want to be sober.

Al Mackey managed to negotiate the back roads from Park Ridge to Madison without incident. He parked Harry Berge's Oldsmobile behind the Quality Courts Inn on Madison's east side and called Barbara from a pay phone. She drove out with his car, and they drove back to State Street, hoping that the chill of a winter's night would protect them.

—— 20 ——

Although Linda Millar remained a mystery, information about Barbara Hoffman accumulated. A tenant at 638 State Street told detectives that Barbara had frequent male visitors. Because she forbade shoes to sully her apartment, it was obvious when she entertained, for footwear would be parked on a mat outside her door. Rubber-soled work boots, expensive leather brogans, tennis sneakers—always men's shoes—were present in the late-night hours when the observant neighbor returned from his waiter's job.

At midnight one night, while staggering down the cavernous hallway after a postwork celebration, he tripped over a man curled up on the tile floor in front of apartment 306. The man snored blissfully, a tweed jacket draped over him like a blanket.

Another tenant reported being awakened by a ruckus in the early morning about two months previously. The woman unlatched her door to complain and spied an elderly gentleman in the corridor, attired in a sport coat and slacks, banging desperately for admission to Barbara's residence. He was hunchbacked, with gray hair and skinny arms that seemed to rattle in the sleeves of his sport coat as he pounded on the door. After minutes of this futility he slumped to the floor, a heap of tailored clothes and wrinkled flesh, and he whimpered. The startled woman thought of calling the police. She shut her door, waited, and when she looked out again the pitiful person had disappeared.

Both tenants were students, and neither could identify Berge or Davies as men they had seen in the hallway or in the building at any other time.

According to Jerry Davies, Barbara changed her phone number regularly. The telephone company confirmed this pattern. In 1977 alone Barbara Hoffman had changed her phone number five times. Jerry Davies had no explanation for Barbara's curious obsession. He simply wrote down the current number on a piece of paper he carried in his wallet, for the number changed too often to bother memorizing.

Under power of a court order, Barbara Hoffman's school records were obtained and studied.

If it is possible to apply mathematical formulas and numerical judgment to as elusive and precarious a concept as intelligence, then Barbara Hoffman had to be classified as brilliant. The Stanford-Binet test, administered during her sophomore year in high school, placed her IQ at 145. Her college entrance examination scores put her in the ninety-eighth percentile of those tested. Straight As were the rule of her scholastic record. She was in the National Honor Society. She spent her junior year of high school in Germany on an AFS scholarship. She was a National Merit finalist. She was fluent in French and German.

In 1970 Barbara graduated from Maine South High School in Park Ridge and was ranked eighteenth in a senior class of 482 students. She matriculated at Butler University, where she received a full-tuition scholarship. She made the Dean's List, joined a sorority, and continued earning straight As. The school in Indianapolis, however, did not suit her. She transferred to the University of Illinois at Chicago Circle and shortly thereafter transferred to the University of Wisconsin.

Madison seemed to have arrested her aimlessness. For two years she was a quiet student who compiled an outstanding academic record. Biochemistry was her major field of study. She earned As in organic chemistry, biochemistry, physics, statistics, and microbiology. In 1973 she was awarded a summer scholarship to the University of Utah to assist in research on protein synthesis. Her transcript reflected the mind of a bright student with a strong aptitude for sciences. Her 3.9 GPA indicated a deep grasp of the subject material and excellent work habits. Her potential was unlimited. Future options included graduate school or medical school or a research position in private industry.

On November 15, 1974, a paltry twelve credits shy of a bachelor of science degree in biochemistry, Barbara Hoffman became a college dropout. A letter seeking a leave of absence due to illness was submitted, and the request was granted. Barbara enrolled for the 1975 spring term but withdrew in April, one month short of the semester's completion. She registered for the fall term with the intention of finishing her degree and quit after five weeks of course work. The spring semester, 1976, followed the same pattern. The dean's office issued Barbara an extension on her leave of absence, but with the comment that the student had been advised to resume her degree program immediately, for requirements were continually modified and continued delay would retard her progress toward graduation. Barbara registered for the fall term, 1976, and dropped out again.

A chagrined dean placed Barbara on permanent leave and declared that future efforts at a degree in biochemistry would have to be undertaken on probationary status. For the spring of 1977 Barbara enrolled as a nondegree student, signing up for a class in abnormal psychology. She withdrew after three weeks. In the fall of that year she enrolled as a nondegree student for another abnormal psychology course, which she quit after one month.

At a smaller educational institution such inconsistency might have earned more careful scrutiny. For the fall term, 1977, the University of Wisconsin–Madison numbered over forty thousand students. In population the campus would have qualified as the eighth-largest city in the state. The machinations of a confused individual easily escaped detection by the bureaucracy. In two-and-a-half years as a degree-directed student, Barbara Hoffman had one meet-ing with her academic adviser. An assistant dean discussed her muddled academic record with her and suggested ca-reer orientation services or psychological counseling if she thought either of those avenues was appropriate. Barbara's response was a polite "no thank you."

For fifteen years Barbara had excelled at school, but in November 1974 she sputtered and stalled. That date coincided with her employment in Madison's massage par-lors.

Pieces of Barbara Hoffman continued to emerge, but rather than clarify, these fragments added to the enigma.

She had formed no strong friendships at work. The women at EDS Federal who shared office space with Bar-bara considered her polite and quiet. She never spoke about her personal life. Detectives working on the inves-tigation were confounded. No one seemed to know Bar-bara. Her apartment held no mementos, no sentimental artifacts. There were no pictures of family or friends anywhere in the apartment; only the pornographic photo-graphs were found. She was perspicacious and poised, and she had scuttled a professional career to satisfy the sexual whims of any horny man who walked through the door. It didn't fit into a neat puzzle.

What about drug use? Vice officers presumed that most women who toiled in the flesh trade used some form of intoxicant to get by. A prescription pill bottle for Dal-mane, a sedative, had been found during one of the apart-ment searches, as had a small amount of marijuana.

Lulling put out word to vice and to other detectives

that the investigation needed a lead on Hoffman. The word he got back was that the streets were mum regarding the Berge homicide and Lulling's only suspect. The skin business in Madison was a closed universe, and much of what happened filtered back to the cops in vice through informants. A murder pulled off by someone in the massage parlor clique would have tongues wagging with speculation, innuendo, hearsay. Someone in a jam would be apt to swap what he or she had heard for leniency regarding a parole violation or for help with a bust or a sentence reduction.

But the silence on the streets was as eerie as the wind howling off the snow-crusted hills of Tomahawk Ridge. No one talked about the murder. No one tried to purchase a favor with a piece of knowledge concerning it. Yet everyone in the city's sex world knew Barbara Hoffman. She was the queen of the parlors, vice had been told, and they were told nothing more.

—— 21 ——

Hockey games on the radio, sausage pizzas and large Cokes, the twang of a pedal steel guitar at Johnny's Packer Inn, and on Fridays after work the ride west on U.S. 14, where two lanes of traffic whizzed to and from Madison at sixty miles per hour, slowing for small towns—Cross Plains, Black Earth, Arena, Mazomanie—accelerating again through the Wisconsin River valley, through a countryside of snow fences and denuded oak trees, where billboards shone under spotlights as round as cow's eyes, touting the wonders of the House on the Rock, or Taliesin, designed by Frank Lloyd Wright, or the Circus World Museum in Baraboo; Jerry Davies pondered his lonely winter and winced. He had been through the motions before. The script varied little each year, but never had it appeared so dreary.

On Fridays he would treat his mother to the fish fry

at a local restaurant in Spring Green. On Saturday nights
he left her home and attended the high school basketball
games: River Valley versus Fennimore or Boscobel or De
Soto. And should the game be on the road, he'd travel the
twenty miles to an opponent's gym. The spectacle as well
as the sport entranced Davies—the ponytailed cheerlead-
ers launched airborne with every score, the players outfit-
ted in gaudy polyester, the tall, gawky center in crew cut
and squeaky shoes, the smattering of applause from
bleachers one-third full, mostly farmers in overalls watching their sons run and shoot. They nodded hello to Jerry.
He nodded back.

It had not been easy before Barbara. It might be impossible without her. Jerry Davies had never realized the
depth of his loneliness until she had fondled his cock and
his heart. When he spurted into her hand, it was like
shedding a skin. He felt new. He remained the same. The
paradox hurt. Things inside him had been irrevocably
altered. His ordinary life appeared hollow without the
thought of Barbara's touch.

When he had sought her company at Jan's he had been
desperate, and through an unspoken admission Barbara
relayed that she was desperate too. She wanted his companionship. Jerry Davies was disbelieving and baffled and
thrilled.

"Barbara Hoffman." Davies rolled the name on his
tongue and tasted flavors he had never tasted before. How
was he to push forward without her company, her voice,
her haphazard affections? His head ached.

On New Year's Day 1978 Jerry Davies drove to his
mother's home in Spring Green. He watched football
games on the TV and feasted on the meal she had prepared.

It was after midnight when he returned to Madison.
In his mailbox was a missive from Barbara. She wrote that
adversity should push them together, not rend them apart.
Would he pick her up in the morning and drive her to
work, as previously? She'd be waiting in the stairwell.

On the second morning of 1978 Jerry Davies's stomach jittered. He drank a cup of instant coffee and painted his underarms with stick deodorant. Perhaps the winter would bring reconciliation and the spring recovery.

— 22 —

Kensington Drive is imbued with the serenity of a country lane. There are no sidewalks to shovel, no curbs to trip over. The houses are two-story and elegant, built of flag-stone or brown brick, and feature bay windows, porches framed with scrolled, wrought-iron railings, bedroom bal-conies. Volvos topped with ski racks or Buicks or Cadillacs or Mercedes frequent the plowed driveways. The tennis courts in the backyards are knee-deep with snow. The quiet is pervasive.

Maple Bluff, which includes Kensington Drive, is an unincorporated village encompassed by the city of Madi-son and a shelter for its property owners from the city's exorbitant tax rate. The village curves along a couple of miles of lakefront and comprises maybe two hundred homes. The community employs its own police force and a public works department whose function is to collect refuse, plow the streets, maintain the village beach, and cultivate the village tulip gardens. There is no intrusion from the city into village affairs. Maple Bluff is an island of affluence and exclusivity, with a population as white as January's snow.

When Ken Curtis purchased the colonial home at 1651 Kensington Drive, the neighbors welcomed him. The presumption was that anyone who could afford to live in Maple Bluff belonged there. Curtis could afford the ad-dress. He harbored no notions about belonging. The new Lincoln Mark IV Continentals—one burgundy, one black—parked in the driveway attested to his success, and the elaborate alarm system installed shortly after he moved in indicated that he had something to protect.

What impressed neighbors foremost was the power

exuded by Curtis's physical presence. At 6'2" and 240 pounds, he appeared constructed of mortar and brick. His thighs stretched the seams of his jeans. His back flared broad, latissimus to the extreme. Biceps bulged at the slightest contraction. Shoulders as thick as cinder blocks were slapped aside an expansive chest, and his neck jutted like a pylon from a mass of trapezius muscle. Curtis did not walk; he swaggered. Intimidation and strength were a part of his carriage. Ken Curtis had watched thirty years come and go, and the experiences of that span had toughened his face but not wearied it. His eyes were icy green. Rather than look at people, he appraised them. A blond beard, well groomed, edged his jaw. His hair was a shade darker and was combed straight back, which revealed the small knot of scar at the left corner of his forehead. In leather jacket and boots, straddling a Harley-Davidson, Curtis would have embodied the quintessential outlaw biker aiming for trouble. In a Brooks Brothers suit he could have passed for a football jock tackling the corporate ladder.

Ken Curtis was neither. T-shirts, sweatshirts, dungarees were his usual garb. Curtis had little book knowledge, but he was smart and loaded with street sense. He owned or co-owned four massage parlors in Madison, including Jan's Health Spa. Moreover, the vice cops suspected him of involvement with drug traffic, fencing stolen merchandise and credit cards, dealing in unregistered weapons, and any of a half dozen other illegal scams. Some people in Madison's law enforcement community regarded Curtis as a punk, a hood with few smarts and a lot of guts. Others held a loftier opinion of Curtis's prowess. Curtis owned a large percentage of the skin trade in the city. He owned property. He knew how to hide and launder his monies. There was nothing small-time about Ken Curtis.

On January 9, 1978, Chuck Lulling pushed the doorbell of Curtis's Kensington Drive home. It was 11:00 A.M. Lazy loops of smoke swirled from the chimney. The upstairs blinds rattled. With a second ring the door opened.

A Hispanic woman in a red sweatshirt large enough to be a cocoon asked what he wanted. Lulling showed her his badge. He wanted Ken Curtis. The woman yawned. "Not home," she said and gently shut the door.

Lulling scratched his chin. He heard her bare feet thump the carpet as she ran upstairs. He waited a minute and rang the bell again. A scowling Ken Curtis flung the door wide and invited Lulling into the kitchen.

"Want some coffee?"

"No, thanks. I've got a few questions for you. It'll take a couple seconds."

Curtis grumbled at the detective. He didn't like having his sleep disturbed. Anytime before noon was an unreasonable hour to him.

"Whatever it is you're asking about," Curtis said, "I don't know anything about it."

Lulling reminded Curtis of his recent arrest for possession of an unregistered firearm.

"My lawyer'll get that tossed out of court," Curtis snorted. "Illegal search. Harassment without due cause. It's pending."

"The matter can be dropped very easily," said Lulling.

"You want a free blowjob at Jan's, Chuck?" laughed Curtis.

"I want to know about Barbara Hoffman," said Lulling.

"Never heard of the lady."

The detective reminded him of Hoffman's working history.

"Girls come and go. How can I keep track? Besides, what's she done that's attracted your interest?"

"You don't remember Barbara Hoffman? Bullshit!"

"And what do you assholes do for me except bust my rocks at every opportunity?" countered Curtis. "I support a goddamn law firm to stay clean. You guys try to nail me with everything illegal that goes on in this town, from dogfights to drug deals, and it sucks."

"You haven't ever seen a pit bull?" Lulling smiled. "You'd mistake cocaine for powdered sugar?"

"Chuck, if I knew anything about Barbara Hoffman, I'd cut a deal. What's she done that's so hot?"

"You don't know her, so it doesn't matter, does it?" Lulling walked to the door. "If your memory returns, Curtis, call me."

Ken Curtis closed the door. He scrambled back to bed, where he snatched the phone from the nightstand and dialed his lawyer, Charles Geisen.

Curtis recounted Lulling's visit. He told the attorney that the detective was desperate for information and, from what Curtis had heard, the cops didn't have enough evidence to move against Hoffman for the Berge killing. He suggested Geisen contact the DA and offer a deal: information connecting Hoffman to the Berge homicide in exchange for a little help for a friend.

— 23 —

On the fringe of Madison's south side was a triangular parcel of city consisting of rickety wooden houses and narrow alleys, backyard gardens and chicken coops, cobbler's shops, bakeries, a junkyard. The area was known as Greenbush. Its denizens were working people—Italian mostly, with a smattering of Irish, Polish, Chinese—men who labored in the construction trade or shoveled coal for Castle-Doyle, women who tended goats, hens, children. St. James Roman Catholic Church and Parochial School offered solace to sinners and an education to kids.

After World War II Madison grew and its boundaries pushed farther south. Cornfields were developed into housing tracts and shopping plazas. Some families left Greenbush for plusher, more prestigious quarters, but many families stayed in the cramped confines, for the Bush was home, a community, a soil where people established roots.

In the late fifties and early sixties, when urban renewal captivated the whimsy of city planners, bulldozers and wrecking balls attacked the Bush under the guise of neighborhood improvement. Tons of concrete were poured. A hospital was constructed. Maple trees and sod were planted in green profusion around boxes of apartment buildings. What emerged was a miniature wasteland, the ghost of a community. Former residents had dispersed throughout the city, embittered that their home turf had been destroyed. Madison's single cluster of ethnicity had been razed.

Ken Curtis and Jim Doyle, Jr., were reared in Greenbush. They were acquaintances as youths, mindful of each other, unaware of present differences that the future would magnify.

Doyle mumbled the Latin as an altar boy. Sports consumed him. He prayed to the apostles for athletic success, and he peeked at the girlie magazines while he sipped a cherry phosphate at Mickey's Dairy Bar.

Curtis squandered nickels on the pinball machines. He stayed away from any activity involving adults. He brawled, drank beer, sloshed in the bogs that bordered Lake Wingra, spearfishing carp for amusement.

At Madison West High School Doyle and Curtis were in the same homeroom but traveled different paths. Doyle concentrated on studies and sports, excelling at both. Curtis drifted. He cut classes and clashed with teachers. Doyle was accepted at Stanford. Curtis faked it as a student, went on to a local technical school, and waited for something to happen. It did. He grew four inches and twenty-eight pounds after graduating from Madison West. Then a buddy introduced him to the inside of a weight room.

While Doyle labored with the books, Curtis cranked iron and packed huge muscle onto his new frame. The bulk added to his belligerence. Curtis went from being obnoxious to being a bully.

Weightlifting and hustling drugs became the twin poles of his life. He entered powerlifting competitions and collected numerous trophies. His ego swelled as large as his pectorals. Occasionally he resorted to thievery, for adventure and profit. Once he hawked hot Sony Trinitrons from the tailgate of a pickup truck for $100 a pop. His boldness and his nastiness earned him a reputation.

Sam Cerro had also been raised in Greenbush. Cerro was a short man, as plump as a Roma tomato, with gray hair very meticulously combed and with stubby fingers ringed by circles of silver that were studded with gaudy stones. He wore baggy trousers, always wrinkled, and Ban-lon shirts. Paternalism and conviviality emanated from Cerro's soul. In a typical gesture he would thrust an arm around a friend's shoulder and whisper a salacious joke or dispense an old Italian adage as if he were sharing a great secret.

Cerro operated a private poker game and a floating craps table. Drugs and stolen merchandise were fields of endeavor. He loaned cash to those people who wished to avoid the traditional banking channels. When sports betting became popular, he ran the local action. Sports gambling developed into Cerro's most lucrative trade.

His livelihood associated the bookmaker with every stratum of Madison society and garnered him a modicum of notoriety. He played poker with judges, took lawyers' bets on college football, drank his beers at the Italian Workmen's Club. Sam Cerro was friendly like a favorite uncle, but he was not consistently smart. Collisions with law enforcement people were troublesome, and his career had been interrupted with arrests for bookmaking, possession of gambling materials, possession of stolen goods, property, and drugs.

When the first massage parlor opened in Madison, it drew Cerro's attention. Though the place eventually folded, he decided the concept was solid if police harassment could be kept at a minimum. What he needed was a competent person to hire the women and kick ass when things got sloppy. He sought someone tough and audacious. Ken Curtis fit the qualifications. Cerro offered the weightlifter a partnership, and Curtis showed no more hesitation than when bench pressing 400 pounds. He gritted his teeth and pushed straight ahead.

Two months later Jan's Health Spa premiered in the

basement of a small shopping center on Madison's west side. A few naive citizens dropped in expecting a gym and exited quickly when greeted by a woman in high heels and lace negligee and a promise of pleasure.

Things went better and worse than each partner anticipated. On about the eighth night of business Curtis pummeled a customer who got obstreperous when he wasn't permitted to sodomize the girl of his choice. It took an emergency room intern an hour and a spool of thread to stitch the horny gent's face back together. Curtis was detained by police but released when the man refused to press charges. A couple nights later one of the masseuses was arrested by an undercover cop for soliciting prostitution, and the massage parlor was closed by official order. A court restraining order had it opened within a week, minus the naughty vixen. The publicity over the arrest provided front-page advertising. Trade was brisk.

The partnership immediately expanded its enterprise. The Rising Sun massage parlor debuted in the shadow of the state capitol to service the uptown activity. The Geisha House opened for the convenience of the east-side clientele. Business in the downtown area was so good that another parlor, on the opposite side of the capitol from the Rising Sun, was opened.

Curtis stocked the parlors with a variety of women— sultry, sweet, sensual, sassy—and procured them drugs to encourage their enthusiasm. Many of the women were recruited from the university campus, answering ads in the student newspaper. On a Friday night giving hand jobs could bring a coed $100 to $150, and if the woman was apt to give other amenities—such as sucking or fucking— she could double or triple that amount.

Curtis augmented his own income with the dissemination of illegal substances. With cash and the proper recommendation a pharmacy of narcotics was available— speed, grass, Quaaludes, angel dust, hashish, cocaine.

The cocaine commerce flourished in particular. Jan's became a hub of local trade, a swirl of back-room barters, where shipments arrived in the middle of the night from

Louisiana, or were driven into town after being flown into a small country airport in Iowa, to be sampled, weighed, cut, and distributed. Wholesale and retail action was conducted in a cool frenzy by Curtis, the calculating weightlifter who never used any of the stuff himself.

For Curtis the parlors were a zany circus in which he played multiple parts: ringmaster, lion tamer, strongman. Most often he was the man on the flying trapeze. Every day brought thrills. His interview technique when hiring a new masseuse was to drop his pants and ask the lady to demonstrate her skills.

If you can't blow the boss, he would tell a prospective masseuse, how does the boss know you can jerk off the jerkoffs?

The ladies, the scams, the profits seemed endless.

Success did not spoil him. He stayed temerarious and mean. One night Curtis heaved a surly customer down a flight of stairs, punched him into the street, kicked him as he tried to crawl away, then mashed his face into the grille of an Oldsmobile until the man gurgled blood and bits of busted teeth. Curtis didn't care about the pain, inflicted or incurred. Pain and pleasure were strategies, methods to achieve what was desired.

Curtis's ability to give and take punishment was legendary among his friends. In the late sixties he was drafted for military induction. One of the favorite ploys of Madison's youth was to swallow a tab of LSD on the day of the physical and thus escape military service because of psychological problems and disorientation. Curtis would never tamper with his head so capriciously, but with his body he would take any extreme. He went to the weight room of the Central Y and ordered a friend to climb the squat rack and drop a hundred-pound dumbbell on his right foot, which mashed the bones in his toes and secured him an exemption from military service.

A couple years later, when Curtis discovered a female massage employee was taking her tricks outside the parlor, he had to set an example of what happened when his rules were defied. He didn't quiz the woman on her scheme. He told her what he had heard, then punched her in the face. Her jaw was broken and had to be wired together.

His volatile temper and bellicose attitude did have consequences: arrests for disorderly conduct, a suspended sentence and probation for battery charges. He packed a pistol under the front seat of his Lincoln, for emergency use only.

By 1976 Curtis was getting fat financially. He was purchasing property and setting up dummy corporations to launder his funds. Where Curtis was careful to distance and protect himself, his partner, Sam Cerro, was reckless. On a muggy August evening in 1976 Cerro tried to purchase $72,000 worth of cocaine from a pair of undercover cops. He was busted. The charges carried a large fine and a maximum twenty years' imprisonment. At age fifty-one jail was a frightening prospect for Cerro, and because of his previous record a conviction might carry the maximum term.

The portly Cerro squirmed. He needed help from wherever he could dig it up.

When Chuck Lulling asked for help on the Hoffman case, Curtis schemed to do his partner a favor.

— 24 —

On January 6, 1978, the snow piled next to the green Dumpster behind 638 State Street was rechecked for evidence of blood. A spot on the bedsheet that had blanketed Harry Berge's body indicated that postmortem bleeding had occurred.

Perhaps on Christmas Day it was too cold for the cops to be thorough. Lulling assigned an officer assisting with the investigation to try again, to sift carefully through the snow no matter how high and tight it had been packed.

His instructions were followed. It was cold, eight degrees above zero, with winds that gusted across the lakes and shivered the city. The snow, which had a couple of additional inches of fresh accumulation, was examined. No blood was found.

— 25 —

It was Jerry Davies who solved the Linda Millar riddle.

Standing in a hallway of the courthouse, his back slouched against a wall, Davies waited to see Jim Doyle. The shipping clerk had used sick time and taken the afternoon off. He needed to talk.

The DA was conducting a John Doe hearing, which was a secret proceeding used as an investigative tool to obtain sworn testimony. Doyle employed the John Doe to get evidence on record regarding the Berge homicide.

He spotted Davies as he exited a courtroom, and they rode the elevator to Doyle's office. Davies spewed his worries in jumbled sentences. He knew Barbara was innocent. It seemed the police kept coming back to her, seeking ways to involve her when she could never have participated in such an act. He hadn't lied to them about the body; thus he wasn't lying about Barbara's innocence.

Doyle didn't challenge the curious logic. In order to change the topic Doyle asked if the name Linda Millar meant anything to him. The sad Davies nodded without thinking.

Doyle repeated the question, and Davies elucidated. Linda Millar, he said, was an alias Barbara had chosen after she'd quit working the massage parlors. She wanted to bury those years and start her life anew. Because she was afraid the old and painful associations would haunt her, she decided that a different name would help cut her ties to the old life. To begin the future, she had explained to Davies, she had to rid herself of the past.

Had she ever actually used her alias? asked Doyle.

Occasionally, Davies replied. Once she'd had him send her an envelope with no letter that was addressed to Linda

Millar, at Barbara's State Street residence, to check whether the post office would deliver mail to the bogus name.

As soon as Davies left, Doyle phoned Lulling with what he had learned. Barbara Hoffman was Linda Millar, who had a savings account, a social security number, a post office box. Harry Berge had died with no will or testament. But two months before he had perished, he had made Linda Millar a joint tenant on his home for "one dollar and due considerations," and he had made her beneficiary of his life insurance policies, which totaled $34,500.

It seemed that Barbara Hoffman had planned Berge's death. Her motive was money.

— 26 —

Barbara Hoffman and Harry Berge were introduced on a lazy winter afternoon in 1975. Barbara was snuggled into a chair at Jan's Health Spa, reading a paperback novel, when one of the girls bolted out of a session with a customer. She cried for the manager to give the man a refund.

"The guy's a fucking weirdo," she said, flustered. "I'll do the usual, but I ain't doing freaky things."

Barbara watched the scene unfold. Three weeks and the girl was already burned out. Probably the angel dust she was smoking had been cut with something weird. That was partly why Barbara herself preferred Quaaludes. The pills were obtained with a prescription, from a pharmacist. She knew what she was getting.

Barbara walked over to the girl and said she'd handle the gentleman.

Down the hallway heat ducts crawled the ceiling like huge silver worms. Wire splicings surfaced and disappeared. Hot air gushed from an open vent. Barbara tapped on a door, stepped into a room with black walls. A blue bulb cast a strange, moonish glow.

A naked man sat in a chair in the center of the room. His skin looked as soft as blue cheese, and the pockmarks on his shoulders resembled mold. His hair was short and as bright as aluminum in the blue light. Black hairs dotted his shoulders and back. Thin dime-store handcuffs were at his feet.

When the man saw Barbara, his expression of dejection did not change. A simple favor, he implored. He deserved to be punished. He tossed an electrical cord across the floor.

Barbara picked up the cord. She locked the man's wrists to the slats of the chair with the cheap handcuffs. Barbara hit him once with the cord. Then she hit him harder. The blue light seemed to crackle as the cord cut his skin.

She cracked him across the shoulders, across the meat of his spine. The tip of the cord whipped around and bit his chest, and he yelped like a puppy. His flesh flushed with creases of scarlet.

After a dozen lashes the man begged her to stop. Defiantly she added two extra.

The man's back was ragged with welts. In two or three spots the skin had broken and a rivulet of blood trailed the curve of his spine. Barbara dabbed the wounds with a towel soaked in cold water. A sigh leaped from the man's lips, and though tears dripped down his cheeks he looked neither sad nor hurt. He looked lonely.

He asked if he could request her next time. Barbara looked at his sagging belly and limp penis and nodded. He told her his name was Harry Berge.

He slid a couple of twenties from his wallet and dropped them on the massage table. He rolled up his electrical cord and tucked it into a back pocket. Then he disappeared.

— 27 —

January 10, 1978, was another hectic day in a series of hectic days for Jim Doyle. The morning was crammed

with meetings. At 2:00 P.M. he would deliver a guest
lecture at a U.W. Law School seminar on legal ethics. A
Democratic party function would ruin the evening. In the
intervening hours were decisions bureaucratic, legal, political.

The old Plymouth that carted him to Monona Avenue
backfired at a red light, skipped gears, lunged forward,
then proceeded along as though nothing unusual had happened. The Plymouth had turned 142,000 miles, and he
wondered if it deserved a new transmission or retirement
to the scrapyard. A clump of rust dropped from the front
fender.

In the basement coffee shop of the courthouse building the DA ordered a large orange juice. He had a vague
notion the juice might calm his stomach. An editorial in
last night's *Capital Times* had added to his aggravations.
The newspaper had lambasted Doyle's frequent use of the
John Doe process, citing two occasions he'd resorted to it
regarding the Berge slaying. Doyle was sensitive to criti-
cism, especially when it was directed by a liberal press that
had endorsed him for DA and whose support he might
need should he run for other elected positions.

The orange juice didn't relieve the ache in his gut.
During his five-minute stay in the coffee shop four people
asked him about the Berge case. Were charges forthcoming? Was Hoffman the prime suspect? Doyle served the
same shrug to each. People were fascinated by the case.
Rumor and speculation abounded. The newspapers fueled
this morbid appetite for details of the murder. Berge's
neighbors in Stoughton and Hoffman's neighbors on State
Street had been interviewed for opinion and gossip.

In fact, after two weeks detectives had gathered only
tatters of circumstantial evidence. Chuck Lulling prodded
and probed, yet the gaps in what the authorities knew
loomed large, and even Lulling admitted they didn't have
enough evidence to consider an arrest.

Doyle shuffled these bleak thoughts to the back of his
head.

Soon he caught a break. Mid-morning, he got a call
from Pat O'Donohue of O'Donohue and Associates, an

independent insurance agency. O'Donohue told Doyle that he'd been following the Berge murder case in the newspapers and that he had documents that related to Barbara Hoffman.

His offering of information was voluntary, O'Donohue asserted. He wanted his name kept out of the newspapers. Not that he had done anything wrong, he added quickly. The situation was unusual. He had been in the insurance business for over twenty-five years, and the situation was unique, he assured the DA.

Pat O'Donohue had reason to be careful. His conduct regarding Hoffman would be subject to review, and to some his actions might appear to be less than professional. He had to tell the authorities about his contact with Hoffman, but he had to minimize his hunger to find her an insurance policy. It was his own greed, and maybe his questionable ethics, that he did not care to discuss.

Doyle sensed O'Donohue's equivocation that morning. He had called to volunteer information, but he had details to hide.

Over the next week Doyle and Lulling pressured the insurance agent, threatening him with subpoena and scrutiny by the state's insurance review board, until O'Donohue finally loosened and divulged all of what he knew.

In November 1976 the Norman Anderson Agency of Madison had received a typewritten and unsigned request from Gerald Davies for a three-million-dollar life insurance policy. Anderson did not sell life insurance, and the lead was shuttled to O'Donohue and Associates, whose offices were down the hall. O'Donohue contacted the interested party. One week later Davies and his fiancée, Barbara Hoffman, appeared for an interview.

As a shipping clerk at the U.W. who'd earned $9,150 in 1975, Davies seemed an unlikely candidate for a three-million-dollar policy. But extenuating circumstances existed. Davies claimed a silent ownership of four Madison massage parlors. A small investment had reaped large dividends, and currently the return from the parlors exceeded his regular income by almost double. His monthly profit was listed as $1,500, a sum expected to increase over the next few years. Davies wanted a large policy in order to defer his tax burden and to build an immediate equity in his estate.

To O'Donohue it was an extraordinary request from what seemed a strange couple. More than once Davies consulted his fiancée when completing the application, and it was Barbara who determined that term, rather than whole, would be the appropriate type of life insurance for their needs. Davies assented and scratched answers onto the questionnaire.

An insurance policy for $3 million might be difficult to procure, he told the couple, because of Davies's unusual investment and the low figure on the tax statement. Nonetheless, he would shop around and do his best.

The fiancée smiled and replied that if he didn't they'd find someone else who would deliver.

The application was filed and the information forwarded to Equifacts, a firm that conducts research for the insurance industry. Equifacts compiled a brief biography of Gerald Davies. His family background was examined. Medical and employment records were checked. Bank transactions and credit ratings were investigated. The single element not researched and verified was his silent ownership of four massage parlors.

A copy of the Equifacts reports and Davies's application for $3 million of term life insurance was submitted to Guardsman's Life of Des Moines, Iowa. It refused the policy. Two other companies also rejected the request. O'Donohue had to convince someone that Davies's financial situation was unorthodox but credible. Not every company would be scared by the massage parlor income. O'Donohue calculated the commission on a three-million-dollar policy and must have decided it warranted his sincerest effort. He spent hours explaining to company vice presidents the massage parlor scene in Madison, explaining that these were legitimate business ventures that his client wished to be discreet about and that Davies's income tax statements were not an accurate reflection of his net worth or of his monthly cash flow. The request was shaved to $1 million and shipped to Guarantee Life of Hammond, Indiana. He reapplied to Guardsman's Life with this reduced figure. Both firms respectfully declined.

Crown Insurance of Buffalo, New York, was next offered the opportunity to underwrite. On February 8, 1977, O'Donohue mailed the application plus a check for $580, which represented the first month's premium. Crown returned the check uncashed. When O'Donohue moaned that all his work was for naught, a part-time agent in the office asked if he might intercede.

Jorge de Zamacona had moved to Madison from Mexico City years ago to pursue graduate studies at the U.W. Madison's liberal atmosphere fit de Zamacona's free spirit, and a variety of interests delayed his academic agenda. There were parties and impassioned discussions about politics and poetry. He saw no reason to rush toward a degree and a return to his homeland. De Zamacona lingered. He worked at a variety of jobs—research assistant, bartender, insurance salesman. He was resourceful, enterprising, with a great many connections. When he asked for a chance with the Davies application, O'Donohue consented.

A flurry of phone calls and inquiries went out from the office de Zamacona shared at O'Donohue and Associates. He contacted a company in Fort Worth, Texas. Transport Life was sent a request for a one-million-dollar policy, which it denied. When he reapplied for $750,000, Transport Life accepted.

Jerry Davies was informed that a policy had been obtained. The annual premium was $13,236.60.

On February 26, 1977, Davies and Barbara Hoffman met de Zamacona at his office and handed him a cashier's check for $6,618.30, one-half the annual payment, and took possession of the policy, which was back-dated to January 26, 1977, to save on a rate increase. The second premium installment was due on July 26, 1977, with a thirty-day grace period. The term life policy insured Davies for $750,000. His estate was named as beneficiary.

The impossible had been performed. De Zamacona had secured an insurance policy for a shipping clerk whose verifiable yearly income, $9,150, was less than the policy's yearly premium. As Davies had no other real assets, except a car and a modest savings account, it seemed absurd. Yet the policy was quite real. O'Donohue was astounded, and he would soon be chagrined. Within weeks of linking Davies and Transport, de Zamacona left town. He had tired of Madison and returned to his native Mexico City to be reunited with his family. O'Donohue doubted the timing was coincidental.

Transport Life paid the field agent the first year's premium as commission on its life insurance policies. The check for $6,618.30 was deposited by Transport Life, which then issued a payment in that exact amount to Jorge de Zamacona. He would receive the balance when the second payment was made. Legally de Zamacona was bound to divide the commission with Norman Anderson, who had received the original request from Davies, and with O'Donohue, whose agency employed him. Instead he had cashed the commission check and fled.

Two months later Transport Life received a request from Gerald Davies for a change of beneficiary form. The documents were sent and returned. On May 10, 1977, Davies officially amended his life insurance policy, designating Barbara Hoffman, his fiancée, as the sole beneficiary.

Though he had vanished from Madison, de Zamacona maintained contact with Davies and Hoffman. He intimated that his personal involvement had been essential in acquiring and continuing the policy with Transport Life. Therefore the second premium had to be paid through him.

On July 26th Davies and Hoffman drove to Chicago's O'Hare Airport. They pulled into the short-term parking area and walked through the heat, humidity, and jet exhaust to the airport's international wing. De Zamacona ambled through customs and met them in the lobby. He accepted a cashier's check for $6,618.30 and issued a receipt. From then on, he explained, the biannual payments could be sent directly to Ft. Worth, Texas. He thanked them, wished them luck on their eventual marriage, and boarded a departing flight for Mexico City.

A week later Barbara Hoffman got a note from Transport Life informing her that her second premium payment had been received.

— 28 —

The revelation of a $750,000 life insurance policy on Davies, owned by Barbara Hoffman, stunned Doyle and Lulling. Transport Life confirmed that the policy was active. Any charges brought against Ms. Hoffman concerning the Berge homicide would not affect the policy on Davies.

Jerry Davies was questioned about the insurance matter, and though he'd forgotten many details, his story matched the version presented by Pat O'Donohue.

Lulling asked if Davies wished police protection, and the shipping clerk stared, as if the detective's words were a foreign language.

"Protection from who?" he asked.

"From Barbara," answered Doyle.

Davies emitted a weird sound, something caught between a laugh and a sob. Lulling bluntly opined that Davies was in danger. Harry Berge, who had signed over his home and $34,000 in life insurance to Barbara, under an alias of Linda Millar, was now dead. Berge's life was a pittance compared to what Davies was worth.

The wire-rimmed glasses inches down his nose, Davies peered out from over the top of the lenses. A blob of shaving cream stuck to his ear behind his left sideburn. He was adamant about not wanting police protection and insistent that it was unnecessary.

Nonetheless Davies was placed under twenty-four-

hour surveillance. It was conducted without his knowledge or cooperation and with strict instructions for discre-
tion, for Lulling did not want to alarm or antagonize him.
Nothing eventful or extraordinary occurred. Davies spent
his time at work, at home, at Barbara's apartment, at Pizza
Hut. He received no visitors and called on no one other
than Barbara.

—— 29 ——

Because Lulling demanded that every resident of 638 State
Street be contacted, two cops made their third visit to the
building and grumbled about their tedious assignment. No
one yet interviewed had seen or heard anything out of the
ordinary on the night of December 22nd or 23rd. What
had been a hopeful avenue of investigation was becoming
hopelessly mundane as they crossed names off their list.
They had learned that Barbara Hoffman was a very private and solitary individual. Occasionally she exchanged
salutations in the hallway with a neighbor, but she never
lingered and conversed, and invitations to coffee and the
building Christmas party were politely declined. No one
who lived there had been in her apartment.

Her neighbor in apartment 305 was John Hunt, an
engineering student who earned his rent by serving as
building janitor. The cops were admitted to his tidy apartment on a frigid day in mid-January. Textbooks and mono-
graphs were stacked neatly on a desk. A Bible rested in
prominent display on a coffee table. Hunt was average in
height, with a slender figure and serious gray eyes.

He knew why he was being interviewed, and he knew
what he had to tell. It centered on the early morning of
December 23rd.

He woke at around 5:00 A.M. on December 23rd, as
was his regimen, and began the day with morning devotions. Seated on the couch, he read from the Bible. The
door downstairs, which opened to the outside, had a no-
ticeable squeak; it was loud, rusty, and he heard it. A few

seconds later he heard the slam of a car door or trunk. He turned, distracted, and looked out the window, which presented a general view of the parking lot below.

It was dark out. Still and cold. The lot was illumined by the spotlight on a telephone pole. Standing next to the door of a black car with a white top was Barbara Hoffman. Hunt resumed his reading of the Scriptures. The outside door squeaked again. He remembered thinking that he ought to rub the hinges with graphite. There was a jingle of keys, and Barbara reentered her apartment.

She exited again, for he heard the outside door. The automobile was started a short time after, and Hunt watched as it was backed toward the green Dumpster. Due to his angle of vision, a portion of the car and Barbara Hoffman were now obscured from view. Bible studies were resumed.

Within the hour Hunt's devotions were completed and he began his janitorial chores. He was removing cleaning fluids and a mop from a first-floor closet when Barbara walked down the steps lugging a wicker basket filled with dark clothing. She kept her head down and avoided eye contact. No words were exchanged, and she exited.

That was what happened the morning of December 23rd. The cops requestioned the salient aspects of his story. His description of the car matched the colors of Berge's Oldsmobile. They asked about illumination in the lot, and Hunt said the only source of light was a seventy-five-watt bulb. But he was certain of what he saw, regardless of the darkness and the early hour.

The cops asked if he'd be willing to tell a court what he had told them, and Hunt said yes.

—— 30 ——

Though Madison's newspapers reported the Berge investigation was at a "dead end," Al Mackey reasoned differently. The police might have been short on leads, yet their attention was focused in a single direction—on Barbara Hoffman.

Mackey didn't know the full extent of Barbara's involvement. It seemed she never told anyone all of anything. The favors she demanded—such as his driving Berge's car back from Park Ridge—indicated that she was in serious trouble. As a friend he told her to seek as good a defense counsel as she could afford to hire, for he feared her problems would exceed his expertise.

Barbara agreed. They made an appointment with Jack McManus.

Barbara had never heard of the attorney Mackey recommended, but he assured her that among peers McManus was regarded as one of the premier lawyers in the state. Because he was effective and efficient, because he did more civil than criminal work, McManus was not the most prominent attorney in town. That honor belonged to Don Eisenberg, who was their next choice should McManus refuse the case.

Jack McManus had a small face. It was wrinkled, leathery, and dotted with feisty eyes. He wore cowboy boots and a string tie. McManus admitted knowing a little about Barbara's predicament. It sounded like a difficult case, both to prosecute and to defend. Then the astute defense attorney got as blunt as a Hank Williams tune. He stared not at Mackey but at Barbara.

He expected her to be charged with first-degree murder, he said. For a case of such importance McManus commanded a retainer of $25,000, payable in advance.

Barbara did not blink. She said the money could be arranged.

McManus had one question before he accepted the case: who was Linda Millar?

Again Barbara showed no reaction. Her brown eyes held steady behind the tortoiseshell glasses. She didn't know anyone named Linda Millar, she said.

Al Mackey was puzzled by the cryptic exchange. With sincerity McManus wished Barbara luck and suggested she look elsewhere for legal representation. Mackey was stunned and sought an explanation. McManus refused to elaborate.

Barbara thanked McManus for his time, and she exited.

Rejected by McManus, Barbara Hoffman brought her plight to Don Eisenberg. He was a large man, 6'4", 200 pounds, who dressed in tailored silk suits, wore a Rolex on his wrist and diamonds on his fingers. He talked tough and fast and sprinkled his conversation with street jargon. His fiery nature bubbled not far beneath the surface of his year-round tan.

No one disputed Eisenberg's flamboyance and bombast. His efficacy and his ethics, however, were sometimes questioned. Depending on the source, Don Eisenberg was either the ace criminal lawyer in Madison, perhaps one of the best in the country, or merely a facile tongue and a huge ego who often failed to do his homework. A garish style, mercurial courtroom outbursts, and victories in two well-publicized trials had earned Eisenberg his notorious reputation.

In 1969 a Wisconsin Menominee Indian named Keith Deer was charged with the slaying of a white man. Deer pleaded self-defense, claiming the man had attacked him and attempted to crush him with a log. The hunk of timber was admitted as evidence for defense, and during his closing argument Eisenberg lifted the stump of wood and heaved it at the jury box. Startled jurors leaped as the log smashed at their feet, and the reality of Deer's fear was illustrated dramatically. The jury voted for acquittal.

In 1974 a University of Wisconsin professor, Dr. Marion Brown, was accused by the federal government of smuggling a quarter of a million dollars' worth of narcotics into the United States from Chile, where Dr. Brown was working on agrarian land use. The trial was held in New York City, and Brown was given no chance by New York observers, who presumed Eisenberg was a hayseed from the Midwest. The hayseed cross-examined ferociously. A government witness testified he had driven from Madison to Milwaukee to complete a drug deal with Dr. Brown. Eisenberg asked how long the trip took and was told four to five hours. Eisenberg hauled out a map and showed the jury that the distance was seventy-two miles and normally takes one-and-a-half hours. Someone was lying. Brown was acquitted on all charges.

These triumphs notwithstanding, Eisenberg did not always win. No defense attorney does. But, according to many courthouse observers, Eisenberg preferred to battle a case in court rather than pursue the plea bargain route, even if it meant arguing a weak defense. Perhaps faith in his verbal virtuosity and courtroom theatrics led him to assume greater risks and to lose cases that more conservative lawyers might have settled out of court.

Undertaking the defense of Barbara Hoffman promised enormous challenges and rewards. Like McManus, Eisenberg had been following the Berge investigation, and his sources predicted she'd be hit with murder one. Already the media had sensationalized the case. The courtroom drama would be intense, the publicity would be fantastic, and Eisenberg seemed to thrive in that kind of charged atmosphere. Press conferences, television interviews, trial pyrotechnics brought out his best. It was as if he relished the pressure as well as the publicity.

After a brief discussion Eisenberg agreed to defend Barbara Hoffman should charges be leveled against her. If he had known he was second choice, a bruised ego might have prevented him from accepting the case.

— 31 —

In early January the DA got a phone call from Charles Geisen, a junior partner in Madison's most renowned law firm—Eisenberg, Geisen, Ewers, and Hayes. Doyle's contact with Geisen had been limited. He knew the lawyer was young, aggressive, and represented Ken Curtis.

The conversation lasted barely five minutes. Geisen

wanted to bargain. He said a client had information that might aid the Berge homicide investigation and that for the proper consideration the client would come forward and tell what he knew. Specifically, Geisen said, the client would provide the name of the last person to see Harry Berge alive and the first to see him dead, the whereabouts of Berge's car between the murder and its discovery by police several days later, several possible motives for the murder, prior aborted conspiracies, and corroborating statements from other individuals.

Geisen sold the package hard. In return for the testimony he wanted the dismissal of a misdemeanor charge—unregistered possession of a firearm—against Ken Curtis. He wanted dismissal of gambling charges that had been brought against Adele Schultz and Leo Hahn, two of Sam Cerro's notorious associates. He also wanted a suspended sentence for Cerro on the cocaine bust last August.

The DA did not hesitate. Geisen's partner, Don Eisenberg, had taken Ms. Hoffman as a client. Any negotiations to benefit another client, for information that might incriminate Hoffman, constituted conflict of interest. As long as Sam Cerro and Ken Curtis and Barbara Hoffman were all represented by the same law firm, there could be no deal. Doyle thanked Geisen for his civic concern and hung up.

— 32 —

It was snowing, and the flakes tumbled thick and vigorous. Students hurried to class, their faces concealed by hoods, knit hats, and scarves, their coat collars laden with the white debris, their boots stomping through the accumulation, slick underfoot. They carted books and backpacks, slide rules and Styrofoam cups of coffee, and they swapped stories of Christmas vacation.

A woman in a green beret and orange earmuffs pedaled a single-speed Schwinn whose fat-tread tires bucked the curb onto the Library Mall. A Caribbean sun beamed from a poster in a travel agent's window. The rays didn't reach Madison.

Ice glazed the windowpanes of Barbara Hoffman's apartment. There was no reason to peer outside. What was out there loomed cold and forbidding. Earlier in the morning she had called her office and said she was sick.

If January 18th was like most other days, Barbara fixed herself a glass of juice and stirred in a tablespoon of vitamin C crystals. She was a sincere believer in vitamin and health supplements and regularly ingested a variety of these products. Her kitchen cupboard was stocked with vials of supplements.

On the kitchen table rested a mimeograph regarding breast implants and silicone injections. Techniques for breast enlargement were compared and contrasted. Barbara had contemplated treatment for years, and now that her employment supplied a comprehensive health insurance plan the old concern was revived. Her small breasts embarrassed her. Ken Curtis had teased that she had tits like a twelve-year-old boy.

A loud knock at the door startled her. The rap repeated, louder, authoritarian. Maybe it was the mailman with a book she had ordered. She answered the door.

Standing red-faced and grim were two police officers, one of them a woman. Their shoes were wet with snow.

"Are you Barbara Hoffman?" The question sounded formal and stupid.

"Yes."

"We have a warrant for your arrest."

The Miranda rights were read, slowly, carefully, and, yes, Barbara understood. They were charging her with the murder of Harry Berge.

The policewoman accompanied her to the bedroom. Barbara changed clothes. She asked if she could take her medication with her—a doctor's prescription for Valium—and was told yes. She asked if they had been following her for the past three weeks, and the cop said she wasn't familiar with the investigation. Had the phone been tapped? Barbara wanted to know. She got the same response.

The phone rang. It was Al Mackey. Barbara explained the situation, and he said he'd meet her downtown.

They led her down the back steps, their heels clicking on the terrazzo tile stairs where Harry Berge's body had thudded.

In the rear lot was a squad car. Barbara was driven to headquarters and arraigned for murder one.

PART II
Departures and Delays

— 1 —

On January 19th, the day after Hoffman's arrest, Sergeant Jerome Gartner was called by Lulling and asked to search the snowbank in the parking lot behind 638 State Street. Although the snow had been searched twice with no result, Lulling was convinced blood had stained the snowbank where Barbara left the body overnight.

Officers Arnold Malesack and Joe Rut accompanied Gartner to the scene. They sifted through the snow piled four feet high along the cyclone fence and next to the green Dumpster. After fifty minutes of diligent scraping Gartner spotted what looked like blood two-and-a-half to seven-and-a-half inches above the ground.

The crew took pictures of the discovery, took measurements to determine its precise location in reference to the rear door of 638 State Street, and collected ten bottles of the substance.

At the lab, when it had warmed up enough to liquefy, the substance was checked with a Hemastix. The positive reaction indicated blood. The evidence was labeled and packaged and sent to the state crime lab for more extensive review.

Within three weeks the state crime lab tested and evaluated the blood. It matched Harry Berge's blood type.

— 2 —

On a frigid January morning Barbara Hoffman was freed from custody upon posting a $15,000 cash bond. Her lawyer at the proceeding was Donald Eisenberg, and he smoothly handled the throng of reporters awaiting her release. Eisenberg, who had played football at Tulane, shielded the slender Hoffman with a shoulder and directed her through the mob like a veteran blocker. People pushed, jostled for a view. The pop of flashbulbs illuminated the hallway. Video cameras recorded the event for the evening news. Microphones were thrust at the accused, and questions were shouted. Hoffman appeared wan and fragile. She clutched the sleeve of her lawyer's suit, and he could feel the fear in the pressure of her fingers.

"We'll hold a press conference in fifteen minutes at my office," Eisenberg announced. He stiff-armed a path to the outside, where he and Barbara burrowed into the backseat of Al Mackey's waiting Cadillac.

After two days of incarceration, chewing Valiums to get her through, Barbara was not prepared for the onslaught of the media. Now she hid in Eisenberg's office, drinking coffee, prepared to duck behind the potted ferns if her privacy was invaded. The citations on his walls—the diplomas, awards, letters of appreciation and merit, a certificate signifying that Donald Eisenberg had argued before the United States Supreme Court, a photograph of a boyish, crew-cut Eisenberg chatting at a cocktail party with John and Jacqueline Kennedy, another posed with Justice William O. Douglas, a framed newspaper headline declaring an acquittal for Keith Deer—were impressive. The wet bar, the exercise bike in the corner, the mammoth oak desk in the middle of the room, cluttered with documents, yellow legal pads, and law books and flanked by a dwarf orange tree that rose from an earthenware jug, added to the lavish ambience. The blinds were shut. Barbara stood in her stockinged feet. The room seemed like a cave, the lamp on the desk a torch, and an observer in an adjoining office who caught Barbara in a moment of contemplation wondered if this place seemed a trap or a tunnel to safety.

Barbara stepped to the door, opened it a crack. Eisenberg's voice rose, stentorian above the noise of the media

throng. Coffee and doughnuts were being served. Eisenberg apologized for the fact that Barbara would not be
answering their questions today, but the trauma of impris-
onment on bogus charges had disoriented and fatigued
her. In a couple of days, he promised, she would permit
interviews.

Eisenberg sounded confident. He joked with the reporters, referred to them by name. The diamonds and gold
that studded his fingers flashed in the TV camera's klieg
light as he gesticulated. Eisenberg derided the DA, contended the accusations were vague and circumstantial, and
predicted the indictment would be dismissed for lack of
evidence. Al Mackey, he pointed out, would assist the
defense.

At that comment the print reporters snickered. They
knew there was room for only one lawyer at a defense
table occupied by Donald Eisenberg.

Soon the coffee urn was empty, the doughnuts eaten,
and the story covered. The party dispersed.

The media attention disconcerted Mackey, and he
looked exhausted by the commotion. Eisenberg seemed
refreshed. Unabashedly he rated his performance as excellent. He snapped the blinds open, tossed off his jacket.
There were legalities to specify and settle. Eisenberg was
a late addition to the case, and there were things he needed
to understand. There were also practicalities Barbara
needed to accept.

In taking Hoffman as a client Eisenberg risked a grave
ethical consideration—conflict of interest. He was legal
counsel to Sam Cerro. One of his junior partners, Charles
Geisen, was legal counsel to Ken Curtis. Cerro and Curtis
owned Jan's Health Spa and other parlors, and the Eisenberg firm had handled the articles of incorporation for
those enterprises. Geisen was listed as acting attorney for
most of those businesses and registered as the agent with
the secretary of state's office.

Furthermore, the law firm had negotiated other business and real estate transactions for Curtis and Cerro.
Barbara Hoffman's employment by these men and her

statement to Davies that she thought the Berge death was related to the massage parlors would have caused Eisenberg serious reflection. Geisen's contact with Doyle one week earlier concerning a possible deal—information provided by Curtis and unnamed others detrimental to Hoffman in exchange for a plea bargain arrangement for Sam Cerro—presented Eisenberg with a predicament. Could the law firm represent Cerro's interests and Hoffman's interests without a conflict?

Courthouse observers familiar with the case speculated about Eisenberg's dilemma. Dropping Cerro as a client would resolve the situation, but the connections with Cerro were deep and lucrative. Declining the Hoffman case would be a great sacrifice. The media coverage promised to be extensive, and it was accepted opinion that Eisenberg basked in the presence of a microphone and a camera lens. His reputation could only be enhanced, and a cursory glance at the complaint against Hoffman would give him confidence he could win. The case was sad, sordid, and sensational. Its components—sex, money, murder—guaranteed prurient interest, regular slots on the six and ten o'clock news, front-page articles, courtroom sketches, a huge gallery, quotes, and press conferences. Many observers felt a victory might catapult him to national prominence and the recognition he thought his abilities deserved. He needed Cerro, he wanted Hoffman, and he decided to keep them both.

To alleviate any concern about a possible conflict, Eisenberg asked Barbara to sign an affidavit affirming her knowledge of the unique circumstances and stating her wishes to retain Eisenberg as her attorney.

Without looking to Mackey for advice, Barbara agreed to sign the necessary papers if it would assure her of Eisenberg's representation. She knew Al Mackey didn't have the stuff to save her. Maybe Don Eisenberg did.

—— 3 ——

For days following Hoffman's arrest Madison's newspapers and television sensationalized the story. "Beneath City's Tranquillity Lies Sleazy Underside" read headlines in the *Capital Times*. The shock and outrage of the community was recorded. Conservatives and religious fundamentalists used the murder charge as an example of the decadence and corruption the massage parlor atmosphere fostered. Ken Curtis and associates incurred a new wave of intense scrutiny and public demands for censure.

In Stoughton, where Harry Berge had resided for the final ten years of his life, the reaction was disbelief. Neighbors emphasized Berge's kindness, his extreme shyness, his lonely routine. Many refused to accept that he and Hoffman had been intimately involved and dismissed talk of his visiting massage parlors.

"If he was involved in that sort of thing, he was doped," remarked an acquaintance.

Others viewed the situation cynically, commenting that if Harry Berge had as intimate a knowledge of the massage parlor world as the newspapers reported, then anyone could be leading a double life. Everyone had taken Berge for as straight and naive as he'd appeared.

Barbara Hoffman was portrayed as a mysterious vixen. No one at work knew much about her. She was competent, quiet, aloof. Residents of 638 State Street were quoted about the number of men who visited her apartment, the odd hours of their comings and goings. Rumors circulated about her sexual prowess and audacity. A couple of female counselors, as the women were referred to at Jan's Health Spa, consented to be interviewed and confirmed that "Barbie" was known as the queen of the parlors. Men adored her touch. She had an aptitude for handling kinky customers. A special "quiet" room had been constructed at Jan's so that the pleasure of pain could be administered without alarming the more traditional patrons, and Barbara was the room's most frequent user.

She had boasted that she earned over $23,000 a year working three days a week at Jan's. Yet no one really knew Barbara Hoffman. She had no close friends. She existed in shadow, permitting only an oblique glimpse. Despite thousands of words, the print and electronic media could not define her, and she coolly deflected all inquiry and examination.

— 4 —

The adversity encountered in the past month, the anxiety regarding the murder charge, had, from Davies's point of view, pushed Davies and Barbara closer together, closer than ever before. A preliminary hearing was scheduled for February 16th, and the immediate goal was to survive the next few weeks intact, until things were cleared and charges dismissed, Jerry Davies told Dr. Paul Slavik at the Group Health Cooperative. He consulted the physician because of his anxiety and stress, and Dr. Slavik gave him a prescription for Valium.

Riding out the turmoil was not easy, and Davies's optimism ebbed. Nights were especially difficult. Visions of December 23rd ambushed his sleep. Moments of that convoluted evening shot into his head, pierced his consciousness like arrows. Some nights he could almost feel his brain bleed thoughts, a scramble of images leaking out of his head and onto the pillow. He saw Barbara scooping clumps of snow over the corpse with her hands; he felt the bedsheets that had enshrouded Harry Berge, creased and as stiff as sandpaper; he saw the dull light of the dashboard on the corpse's frozen, stubby toes.

Some nights he lay awake pondering Barbara's predicament. The machinery of circumstance had run amok. It would grind him and Barbara, crush their hopes like tiny peppercorns, and Barbara would be assigned a jury of her peers.

"I'm anxious like I never was before," Davies told the

doctor, during a second visit. Worry had written its signature. The crinkled mat of Davies's forehead, the pensive eyes, the cheeks grown gaunt were indication enough that things were not right.

The physician renewed the prescription for Valium that he had issued one week earlier. He didn't increase the dosage—two-milligram tablets to be taken as needed—but he upped the quantity from ten to thirty pills. Davies needed to relax.

It was neither a lie nor a self-deception that his relationship with Barbara had improved. She had taken an indefinite leave of absence from EDS Federal. Davies used accumulated sick days to take time off from work. From New Year's Day through the preliminary hearing in mid-February they spent more time together than in the prior six months combined.

— 5 —

Less than two weeks after Barbara Hoffman was released on $15,000 bail, the twenty-four-hour protective surveillance on Jerry Davies was suspended. The decision infuriated Chuck Lulling.

The state's case against Barbara Hoffman, Lulling reasoned, was anchored on the testimony of a timorous Davies. His statements verified that Barbara said there had been a body in her apartment, established its location in the parking lot, and detailed its journey out to Tomahawk Ridge. Davies also confirmed Hoffman's elaborate efforts at concealment of the deed and at erasing their connection to the body. Her subterfuge with the invention of Linda Millar was bolstered by his words. His rendering of the history of their love affair cast serious suspicion on Hoffman's character, and the insurance policies added an invidious motivation for her involvement with both him and Berge. Like a skillful hunter, Hoffman had set Berge up, and Davies was her next prey.

Without Davies, however, the charges withered from solid to circumstantial. Anyone as intelligent as Hoffman would be cognizant of Davies's value to the prosecution. What he remembered or forgot or misconstrued would make a major difference in how the case was presented and judged.

The insurance policy blended an unsavory spice into the stew. It provided an incentive to do more than merely warp Davies's recollection of the past. More than $13,000 had already been invested in the shipping clerk from Spring Green. Because it was term life insurance rather than whole, the money was irretrievable unless Davies perished. Then Hoffman would reap a windfall. The temptation to eliminate a damaging witness and to secure a bundle of insurance bucks with the same lethal maneuver had to tantalize Barbara's imagination. Manipulation of Davies's emotions and memory was safer but not certain; killing guaranteed a double reward.

If nothing else, the idea merited consideration. It had to have crossed her mind. Lulling's experience indicated that sinister notions beheld a life unto themselves and, if pushed and prodded around the psyche long enough, gathered an impetus and achieved an actuality that was played through to its tragic conclusion. Furthermore, the Transport Life policy was due for renewal January 26th, and a one-month grace period was allowed. Barbara had to produce $6,168.30 or forfeit the policy—or see to it that Davies died.

A concerned Lulling enlisted Jim Doyle's support for continued protective surveillance. The DA agreed that Davies's blind devotion to Hoffman made him vulnerable. Together they campaigned for a resumption of full-time surveillance.

Their efforts were quickly stifled. Economic constraints and budgetary cutbacks were cited as the reasons their appeal was denied. The city could not afford to have three officers sit and guard a man who claimed he was not in danger.

Angered by the decision, Lulling assumed a personal

vigil over Davies. On frigid winter nights he huddled in his car, puffing on his cherrywood pipe, the car heater keeping the frostbite from his toes, and waited for Davies to exit 638 State Street and drive home. When Davies went to bed, Lulling stuck a peanut shell under the rear tire of the Chevy, which the detective checked every morning on his ride to work. If Davies went out, Lulling knew about it.

The veteran detective's intense involvement stemmed from a sense of obligation to his job, not from any special affinity for Davies. Jerry Davies was a fool for dating Hoffman in the aftermath of the Berge homicide, and Lulling had told him exactly that. Nonetheless, Davies was a fool who had to repeat his story to a judge and a jury.

— 6 —

During Barbara's tenure as a masseuse at Jan's one of the part-time managers was a genteel fellow named Bruce Dalby. Tall, blond, conspicuously handsome, Dalby looked as if a California beach, not a sleazy massage parlor, would constitute his natural habitat. He had ink-blue eyes and an insouciant smile, wore oxford shirts and tennis shoes. He was a friend of Ken Curtis's; however, the snarl and the bulging muscles that seemed a requisite of Curtis's buddies were conspicuously absent in Bruce Dalby. Weightlifting and fisticuffs were of no concern. His interests were more esoteric—the contrasting qualities of Mexican, Hawaiian, and Jamaican pot, the plot twists of a Dickens novel, the proper topspin on his forehand volley.

Though thirty years old, Bruce Dalby still lived with his parents in Nakoma, an exclusive area that edged the University of Wisconsin Arboretum on the city's west side. His parents' aristocratic pretensions nauseated him. Yet he accepted the spoils of their wealth—the country club memberships, the Mercedes for graduation from college. Dalby respectfully disrespected his family. His drug use was kept discreet. He possessed the remarkable ability to sit at a family dinner zonked on hashish and not slurp the French onion soup, or drip the hollandaise onto his shirt, or gobble the mocha torte in a sugar-craving frenzy.

Whenever his parents were out of town, Bruce Dalby threw bawdy celebrations. On a Saturday in July 1975 Dalby hosted an anniversary fete for his parents, who were five thousand miles away on a European vacation. Barbara Hoffman was working at Jan's that night, and she and Liza drove to Nakoma after their shift.

Still buzzing from the narcotics consumed during work, Barbara and Liza meandered through the crowd. The crumbs of an anniversary cake lay on a marble tabletop. Ice cream melted in china bowls. In the kitchen they joined a small group that was snorting coke. Wine, Quaaludes, and cocaine mixed fine. Liza vanished among the revelers. Barbara roamed the house.

Behind the leaded-glass doors of a den she spied Ken Curtis, or rather his back, which was broad and unmistakable in a tight-fitting T-shirt. His legs, exposed by gym shorts, were muscular but skinny compared to his ponderous upper body. Curtis was surrounded by a clique who treated him with deference, listening carefully when he talked, directing comments for his approval.

The conversation spun aimlessly. Behind damask curtains a chubby woman was performing fellatio on a fellow whose face was hidden. The party had slowed. People were either fatigued or catching their breath for the next outburst.

Ken Curtis called Barbara over. He whispered to her, watched the curiosity in the freckles of her delicate face as she contemplated his offer. She nodded.

The windshield of the Lincoln Continental bent the moon and refracted its creamy rays across the dashboard, across the patch of upholstery where Curtis shimmied out of his gym shorts. The scent of the pine trees drifted through the windows. Talk seemed superfluous, so nothing was said. Barbara kissed at him playfully, and he dodged her. He offered his neck, his cheek, his chin, but denied her his lips. She kissed the thick expanse of his chest, felt the strength and tightness of his shoulders and back. He guided her descent into the beam of moonlight that washed his belly and hips.

Her fingers coaxed Curtis rigid. Barbara took his cock to her lips, slid it against the roof of her mouth. She lapped at the shaft with brisk rushes of her tongue as if it were a brush slapping paint on canvas.

Curtis muttered approvingly, and his prick swelled fuller in appreciation of her art. He lifted the hair out of her face and watched as she took him deep into her mouth. In the leap of passion she had neglected to remove her glasses, and the lenses crushed into a jungle of pubic hair. His callused hands rubbed her shoulders as she raked her teeth gently along the length of his prick.

Her mouth pumped up and down, as if she were chasing something, madly sucking his cock. The muscles of his body contracted. The heat poured off his skin. Her teeth and tongue took turns teasing. The patch of moonlight spilled, salty and sticky and white.

Hoffman and Curtis became lovers, sort of. There was little romance involved. When Curtis desired her company, which usually meant her sexual favors, he called. They might spend an hour together in the afternoon or in the evening. Should Curtis decide he wanted to stay the night in her apartment, Barbara willingly complied and arranged for Matt Bradley to stay in a motel room. Their relationship was fierce, fiery, and carnal. One thing it did not include, however, was kissing. Curtis never pressed his lips to Barbara's; a kiss was something he would not share. No matter how Barbara pleaded, he withheld this simple act of affection.

— 7 —

On February 16th a preliminary hearing was held before Dane County Court judge William Byrne.

Senior Assistant DA John Burr, aided by Chris Spencer, handled the prosecution. Doyle had chosen Burr to argue the case for the state because of his experience and thoroughness. He had been a prosecutor for a dozen years. He was diligent and able; he did his homework carefully and never entered court unprepared. In a case largely based on circumstantial evidence these qualities would prove invaluable. Furthermore, Burr's solid and reasoned style would show a sharp contrast to Eisenberg's theatrics. Rather than fluster Burr's even temperament, Eisenberg's belligerent demeanor would goad the assistant DA's competitive juices. Burr would not be intimidated or cowed inside a courtroom, or so Jim Doyle predicted.

The problem with giving the case to his senior assistant was that a deep animosity existed between Burr and Chuck Lulling. The two men had worked together in the past and had clashed. Both toted sizable egos and long memories, and they avoided contact. Like stubborn children, Burr and Lulling did not speak directly to one another. Spencer or Doyle acted as intermediary in coordinating the investigative and legal aspects of the case.

Except for the crush of media attention—the TV cameras and the flashbulbs and the reporters barking questions in the hallway—the prelim hearing was routine. A reticent Jerry Davies plodded through the events of the night of December 23rd and the morning of December 24th. His answers to Burr's questions were short. His tone was clipped, fractured. He kept poking at the bridge of his glasses, his brown eyes downcast, fighting to avoid the unrelenting gaze of his fiancée. The tale did not vary from what he had confessed to Lulling on Christmas Day. Yet Davies's appearance and attitude worried the prosecution. His resistance was ebbing. He was going through the motions, obsessed by the consequences.

Other witnesses testified regarding Berge's change of beneficiary on his life insurance plans—naming Linda Millar the beneficiary—and his putting Linda Millar's name on the deed of the house. Evidence was presented to demonstrate that Linda Millar and Barbara Hoffman were one and the same person.

Pathologist Billy Bauman, who had conducted the autopsy, reported that Harry Berge had died from five blows to the head and neck area. Aspirated vomitus may have also contributed to the death.

Donald Eisenberg argued several motions for dismissal, and all were rejected.

The inquiry concluded with Judge Byrne's ruling that probable cause had been proven. Barbara Hoffman was ordered to stand trial on charges of first-degree murder.

— 8 —

The pressures of loyalty and conscience battered Jerry Davies. He was tossed like a sailless skiff adrift in Lake Mendota's choppy waters on a gusty spring day. When the thought occurred that he might capsize, he rushed to Dr. Paul Slavik for a refill of the Valium prescription.

In an effort at stability Davies called an old friend. Chuck Richardson was a boyhood chum who had married and settled in Madison. He and Davies had maintained infrequent contact. They drove for an hour or two one winter afternoon, Davies's Chevy crunching the salt-strewn streets, a U.W. Badgers basketball game on the radio, and they reminisced about their youth in Spring Green. They swapped stories about BB gun battles in the rows of feed corn; about their first taste of beer—Huber—brewed in nearby Monroe; about their seasons of high school football. Jerry had been a flat-footed defensive back and Chuck a roly-poly lineman.

The present was overwhelming, and the past—fixed, immutable, safe—offered a soothing retreat. The recollections ameliorated Davies's upset. He hinted to Richardson of his current troubles but shied away from a frank discussion. He seemed satisfied to talk of things vaguely, to start a sentence and let it trail off into silence. Richardson did not press. He listened, but did not probe. Some things were impossible to talk about.

Chuck Richardson and his wife had read of the tragic affair in the newspapers and were stunned by their friend's connection to Hoffman and the massage parlors.

A person as shy around women as Jerry Davies entering a massage parlor was unimaginable, commented Chuck's wife. Davies was so ill at ease that in restaurants he stuttered when he gave the waitress his order.

Richardson concurred. Not once could he remember his buddy attending a dance or going out on a date. Davies had told him he was just too bashful to meet women. Now Jerry mentioned their marriage plans if Barbara was acquitted.

The Chevy pulled into the Richardson driveway. Chuck hunted for a sagacious word to impart. He couldn't find anything to utter except "good luck" and an invitation to visit again. Davies smiled and drove away.

—— 9 ——

The premium payment on the Transport Life policy was due, and Barbara was in a dither. De Zamacona's final instructions before he'd vanished back to Mexico were to send a check directly to the home office in Texas to keep the policy active. But Barbara did not have $6,618.30. If she didn't raise the necessary cash, Davies's monetary value plummeted from $750,000 to the paltry $20,000 in insurance he owned prior to their meeting, which rose only slightly, to $35,000, in case of accidental death. Furthermore, the money already invested would be lost. She scrutinized the policy and solicited Al Mackey's advice.

She brought him the Transport Life policy. He rummaged his pockets for bifocals, slid the frames onto his nose, and after a half hour of study his announcement was unequivocal: call the company, ask if they will refund the premiums, and cancel the policy.

Barbara didn't like the counsel, but she didn't see another way out. She instructed him to act as her attorney and proceed.

On February 24th Mackey phoned Dave Wallace, director of claims for Transport Life, and inquired if the company knew of the charges against Barbara Hoffman.

Rumors had circulated, Wallace said.

Mackey explained the situation and wondered what effect it would have on the policy.

No effect, said Wallace, unless Davies made a written request that his life no longer be insured in favor of Ms. Hoffman. Only then would action to cancel the policy be pursued.

Did this imply that the policy could be rescinded and a refund granted? Mackey questioned.

The insurance executive explained that a full refund was not possible. The cost of underwriting had been incurred, records had been set up, commissions had been paid, and Davies had received a full year of coverage. Wallace said that Transport Life would remit $2,000, provided that the policy was in its office by February 27th. Mackey agreed.

The compromise did not please Barbara. She presented the problem to Don Eisenberg.

A clerk in the firm studied the policy. In his opinion it contained little investment value, for term life was designed as life insurance protection and not for an investment return. Furthermore, it was questionable whether the beneficiary of the policy could collect while under indictment for murder.

On February 27th Eisenberg called Wallace. Under a persistent cross-examination the claims director confirmed that these points were probably true. Wallace also told Eisenberg of the negotiations with Al Mackey.

Eisenberg told Barbara that his strong recommendation was to relinquish the policy. When she protested, he stressed that the policy could be damaging to her in court and that there were some obstacles that not even his immense talents could overcome.

Barbara reluctantly agreed to heed Eisenberg's advice. Eisenberg called Wallace later the same day and said the $2,000 refund for forfeiture of the policy was acceptable, but the deadline was too tight. Wallace extended it by a few days.

One of the fine points Barbara's lawyers had overlooked, or perhaps considered of no importance, was a clause that explained that in the event of a suicide the policy was void and the premiums refundable in full.

Jerry Davies had been convinced of his responsibility for the third installment, and he attempted to raise the staggering sum of more than $6,000. On February 27th he sold a Konica camera to a used-merchandise shop for $350. A few safe stocks, purchased years ago, were cashed. Fifteen hundred dollars was borrowed against three life insurance policies he owned through work. When the loan was procured, Davies also asked the agent, Phil Sprecher, for a change of beneficiary and ownership form. He wanted to make a change in these insurance policies.

Sprecher had been acquainted with Davies for over a dozen years, and he asked for an explanation. Davies replied that he was unofficially engaged to Barbara Hoffman and wanted to assign her the policies. Sprecher advised against it. Twenty-two years Davies's senior, he spoke paternalistically and cautioned the young man to wait until after the wedding before altering the legalities of his insurance. There was no need for haste.

Davies took the necessary forms home and promised to sleep on the change.

On March 2nd Dave Wallace received a parcel from Eisenberg that contained the Transport Life policy on Jerry Davies. Hoffman was forfeiting the policy. Two days later, however, Wallace received a personal check from Barbara Hoffman for $6,618.30, the premium payment on the surrendered policy. A confused Wallace immediately phoned Eisenberg, who was startled by news of the payment. The lawyer apologized for the mix-up. He promptly called his client.

When Barbara entered his office that afternoon, Don Eisenberg bristled. In a tirade, he said he demanded trust from his clients; he demanded honesty. Didn't she understand the situation? Without his courtroom acrobatics, without his strategic defense and magnificent oratory, she would spend, at an absolute minimum, the next eleven years and four months of her life in a cinder-block cell at the Taycheedah Correctional Institute for Women. The bullshit had to cease. She had to get her head together, or her ass was going to sit in cold storage for a long, long time. And if she didn't care, if she kept trying to hinder her own case, she could find a new lawyer. He despised losing and was not about to be defeated by the asinine antics of his own client.

Barbara was terrorized by the harangue. Tears spilled from behind the tortoiseshell glasses. What she could not tell Eisenberg, what she could not explain for herself, was why she had written a check to Transport Life for $6,618.30 when the balance in her bank account was $14.58.

A stop-payment order was issued for the check to Transport Life, which would have bounced anyway, and the deal negotiated with Wallace was completed when Eisenberg received a check for $2,000 and a notification that the policy was forfeit.

Davies, meanwhile, proceeded with the changes in his Central Life Assurance plans.

Davies mailed the proper forms to Phil Sprecher on March 6th. Two days later he phoned to be certain the paperwork had been done. The next day Sprecher got a note from Davies requesting confidentiality regarding these transactions due to the adverse publicity Barbara had unjustly been subjected to by the media. To alleviate Sprecher's concern, Davies included the following statement.

I have, of my own free will, as an act of love, trust, and affection, without any influence from Barbara Hoffman or from any other individual, made the

changes in ownership and beneficiary clauses of my
insurance policies with Central Life Assurance Company.

The statement was dated March 7th and signed by
Gerald Davies.

Central Life adjusted the policies according to Davies's
request.

—— 10 ——

It was early afternoon before the February sun finally
broke through a sky the color of ice. Winter's gray fell
away in pieces and revealed an expanse of deep blue
whose texture hinted at transition and whispered of an
early spring. Snow melted flake by flake in a slow, incessant dripping.

Jerry Davies steered the back roads to Spring Green,
a circuitous and hilly route, traveling past dairy farms,
past homesteads with homespun sobriquets. "Oleo Acres,
One of the Cheaper Spreads," read a sign in a front yard.
Barbara Hoffman stared out the passenger window at a
countryside composed of whites, beiges, browns, austere
and angular and enlivened by the sun. Jerry drove up and
down the valley roads, smiling like a puppy at the thought
of introducing her to his mother; yet, at the same moment,
in the happy profile, there was a twitch of reservation, as
if he was afraid to expose his origins because they might
be found lacking.

It is a safe guess that Barbara neither loved nor
loathed Davies. Those emotions require time and energy,
commodities she didn't squander on him. He was chosen
for a reason. She grasped where Davies was malleable and
sensed where he might snap. His psychological profile was
similar to Harry Berge's, and perhaps Barbara perceived
him as a younger edition of Berge—lonely and timid, fear-
ful of women and mystified by their subtle powers, desperate for contact, petrified by contact.

The trip to Spring Green with Davies might have satisfied a perverse interest Hoffman had in other people's pasts. More than a couple of times she drove with Harry Berge to his home in Stoughton. More likely her consent to meet Davies's mother was an effort to placate and manipulate the man whose testimony could decide her fate.

Visiting Davies's home that afternoon must have provoked thoughts of her own upbringing in Park Ridge. Whereas the Davies household was mired in rural poverty, the Hoffman household was modest and ordinary, proper and ambitious. Her father was an engineer, her mother a school secretary. All three of their children had attended college. The Hoffmans were suburban and solidly middle-class. But something in this happy family scene must have disturbed Barbara. Perhaps, like many children of her generation, she felt her parents' life reeked of stagnation and phoniness. Maybe she felt that the opportunities and aspirations that had been foisted on her led to a slow and certain suffocation. Maybe it was too easy. Maybe when there is nothing to want for, there is also nothing to want. Barbara drifted away, and once she enrolled in college she was gone forever. She returned once a year, at Christmas, because her parents insisted on the ritual. She granted them this one shallow formality.

For dinner that afternoon Ruth Davies served a tuna noodle casserole. She was impressed by Jerry's fiancée. The girl was quiet but pretty, prettier than she had expected Jerry would find. Ruth didn't know about Barbara's arrest. Barbara smiled obligingly when Ruth gave her a tour of the humble home. Without Ruth's commentary the tour would have taken a minute or two, no longer. The Davies home formed a stark contrast to the suburban luxury in which Barbara had been reared. It was the smallest, shabbiest dwelling in Spring Green.

The living space was cramped and dilapidated, constructed with a variety of materials—cinder block and barn board, mostly; five tiny rooms and a pantry, and in certain spots the window jamb was no longer flush with the wall, and plastic had been stapled over the openings to defend against the elements. Barbara's house in Park Ridge had closets bigger than the bedroom that had serviced the three Davies boys, replete with a hole in the floorboards that gave sight to the earth beneath.

The bathroom had been added when Jerry was three, Ruth said.

Whether out of shame or weariness or because he was ready to depart, Jerry intervened and declared it was time for them to return to Madison. Perhaps Barbara's boredom had become palpable. Maybe his mother's desperate craving for companionship had broken through. He fetched their parkas, and abruptly they left.

Ruth Davies stood at the door, oblivious to the cold, thin and erect in her apron, fingers knotted around her teacup. She watched the taillights jitter as her son's Chevy bucked the railroad tracks. One of the lights winked as the car joined the country road, and then the lights dwindled into twin embers and were extinguished by the night.

— 11 —

It was March 27th, Easter Monday. Anita Clark drank her morning coffee and checked the day's schedule. A verdict was due in the Sam Cerro drug trial, and her sources predicted "guilty." Cerro had been charged with purchasing $72,000 worth of cocaine from undercover cops. Her errands included a couple of interviews, and as she reviewed the court calendar she noticed that the Hoffman arraignment was scheduled for April 7th, less than two weeks away. Anita Clark was the best crime reporter in Madison, and she'd been assigned to the Hoffman trial.

Someone from the mailroom, eyes puffy with a hangover, strolled over to her desk with an envelope. It came an hour ago, he complained, as if the letter and not yesterday's beer were the source of his headache.

The letter was postmarked Saturday, March 25th, from Madison, and had no return address. Anita opened it carefully. The missive was handwritten in blue ink, on unlined paper, and the scrawl rose as it traveled the paper from left to right. There was no salutation. She read slowly:

> I want to write these letters because I want to set the record straight. I was scared, I was jealous, Barb is innocent and I wrecked her life. All those stories I told about Barb are false.
>
> She never had anything to do with a body at all. She never did. I went crazy, I was so scared. The police scared me. I was crazy and I didn't know what I was saying.
>
> Then I had to keep telling the same story or they would charge me with a crime. Now they did it to Barb instead and I don't know what to do anymore except to tell the truth. I'm not crazy anymore and I'm not scared. I want to tell the truth, I'm not afraid to go to jail. Barb never had anything to do with a body at all. I swear it and they can do what they want to me.
>
> Sincerely,
> Gerald Thomas Davies

Anita Clark was stunned. A desperation leaked from the letter. She reread it. Desperation and futility and resignation; Jerry Davies was exonerating Barbara Hoffman and implicating himself for the Berge murder. For a reason she could not explain Clark had not a doubt about the letter's authenticity. She picked up the phone and called the district attorney.

Forty minutes later Clark and Doyle and John Burr buzzed over the letter like bewildered bees. They were cognizant that Davies had been dating Hoffman despite their warnings. When February 26th had passed and the thirty-day grace period on the Transport Life policy had expired, Doyle had quit fearing for Davies's physical welfare. Since the initial interrogation by Lulling, however, it had been a constant worry that the fragile shipping clerk might recant. His testimony, in John Doe hearings and at

the prelim, was firm and unequivocal. But the arraignment was a mere eleven days away, and the impending
reality of a court trial, the impending reality of his fiancée's serving a possible life sentence in jail, had apparently
eroded his fortitude. Undoubtedly Barbara had exerted
pressures subtle and severe. Panic was what they decided
the letter was about—panic, perhaps coercion.

Chris Spencer knocked on the DA's door, waving an
envelope he'd just received in the post. The letter to the
assistant prosecutor was identical in every syllable to the
one Anita Clark had received. It was not a photocopy but
a second longhand copy.

The prosecutors speculated about the implications of
the letters and the appropriate response. They considered
contacting Davies immediately. But Davies was fragile.
They did not want to risk antagonizing him and losing his
cooperation, so they opted to wait.

Let matters rest for a day or three, Doyle decided. In
the meantime they needed to devise a strategy to counter
Barbara's influence. Davies's testimony already on record
could not be erased. But they needed him solid. With him,
their case was precarious. Without him, it was lost.

—— 12 ——

The bathroom ceiling fan whirred noisily, and the metallic
prattle echoed through Jerry Davies's apartment at 2305
South Park Street. The place seemed abandoned. The
drapes were open, permitting a peek at a gray afternoon,
at a clump of winter grass, at a quartet of evergreen trees,
and beyond the evergreens the mud-streaked macadam of
a motel parking lot.

It was Monday, March 27th. Meticulously arranged
on the dining room table were three grocery bingo cards
from Kohl's and a collection of corresponding numbers on
cutout paper squares. Jerry Davies was one coupon shy of
winning a cartful of groceries.

The kitchen was sparse and neat. A trio of wooden bowls rested in the sink, water and a spoon in each. An ice cream scoop lay on the counter. The icebox was as bare as the apartment, holding only a can of soda, a cellophane package of sliced bologna, and a stick of margarine, with a half gallon of Schoep's butter brickle in the freezer. The thermostat was pushed to a clammy seventy-nine degrees. The air conditioner fan hummed faintly in the living room.

The bedroom smelled of air freshener and dirty socks. The walls were pale blue and empty, except for a University of Wisconsin hockey schedule taped above the dresser and a newspaper photograph of Barbara Hoffman pasted next to the bed. The monocle of a portable television set stared from a TV stand. A crescent of tin foil arced from the antenna.

The place was in perfect order, as if someone were readying to move out or had just moved in. The stillness was broken by the dissonance of the bathroom fan, which was unceasing. Its pitch altered, from sibilant to shrill to choppy, a sound like the rotary blades of a helicopter—whap, whap, whap.

The noise did not disturb Jerry Davies, who lay in the bathtub in six inches of tepid water. The heels of his feet were propped on the porcelain next to the faucet valves. His shoulders slumped at the back of the tub. His head was relaxed, leaning back against the dull blue wall tiles, and tilted, so that if it were not for the ceiling and roof above, he would have been gazing at the heavens. Davies's hands were folded and held his penis. Where the skin dipped below the water it was splotched white and wrinkled. Where the fingers poked above, the tips were shaded purple. The toes too exhibited an edging of purple, and the chrome tap handles mordantly mirrored the discoloration. Davies's mouth showed lividity. A purplish tint rimmed the nostrils. His guileless brown eyes were open. Death had given him what life had refused—an appearance of serenity.

Davies's body was discovered on the afternoon of March 27th.

The tenant who lived above Davies's apartment had been annoyed by the clattering of the bathroom fan. He reported the irritating noise to the maintenance man. The maintenance man and the resident manager entered the premises at 3:20 P.M., expecting to slap a wall switch and exit. Instead they shuddered at the sight of a corpse.

Steve Urso was one of the first officers on the scene. Because he was Chuck Lulling's nephew, he immediately realized the significance of Davies's death and called his uncle and the DA with the news.

Rather than gruesome, Urso thought the setting oddly surreal. The fan gurgled stridently. The bathroom appeared clean, peaceful, with Davies in a state of contented repose. Rigor mortis had set in, and Davies's skin looked shiny in the Kohler tub, like a piece of wax fruit on a platter. Discoloration blotted the appendages, and what was underwater was tinted white. A melancholy smile seemed pressed on the livid lips. A trace of spittle had hardened at the corner of the mouth. The cocked head pondered heaven, and in what struck Urso as a poetic counterpoint, blunt fingers cupped the penis.

By 3:50 P.M. the place was swarming with police. An emergency medical service crew had come and gone. Doyle and Lulling and Spencer toured the scene of the tragedy. Captains and lieutenants chatted in the hallway. Everyone wanted to witness the poor fool who had been beguiled and destroyed by love.

Sergeant Peter Brown took photographs. Each room was dusted for fingerprints. Personal effects were confiscated from the bedroom closet and desk and dresser drawers. A rent check for April was sitting atop the bureau. The coroner and deputy coroner inspected the body.

Davies was clean—no marks, no bruises, no abrasions. There was no indication of struggle anywhere in the apartment. Dry towels and slippers waited for him to emerge from the bath. An uncapped plastic vial sat alone atop the toilet tank. The prescription was dated March

Gerald Davies, circa 1976 (Dane County Sheriff's Department)

Former Madison police detective Chuck Lulling, who headed the investigation of the Berge murder (Bill Fritsch/*Madison Magazine*)

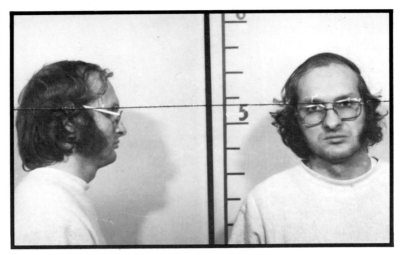

Police mugshots from Jerry Davies's arrest on Christmas Day 1977 (Dane County Sheriff's Department)

Gerald Davies's car (right), which was used to transport Harry Berge's body to the snowbanks on Blackhawk Road, in front of Davies's apartment complex (Dane County Sheriff's Department)

The Rising Sun, one of the parlors owned by Ken Curtis. Barbara worked here part-time. (Karl Harter)

The Kollege Klub, the basement bar where undercover police observed the encounter between Jerry Davies and Barbara Hoffman shortly after Davies had implicated Hoffman in the Berge murder (Karl Harter)

I have of my own free
will, as an act of love, trust, and
affection, without any influence
from Barbara Hoffman or from
any other individual, made the
changes in the ownership and
beneficiary clauses of my insurance
policies with Central Life Assurance
Company.

March 7, 1978
Gerald Thomas Davies

Davies's letter to insurance agent Phil Sprecher signing over his Central Life Assurance policies to Barbara. She later got $10,000 of this money.

I want to write these letters because I want to set the record straight. I was scared, I was jealous, Barb is innocent and I wrecked her life. All those stories I told about Barbara false. She never had anything to do with a body at all. She never did. I went crazy, I was so scared, the police scared me, I was crazy and I didn't know what I was saying. Then I had to keep telling the same story or they would charge me with a crime. Now they did it to Barb instead and I don't know what to do anymore except tell the truth. I'm not crazy anymore and I'm not scared. I want to tell the truth. I'm not afraid of going to jail. Barb never had anything to do with a body at all. I swear it and they can do what they want to me.

Gerald Thomas Davies

Davies's alleged "suicide note"

Barbara Hoffman at a pretrial hearing in 1978 (Rich Rygh/*Capital Times*)

705515

DELIVERY RECEIPT ◆ *Motor Transport Co.* ◆ PRO 30661718
DUNS 00 794 7104   SCAC MOTR   4101 W. BLUE MOUND RD. - MILWAUKEE, WIS. 53208

CONSIGNEE
J DAVIES   2305 S PARK ST APT 7 MADIOSN WIS   DATE 5/11/77P

SHIPPER
LAABS INC   911 N 27TH   MILW WIS 53208

ROUTE CA PRO & DATE

NO. PCS	DESCRIPTION OF ARTICLES TRANSPORTED		WEIGHT	RATE	CHARGES
1	POTASSIUM CYANIDE POISON		3		
1	SODIUM AZIDE -POISON	MAY 23 1977	7	M	12.84
			10	PREPAID	
2 TOT PCS					

THIS BILL MUST BE PAID WITHIN SEVEN DAYS AS PRESCRIBED BY LAW.   RECEIVED IN GOOD ORDER FIRM   (SIGNATURE IN FULL) BY

Receipt for the cyanide shipped to Davies

Don Eisenberg arguing one of many motions in the Hoffman case (© 1979 Brent Nicastro)

Barbara Hoffman and her lawyer, Don Eisenberg, at a
January 1979 pretrial hearing at the City-County Building,
Madison (Rich Rygh/*Capital Times*)

John Burr, assistant
district attorney of
Dane County, at the
Barbara Hoffman
trial, 1980 (Rich Rygh/
Capital Times)

Jim Doyle, district attorney of Dane County, 1978 (David
Sandell/*Capital Times*)

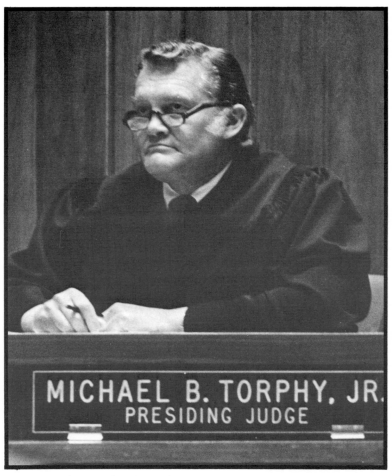

MICHAEL B. TORPHY, JR.
PRESIDING JUDGE

Circuit Judge Michael Torphy, who finally presided over the case in June 1980 (Rich Rygh/*Capital Times*)

Sam Cerro, owner of a Madison massage parlor: his complicated plea bargain on an unrelated matter allowed for key testimony in the Hoffman trial. (David Sandell/*Capital Times*)

The courtroom, June 1980 (David Sandell/*Capital Times*)

Barbara Hoffman and Don Eisenberg at the courthouse (David Sandell/*Capital Times*)

The verdict is delivered, June 28, 1980. (David Sandell/*Capital Times*)

13th and read "2 mg Valium, 50 tablets, taken as needed, for Gerald T. Davies." The bottle was empty.

Hair samples were collected from the rim of the tub, the sink, the toilet seat. A red Ace comb, the towels, the bathroom rug, a jar of bathtub water were collected for testing. The body was transported to the morgue for a morning autopsy.

It was about 6:00 P.M. when the phone rang. Doyle and Spencer had long since departed. Lulling and Lieutenant Joe Reuter were driving to Spring Green to inform Ruth Davies of her son's death. The phone rang a second and a third time. The lab crew suspended its work and waited, as if the call were a portentous event.

Urso picked up the receiver. "Hello."

A woman's voice, quite surprised, uttered, "Jerry?"

Urso identified himself, and the caller fell silent. He discerned the soft patter of her breath for a full thirty seconds before she hung up.

Five minutes later the phone rang again. Urso answered. This time the sound of her breathing was all he heard. He didn't question; he simply listened—for thirty seconds, a minute. The line went dead.

— 13 —

On Monday, March 27th, Sam Cerro was found guilty of attempting to purchase cocaine from undercover agents at a City of Madison parking facility.

The maximum penalty included $45,000 in fines and up to fifteen years in prison. Sentencing was postponed until a later date.

— 14 —

The Davies autopsy was performed by Dr. Billy Bauman at 9:30 A.M., March 28th. The body showed no signs of

physical trauma. A slight scratch on the neck was undoubtedly a nick from a razor blade, for Davies was clean
shaven when he'd settled into the bath. A yellowish-
brown bile had been secreted from the mouth and nasal
passage. No bruises, no abrasions, no blood marred the
skin.

Internally a myocardial hemorrhage was discovered
on the anterior wall of the heart, but it was determined to
have been minor and nonfatal. The lungs, however, had
suffered harsh abuse. Their weight was more than twice
the average, having increased from a normal 900 grams to
1,890 grams. The reasons were severe pulmonary congestion, edema, and hemorrhage—symptoms consistent with
asphyxia due to drowning.

The examination lasted until 12:09 P.M. Bauman
found nothing else that appeared contributory to expiration. Lung, liver, kidney, brain, urine, and blood samples
were obtained and transported to the state crime lab in the
hope that a careful analysis might detect a chemical cause
for Davies's death.

Otherwise Bauman was baffled. It didn't seem plausible, yet for lack of anything better the initial conclusion
was death by accidental drowning.

— 15 —

Every resident of the Woodview Apartments, the complex
where Davies had lived, was questioned, and not a single
individual had seen anyone enter or exit Davies's flat the
entire Easter weekend. In fact no one could recall their
neighbor ever having a visitor during his three years at the
complex.

A check of the premises did not hint at any disturbance. Nothing appeared stolen or missing. Latent prints
gathered in the apartment matched the identification
marks of two people—Jerry Davies and Sergeant Peter
Brown, the officer who had taken photographs of the

scene minutes after discovery of the body. None of the latent prints could be matched to Barbara Hoffman. An empty envelope, mailed to Linda Millar in care of Jerry Davies, with Barbara's return address, was tucked into a dresser drawer. Barbara's phone number and social security number and the post office box assigned to Linda Millar were written, in deliberate and legible script, in an address book next to the phone.

These findings, however, did not mean she had been present on the fatal Easter weekend. The sofa, the carpet, the bathroom tiles were scrutinized, yet not a strand of her hair was found. If Barbara had been there, she had been invisible and had left no trace.

— 16 —

The pathologist estimated the time of death to be between 5:00 and 7:00 P.M. on Saturday, March 25th. Dr. Bauman emphasized that this estimate was a very rough approximation. The humid environment and the water had hastened postmortem decomposition. These factors complicated matters and made a firm answer about when Davies had expired impossible to a degree of scientific certainty.

— 17 —

Frustrated by the inconclusive autopsy, Dr. Billy Bauman decided he wanted another opportunity to review Davies's body before it was laid to permanent rest. Davies was simply too clean. Any circumstance but the most bizarre or extraordinary would have left an indication, a clue as to what had happened. Yet Davies was perfect, as if he had fallen asleep contemplating his woes and chosen not to awaken and confront them. Maybe that was what the shipping clerk had wished, but it demanded more than wishing to make it so. It required an ingestion or an injection.

The pathologist chased that reasoning. To him it appeared to be a suicide by means of an exotic drug or poison. All other possibilities had been carefully screened and eliminated.

On March 30th Bauman and Detective Robert Doyle drove to the Richardson Funeral Home in Spring Green for a last examination of the corpse. The embalming had been completed, and Davies's skin looked like processed cheese.

Davies's inner and outer ears were searched for puncture wounds. The inner ear canal was probed for puncture wounds or the residue of a foreign substance or liquid. Bauman's intimate search found nothing odd or unusual. He reexamined the body for any mark or cut or bruise he might have overlooked during the autopsy.

Bauman's guess was that Davies had committed suicide by injection of a deadly chemical. Because Davies had not been found until two days later, the chemical had been absorbed into his system and was difficult to detect.

Bauman hunted for the wound of a hypodermic needle. Between the fingers, between the toes, under the arms, every fold of his skin was assiduously inspected. Due to postmortem degeneration and skin slippage, any findings would have been scientifically inconclusive, but they would have provided a possible framework for research with the biopsy samples.

After an hour and the discovery of no puncture wounds, Bauman quit the search. It was futile. Davies was clean.

— 18 —

April 1st was not chilly and not warm, somewhere between coat and sweater weather. The sunshine was deceptive, for the ground remained damp and cold from the winter's long cover.

Ruth Davies wore a heavy tweed coat, black with weaves of charcoal and navy, tattered at the elbows, frayed at the collar and hem. The buttons didn't match. The coat drooped over her shoulders like a tent. A minister droned on about her son, praising virtues Jerry never possessed. Ruth felt the cold of the earth rise up through the soles of her shoes. Her other boys, Tom and Bob, had served as pallbearers, along with their father, Leo, and Chuck Richardson, Jerry's boyhood chum. Two men from the funeral parlor assisted in carrying the casket because the family had no one else and Jerry had no other friends. The cop from Madison with the walrus mustache and the assortment of pipes was present. Ruth's daughter had driven up from downstate Illinois. It was the first time in nineteen years that the family had assembled, and Ruth Davies tried not to dwell on that thought or it would make her almost as forlorn as Jerry's death had.

Her children had scattered like seeds hurled by the wind. Now Jerry had also departed—Jerry, who was the only one to remain behind and care for her.

They were lowering her son into a hole in the earth. The rollers squeaked. The minister chanted a final prayer. Her daughter wept. Birch trees on a distant hillside looked like stark, shiny ghosts. Ruth heard the lead car of the funeral procession start its engine. She stared at the meager gathering. Her lips were blue and felt as cold as stone. Her eyes brooded, as tough and dark as black walnut shells.

—— 19 ——

The cause and circumstance of Jerry Davies's death puzzled everyone connected with the investigation. As incredible as accidental drowning in a bathtub appeared, the alternative theories seemed no less bizarre. No one had seen or heard a visitor enter or leave Davies's apartment. A thorough search had turned up no evidence of anyone else's presence. There were no indications of foul play. Nothing was amiss in the apartment or with Davies, other than the fact that he was dead.

The obvious causes were discounted immediately. There were no bumps or contusions on his skull, so he did not trip and bang his head. He did not suffer a heart attack. His lungs had filled with fluid, as if he had drowned, and he had died from lack of oxygen.

The dearth of evidence concerning interference from an outside party and the empty pill bottle on the toilet suggested suicide. However, Valium was a peculiar weapon for self-destruction. Neither the pathologist nor the coroner knew of a single instance in which an over-dose of Valium had resulted in death, and a quick check of medical records showed no recorded cases in state history. Official conclusions from the state crime lab would not be submitted for weeks, but initial tests of the residue in the vial indicated no alien substances were present.

Nevertheless the suicide theory gained wide support. Davies was fragile. Davies was in an excruciating predica-ment. The trial date was approaching. The pressure drew him taut, and he snapped. No other explanation was rea-sonable.

Were the letters that Anita Clark and Chris Spencer had received on the morning of March 27th suicide notes? No one had guessed it at the time, but hindsight changed the context of the words. Moreover Davies had mailed two other letters—identical in form and content—to Stan Davenport, who was captain of detectives and technically in charge of the Berge murder investigation, and to Don Eisenberg, Barbara's lawyer. In retrospect it appeared that Davies had wanted to correct the record and provide an unequivocal public statement regarding culpability and innocence and Harry Berge's murder. A cursory evalua-tion by a state handwriting expert showed that the four letters were written by Davies, probably in succession and without apparent stress. Did he pen the letters, post them, then return home and kill himself?

With a single dramatic gesture, Davies had freed his

fiancée and terminated the agony they both had endured. At least that was the speculation.

Maybe Davies's desperation went deeper than that romantic scenario of suicide. Perhaps the image of Berge in the snowbank was the nightmare Davies couldn't escape. The ugly vision was compounded by the insidious thought that his sweetheart, despite her persistent denials, had committed the brutality. Davies had acted to police as if he believed Barbara's proclamations of innocence, but maybe even gullible Davies had suffered moments when doubt chewed through the shell of trust he had constructed around her. His predicament contained no solution. The harder Davies delved for a way out, the more his head hurt. A properly arranged suicide exonerated Barbara and liberated Davies from his own torment.

Could Davies have plotted it and carried it through? Chuck Lulling argued fiercely against the idea that Davies's death was a suicide. Could the fragile and frightened Davies coolly gobble a handful of pills, slide into a tub of warm water, and placidly await death?

The consensus said suicide. Lulling stuck with his intuition. Suicide was inconsistent with Davies's character, he told Doyle. Lulling smoked his pipe. He had discussed the case for hours with his wife, exploring the possibilities, critiquing his own theories, listening to Marian's reactions, and reconstructing the tragic event. Now he replayed his opinions for Doyle, for no one else was interested, and the investigation seemed stymied.

The veteran detective had based his views on his visceral reaction to Davies and on a clever interpretation of the apartment. Does a man intending to commit suicide lay out two clean towels and bathroom slippers next to the tub? Does he shave before killing himself? Does he worry about his collection of grocery bingo cards? Does he write a check for next month's rent? These nuances disturbed Lulling.

If Davies was so concerned with Barbara, why didn't he leave a will? Why didn't he leave a suicide note? Davies was not spontaneous. He would have left some message of explanation for his mother and for the only other woman he had ever loved, Barbara Hoffman. Yet there was nothing.

Reread the letter, said Lulling. Why wasn't it dated? Suicide was nowhere mentioned or implied. The letter was not a pathetic farewell; it was one awkward attempt at exculpating Barbara. Why fear jail if he didn't intend to survive the weekend? Why say "They can do what they want with me" when he knew he'd be dead before anyone read the letter?

The attempt to assume blame for killing Berge was transparent, said Lulling. Jerry Davies was timid and desperate and adrift in the world, but he was not intemperate. He did not slay Harry Berge in a fit of jealous rage, and he did not end his life by an act of utter despondency. He'd been murdered, quite neatly, quite deliberately—by Barbara Hoffman.

Lulling admitted the assertion was bold, but so was Hoffman. Only someone of supreme confidence and with a supreme sense of superiority would attempt such an audacious deed given the circumstances. Barbara was convinced of her cunning, of her acumen. It did not matter that the $750,000 insurance policy had been rescinded. It did not matter that Davies's testimony would be dissected by Eisenberg's scathing tongue. Barbara was compelled to exert her own control. Her extreme self-reliance would not let her do anything less.

The letters were devious and perfect. Driven by jealousy, Davies murdered his rival for Barbara's affections. He shoved the blame on Barbara because it was his obsessive love for her that had provoked his outburst. He had to hurt her too. When he saw the devastation he had wrought, he became penitent. Things had to be settled and the guilt reapportioned. Davies confessed, yet he wasn't strong enough to live with the burden of what he had done. With Barbara cleared of wrongdoing, he killed himself.

That was the interpretation Barbara wanted. With one

daring act she had eliminated the chief witness against her and had pushed the Berge murder case into hopeless confusion.

It was a calculating and appalling deed, and unless something drastic occurred in their favor, Lulling said, it might succeed.

Doyle stared at the detective through a screen of pipe smoke. Lulling's opinion was passionate and radical, but the DA did not disagree.

— 20 —

Television crews from the local network affiliates wrestled for position on the second floor of the City-County Building outside the courtroom of the Honorable P. Charles Jones. It was April 7th, and the arraignment of Barbara Hoffman for Harry Berge's murder was scheduled for 9:00 A.M.

The cameras focused on the elevator doors opposite the courtroom. Tech men conducted lighting and sound checks and guzzled coffee from Styrofoam cups. Yards of black cable spooled at the base of their tripods. Klieg bulbs burned like miniature suns in the dim hallway. Reporters gossiped in amiable tones, speculated on the mystery of Davies's death and the pall of doubt it cast over the case. Courthouse observers lingered—lawyers awaiting a hearing, secretaries late for work, bailiffs, office clerks, people with other business who hoped to snatch a glimpse of the notorious Ms. Hoffman.

At 8:53 A.M. the elevator doors whisked open, and Barbara hesitated, as if temporarily paralyzed by the attention. There was a cacophony of voices. Flashbulbs popped, and blue light soaked the hallway like rain. Her brown eyes registered surprise behind the tortoiseshell glasses. Don Eisenberg shielded her with his left arm, prodded her forward, and scowled at the cameras.

Questions from news reporters were brushed aside.

The crowd tightened and the space shrank as people shoved closer for a peek at the defendant. Photographers climbed onto the hallway benches to capture Barbara's expression of bewilderment. Eisenberg castigated a cameraman who ventured too close. Someone hollered for Barbara's comments. Her attorney answered with a barrage of expletives guaranteed to be deleted from the evening's news footage. An associate grabbed the door, and they scooted out of the media assault.

After the maelstrom in the hallway the courtroom seemed like a sanctuary and a tomb. It was gloomy and quiet. Doyle, Burr, and Spencer conferred in hushed tones at the prosecution table. Anita Clark jotted on a notepad in the front row.

Judge Jones entered. He announced the case as the *State of Wisconsin* versus *Barbara Hoffman, aka Linda Millar.*

Eisenberg immediately protested. "Your Honor, there is no 'also known as.' Her name is Barbara Hoffman, and that's it."

Before Jones finished reading the charges, the defense attorney rose and objected to the cameras and the media blitz in the hallway. He labeled it "cruel and unusual punishment for Barbara" and asked that more civilized arrangements be established for her entrance and exit from the courtroom.

Jones nodded, and the proceedings continued.

Eisenberg objected frequently. He formally requested that the case be returned to county court for another preliminary hearing, arguing that the Davies letters constituted new evidence. The letter was an ostensible admission of guilt.

Jones noted the challenge but issued no ruling. He asked for a plea from the defendant.

Again Eisenberg protested. He declared that the criminal complaint against Barbara—which accused her of bludgeoning Harry Berge about the head and neck with a blunt instrument, thus causing his death—contained numerous and reckless misinterpretations of fact. The defendant would not enter a plea, said Eisenberg. She would stand mute before the court.

The judge sighed at the bombast. He ruled that the court would enter a plea of not guilty for Ms. Hoffman. No trial date was set, because the defense indicated it would be filing motions for a new prelim, for dismissal, etc., within the thirty-day deadline, and rulings would be made accordingly. The arraignment was adjourned. Barbara Hoffman had remained silent throughout.

Judge Jones permitted her to exit through his chambers to avoid harassment and for her personal safety. As she left the courtroom, she turned and stared—it was all men: her lawyer, the prosecution lawyers, the judge, the bailiffs. She was surrounded by men, somber and earnest, dispatching justice in accordance with a system they had created and perpetuated. The only women were Anita Clark, buried in her notes in the front row, and the court stenographer, whose red nails punched the shorthand keys and who could have been earning twice her income on half as much work if she traded her polyester suit for a lace negligee.

Eisenberg held a press conference in the hallway. Rumors linking Barbara and the massage parlors were strenuously disavowed. With TV cameras registering his every word and gesture, Eisenberg passionately and eloquently predicted that the spurious allegations leveled at his client would be squashed and her good name and reputation restored. He denigrated the police work on the case. Jerry Davies, he insisted, had been bullied into making statements, and what was obviously a suicide note corroborated Davies's guilt. The court had no alternative but to dismiss the charges for lack of evidence. A suit by Ms. Hoffman, Eisenberg informed the media, was being contemplated.

— 21 —

Later that day Don Eisenberg called Phil Sprecher, the agent who had sold Jerry Davies life insurance, and asked about settlement of the three small policies totaling $20,000 with Central Life Assurance. A month ago Davies had named Barbara Hoffman beneficiary of the policies. If the death was considered accidental, the policies paid $35,000.

Sprecher replied that the necessary forms would be mailed out immediately.

—— 22 ——

A blend of moonlight and the phosphorescence of the street lamp; from the darkness of the kitchen Liza peered at a patch of tulips in a neighbor's backyard. Every day of April she had watched the perennials bud and blossom, but at that moment the flowers appeared surreal, a collection of scarlet china cups balanced on green crepe-paper stems. It was too late to be talking on the telephone. The spiral cord stretched across the kitchen as if a lifeline extended to a drowning soul.

The glow of orange from Liza's cigarette was the only light in the house. Into an earthenware saucer she flicked the ashes, then hoisted a mug of herbal tea to her lips.

The clock on the stove read 2:35.

"Where did I go?" Barbara asked, talking about last December. "What did I do?"

The words echoed in the plastic cavern of the telephone receiver. Liza had been through these agonizing conversations before. Barbara struggled to remember, as if she were trying to recount a brief journey that had been forgotten, as if she were trying to recount a summer vacation from her youth. Barbara recited scenes without sequence or order. Forward and backward, her mind jumped. Names and incidents were recalled like pieces blindly pulled from a hat.

The chatter made Liza uneasy. Barbara tossed around names that Liza had read in the newspapers, names that belonged to men who were dead. Liza stared out the window. She saw photos clipped from the front page of the newspaper, photos black and white and fuzzy in the moonlight, and the photos were propped in the china cups that were really tulips. Liza saw dozens of portraits of two melancholy men, Berge and Davies. The photos could have been of the same individual at different periods in life— young man sad and old man sad, or father and son and loneliness.

Liza lit another cigarette. She interjected with pertinent advice about the benefits of sleep and relaxation. A poster on a campus kiosk had advertised a lecture on transcendental meditation. Perhaps they should attend, suggested Liza. They could both use some quiet in their lives, she added, but Barbara withheld a reply. Was Barbara contemplating the idea or being silently scornful?

Liza blew a line of smoke into the darkness and chuckled at a remembrance from the days at Jan's Health Spa.

Liza used to tease that Barbara had perfected a scornful glance and that it was her most frequent expression. A method of maintaining adequate distance, Barbara had laughed, but it was not a joke. Liza remembered how different Barbara was from everyone else in that environment. Barbara's patrons treated her regally. They brought her gifts and trinkets, issued dinner invitations, acclaimed her talents to whoever listened. On Sunday nights men waited hours for thirty-five minutes of her tongue and touch. Her popularity, however, was not universal. The women who worked with Barbara did not view her with the esteem accorded to royalty.

It would have been easy to regard Barbara's disfavor as jealousy due to the attention, or resentment because of the generous tips she earned, or insecurity, for obviously Barbara knew something about men, or was willing to do something to men, that the others didn't. Liza had discerned another dimension to the dynamic. Shy and aloof, Barbara discouraged contact from other women.

As contemptuous as Barbara had acted of the massage parlor atmosphere and its denizens, the small, strange world had affected her profoundly. The drug abuse and the sexual disparagement had jostled her head. Perhaps resistance to the bizarre and the perverse melted, not from any sense of liberation but from an evaporation of self-respect. It was as if discordant elements in Barbara's personality, which had been submerged deep below the surface, bubbled free. Barbara had always been fascinated and intrigued by abnormal psychology, taking classes at the U.W., doing reading and informal research. Sometimes it seemed to Liza as if Barbara were conducting experiments on herself, testing limits, treading into uncharted areas. Liza had wondered if Barbara was training herself or punishing herself or losing herself.

The tiny cosmos of drugs and sex that revolved around Jan's did not unravel Barbara, Liza had long since decided; rather it accelerated a fragmentation that had begun years ago. What the experience at Jan's did was grab the loose shreds of her psyche and yank. When Barbara quit the parlor, she departed frazzled and disturbed. Her sense of self and reality were as askew as clippings of yarn thrown across a floor, which didn't make her much different from the other women hopelessly orbiting that crazy universe.

Liza's tea was cold. The moonlight had shifted, and the china cups appeared cracked. The phone cord was wrapped around her forearm, serpentine.

Liza wanted to hang up, but she couldn't. She tugged another cigarette from what three hours ago had been a new pack and was now a couple of loose sticks.

Why did she participate in these marathon conversations, which were really Barbara's maddening monologues? Liza gazed at the shadows of her kitchen, at a bulb of garlic on the counter, at potatoes the shape of rocks, at a toaster cover that looked like an Easter bonnet her mother had worn one spring, at the rack of McCormick spice tins in rows as neat as teeth.

Barbara talked. Liza turned to the window. It was April and a time for recovery and resurgence. She watched the smoke crawl from her cigarette. The tulips quivered in an early breeze.

—— 23 ——

The day after Hoffman's arraignment for the murder of Harry Berge a toxicologist at the state crime lab in Madison, following the sensitivities of his nose, made a startling discovery regarding the death of Jerry Davies.

Since March 28th, Kenneth Kempfert had been examining selected materials from the Davies autopsy, trying to ascertain if something of a chemical nature had contributed to Davies's expiration. Lung, liver, urine, kidney, brain, and blood specimens were subjected to standard tests, but no abnormalities were found. The negative results surprised the police investigation team and added to the aura of mystery that hovered over Davies's sudden and inexplicable demise.

For Kempfert it meant further inquiry. He delved deeper, using more sophisticated and elaborate techniques. Samples of blood, urine, and liver were analyzed for the presence of drugs and other extractables. It was a tedious process. A separate test had to be administered for each suspected foreign substance, and there was no hint as to what, if any, lethal toxins might be involved. Ordinarily Valium would not have been considered, but because of the vial in the bathroom it was checked. A specialized extraction process designed to maximize the detection of diazepam—Valium's generic name—was utilized with the blood samples. The gas chromatograph registered no significant traces, although a short peak in the graph indicated that diazepam of a therapeutic dosage may be present. Low levels of caffeine were found in the urine and the stomach contents. The county pathologist had already determined that the stomach contained food elements which very likely constituted chili. However, a milligram or two of diazepam, combined with coffee and chili, were not intrinsically fatal.

Kempfert expanded the search. Systematically he evaluated the blood for other chemicals and toxins, such as carbon monoxide, arsenic, botulinym, lead. A list was compiled and checked. He even tested for an exotic snake

venom because of an article he'd read in the evening newspaper. None of the potentially poisonous substances
graded out positive.

Every day Chuck Lulling telephoned or visited the
University Avenue lab, anxious to know of the latest findings. It got so that Kempfert recognized the sound of
Lulling's footsteps and the smell of his pipe tobacco. He
could also read the impatience and fatigue on the detective's face. The skin edging the eyes no longer appeared
wearied with wisdom but looked cracked with age. Lulling's mustache was predominated by gray, whereas only a
few months previous it had seemed stocked with a profusion of black. The belly sagged rounder. The shoulders
slacked.

Lulling had less than a month before retirement, and
the notion of going out a loser in the Hoffman case ate at
his gut. He was acutely aware that Kempfert was no magician. He was a scientist whose meticulous efforts could
break the case. Yet Lulling wanted magic. He pestered and
cajoled Kempfert because he knew the power of the laboratory. He knew the lab could discern the subtle and the
sinister.

Thus Kempfert elaborated his examinations, earnestly
testing the tubes of Davies's blood, chasing a phantom
chemical culprit. Other projects were neglected or rele-
gated to the rest of the lab crew. As the days and tests
passed without offering an answer, Kempfert himself
wondered if Lulling was prodding him in an endless pur-
suit. The list of fatal drugs was long enough to be infinite.
Maybe accidental drowning was not as absurd as it had
initially seemed.

Over the last couple days of lab work Kempfert's nose
had twitched with the vague hint of a smell that was queer
but familiar. The odor's association eluded him until the
morning of April 7th, when he realized that the scent was
burnt almonds. He intuited that this smell was important,
and that evening, at home, its significance hit him. Cyanide was characterized by an odor that resembled burnt

almonds. Too hearty a snort and the fumes could cause illness or death. But how had such a strong smell gone undetected by Billy Bauman, who had extracted all the samples Kempfert handled and who had conducted the autopsy?

The toxicologist paged through the medical literature. Approximately one-quarter of the population, due to a minor hereditary defect, does not perceive the smell of burnt almonds. The odor had eluded Bauman due to a quirk of nature.

Kempfert's excitement barely permitted sleep. The next day he got to work early and ran the procedure for identifying cyanide. A small portion of Davies's blood was mixed with two different reagents. A violet color appeared, which indicated a degree of saturation in the blood. Then he took a second sample and placed it in a small dish called a Convay diffusion chamber to ascertain the amount of cyanide in the blood. The measuring was done by ultraviolet spectrophotometry. Once inside the body, the exact form of cyanide—sodium, potassium, or other—could no longer be determined, but that was irrelevant. To substantiate his results Kempfert examined a sample of the stomach contents, evolved hydrogen cyanide gas, and identified it by infrared spectrophotometry.

When the test and retests were completed, he phoned Lulling with the news. Davies had not drowned. He had been killed by an ingestion of cyanide. His blood contained approximately three hundred milligrams, which was twice the lethal dose.

Lulling was stunned. He thanked Kempfert for the fine job, advised that he speak to no one but Doyle concerning the discovery, and treated himself to a fresh bowl of pipe tobacco. After a few minutes of reflection he drove to the medical library at the university and read everything he could about cyanide poisoning. In the middle of his research he wandered out to the pay phone in the hall and caught the toxicologist as he was leaving the lab after a ten-hour day.

"Tomorrow," Lulling said, as if the request were a command, "you should retrieve Berge's blood samples and check them for cyanide too."

The samples obtained from the Berge autopsy were in storage and sealed. Kempfert received authorization and repeated the test for cyanide on Berge's blood and stomach contents.

The results were positive. Berge's blood contained over thirty-seven times the lethal dose of cyanide.

— 24 —

On April 12th Robert Shunk, a document examiner and handwriting expert for the state, submitted his final conclusions. The letters signed by Davies and posted to Anita Clark, Chris Spencer, Eisenberg, and the police, letters that absolved Barbara Hoffman of participation in the Berge murder, were written by Jerry Davies. Each copy was done individually and with the same pen. The letters were written at normal speed and without any sign of duress or unnecessary hesitation.

— 25 —

It was chili, Chuck Lulling decided. Barbara Hoffman brought her fiancé a hot chili dinner on a snowy Easter weekend, a loving, thoughtful gesture except for one minor detail—the chili was laced with cyanide.

Chili was the perfect food for her scheme. The sublime taste of the secret spice—cyanide—would be buried under sprinkles of cayenne pepper, cumin seed, salt, chili powder, and Tabasco sauce. It was served steaming hot and spicy hot. The reaction would be swift, without time for reflection or panic, without a moment of hesitation during which Davies might dwell on the nature of each

fatal spoonful. No one would suspect chili. Add carrots
just in case, because nobody puts carrots in chili.

Furthermore, the secret spice would leave no trace. It
would remain undetected unless specifically tested for.
And why should anyone even think of it? Berge had been
whacked in the cranium with a blunt object, probably a
frying pan. The criminal complaint read "bludgeoned
about the skull and neck, resulting in hemorrhage and
edema and death." Lulling regarded Barbara as audacious
and sinister. She would have thought, if the cops couldn't
get Berge right, how would they ever guess chili? The
image of Barbara, smug and confident, infuriated him.

Lulling visited every restaurant and fast-food joint
from State Street to the end of South Park. Every eatery
that served chili was asked a simple question: did it put
carrots in its chili? The answer never varied. None of
them used carrots in their recipes. For Chuck Lulling that
confirmed his visceral suspicion. Barbara Hoffman had
cooked her fiancé dinner on a snowy Easter weekend—and
spiced the meal with cyanide.

— 26 —

The single outlet for cyanide in the Madison area was the
Hydrite Company in Cottage Grove, a firm that distributed the chemical in two hundred-pound drums to three
local companies involved in the metallurgical industry.
Hydrite did not sell the compound in quantities less than
the sealed drums, nor had it received any request to do so
in the last six months. It seemed improbable that it would
have been the source for the material that killed Berge and
Davies. Police subsequently contacted every pharmacy in
the city, but only one, Prescription Pharmacy, had cyanide
on the shelf, and the jar had not been disturbed for over
three years.

A check with the university showed a different situation. The University of Wisconsin–Madison bought cya-

nide at $3.39 per pound for use in laboratory instruction, research, and experimentation. Both potassium cyanide and sodium cyanide were stored in numerous labs in the university chemistry and biochemistry buildings.

On April 13th Officer Joe Rut surveyed the facilities at the U.W. and discovered chemical storage shelves immediately off the main hallway and in places where the contents could be accessible to whoever wandered by. Twenty-one labs held cyanide in the chemistry building. Three pounds of cyanide were found in the biochemistry labs, and another three-and-a-quarter pounds were found in various labs in the molecular biology building. Forty-eight containers of cyanide were dusted for fingerprints in hopes of matching a latent print to Barbara Hoffman or Jerry Davies, but all Rut got were smudges and partials, and nothing matched the victim or his suspected killer.

The next day Lulling and Urso interviewed Dr. Bruce Selman, a professor of biochemistry. Dr. Selman informed the detectives that one-quarter pound of potassium cyanide was missing, and presumed stolen, from the chemical inventory of his lab. A check of the records indicated that it had been received in November 1976 and had been missing for at least one month prior to the current date.

Later the same day they spoke with U.W. professor David Nelson, who stated that he'd taught Barbara Hoffman in a biochemistry course, and according to his notes, cyanide was discussed on a minimum of two occasions and was mentioned because it presented a classic example of how a toxic agent can disrupt and interfere with the normally functioning human organism. Ms. Hoffman had earned an A in his class.

Also interviewed was Professor Robert Burris. Barbara had taken a plant biochemistry course he offered in the fall semester, from September 1975 to January 1976. Cyanide was covered in the course. He remembered her as shy and extremely bright, and he remarked that she didn't ask many questions, because she knew all the answers. Her grade for the course was an A.

Talks with security personnel, other professors, and

graduate students and research assistants who frequented the chemistry building established that Barbara had visited the facility as late as the fall of 1977, even though she was no longer enrolled as a student. Lulling and Urso showed pictures of her, and several people were positive about seeing her on the premises.

Every indication was that Barbara Hoffman had pilfered cyanide from the university. Her work as a student majoring in biochemistry had demonstrated to her the severe and lethal nature of the compound, had shown her where it was stored and its accessibility, and her presence in the labs would not be regarded as suspicious or out of the ordinary. Nevertheless the assumption that she'd obtained the cyanide from a chemistry lab was entirely circumstantial. No one had seen her snooping about, caught her with the deadly substance, or heard her discuss its potency and effects.

— 27 —

On April 19th articles procured from Davies's bathroom—an Ace comb, towels, soap, toothbrush, bedroom slippers—were tested for traces of cyanide. Sections of the drainpipe in both the bathroom sink and the tub had been removed and were also examined. All results were negative.

— 28 —

The eggs were over easy, the steak medium-rare, the hash browns of the prefabricated variety—potatoes frozen into a block, then deep-fried to resemble a square of varnished oak.

"Fucking hash browns taste like sawdust," Ken Curtis grumbled. He sat alone in a booth at the Embers Restaurant. His broad frame filled a seating space designed for two. It was four minutes past midnight.

Curtis glanced around the restaurant for his connection. Maybe the old man wouldn't show.

Across the four lanes of East Washington Avenue, ground lights bathed the headquarters of American Family Insurance with bright, milky beams. Curtis pondered insurance money and sex and the silly contortions of ambition. The scam would have succeeded except for lousy timing and a stroke of impatience. The idea was sinister and brilliant. It showed boldness and ingenuity, and Barbara might have gotten away clean if Berge hadn't died on her.

Killing Berge was an amateur move, Curtis decided. Recruiting Davies to get rid of the body had compounded the mistake. It was an error that cost her three quarters of a million dollars. But the damage could have been confined to her pocketbook. Had Barbara been as smart as she boasted, things could have been controlled. Losses would have been minimal. Hiring Eisenberg was astute. However, Barbara couldn't stay straight long enough. She thought she could evade the Berge charge and still collect the windfall on Davies.

Sam Cerro's bust was a bad break for Barbara. She didn't know it, but it ended her hopes of beating the Berge rap. The irony was that she had no connection to Cerro, no way of understanding their bond.

It seemed to Ken Curtis that Barbara had sealed her fate when she killed Davies. With Davies alive the DA acted uninterested in the tales Curtis had to sell. His information was superfluous. But with Davies dead the balance tilted. Without Davies, Curtis reasoned, the prosecution's case had an empty middle, a huge void where the center should have been, and acquittal was likely. Why else would Lulling be willing to cut a deal? Curtis sensed his information was crucial to convicting Hoffman or at least to keeping her in court long enough to let a jury deliberate.

Give-and-take held the world together. It got people

what they wanted, and those that bullied the nastiest and bartered the best got the most. These were axioms Curtis lived by, axioms that helped him prosper. Barbara was so smart she was dumb. She ate too many Quaaludes, swallowed too much wine, tried to manipulate too many men. It never occurred to her that maybe she was the one being manipulated.

The folly of a vixen with a middle-class upbringing, he smirked. He liked to fuck her in the afternoon. For a brief spell it became habit, visiting apartment 306, scoring a quickie if she was home alone, then going about his business. Whatever naughty desire Curtis conjured, Barbara performed. They did everything but kiss. Despite how she'd plead, Curtis refused to kiss her.

When he grew accustomed to her sexual tricks, when he recognized that beneath the intelligent tongue was desperation, and insecurity fathoms deep, he changed the rules with her. He spurned her advances. Until a year ago he still visited, infrequently, still chatted with her, still let her suck his cock, still had her convinced that he was the one performing the favor.

Curtis's thoughts switched tracks when Chuck Lulling and Steve Urso entered the Embers Restaurant. It was 12:31 A.M.

Urso was present because Curtis had insisted on it. They had grown up in the Greenbush together, played basketball as kids in the Y league, been classmates at Madison West High School. Curtis considered Urso a known quantity. He could gauge Urso's responses. He had a notion of whom he was working with, the motivations, the possibilities, the respect. Curtis viewed Lulling with distrust. Even those friendly with him knew that he was a cop from the old school who made up the rules as the game was played out, who had no qualms about amending the rules in his favor at any time and without notice.

The detectives joined him in the booth and ordered coffee.

"Fucking cops are boring," Curtis said. "They always

order coffee. Is it part of the job, or what?"

"If we weren't cops, we'd be able to afford breakfast too," replied Urso.

Lulling stuffed the bowl of his pipe with tobacco from a leather pouch. The meeting with Curtis was unauthorized. Doyle had nixed it, but the DA's position was compromised by the ethical standards of his profession. Lulling had no such restrictions. So he defied orders and arranged the conference.

With Davies dead they needed the information Curtis had been willing to trade back in January. The investigation had stalled, and they were in desperate need of a break in the case. Lulling thought Curtis might provide it.

The senior detective started by announcing that Sam Cerro would have to serve time. Lulling's words were interpreted as a statement of fact rather than as a negotiating ploy. Curtis said the time was not to be served at Waupun, the state's maximum security prison.

Lulling nodded through a puff of sweet gray smoke. He offered a deal: six months' time and four years suspended for Cerro in exchange for what Curtis knew and his testimony in an open court.

"The time gets done at Oakhill," Curtis said, referring to the minimum-security facility a dozen miles outside Madison.

"I ain't the fucking judge, Ken."

"You know how to jerk 'em off, though, don't you, Chuck?" Curtis smiled.

"Now, what exactly am I getting in exchange?" asked Lulling.

Curtis waved away pipe smoke and leaned forward.

"When was the last time your wife sucked your cock clean, Chuck? Whether it was last night or fifteen years ago, she ain't never sucked it like Barbie, because Barbie is the best blowjob in Madison. Her fucking mouth is a miracle, man, except when she talks. She did herself in. She fucked up with her mouth. She talked too much."

Urso scribbled notes. A year, maybe fourteen months

ago, Curtis's roommate, Larry Sawyer—whom the detectives immediately recognized as a local drug peddler and hoodlum—attended a party at Bruce Dalby's house in Nakoma. People were having a happy time, dancing, getting high on sundry drugs, and soon they were having a happy time without their clothes on. The party splintered, and after a haze of coke and carnality Sawyer found himself in a bedroom with Barbara Hoffman and a few other naked bodies. Barbara had been mixing Quaaludes and wine, a favorite combination.

When Barbara got high, she liked to talk. It was some kind of release for her, Curtis explained.

Barbara boasted that in a couple of months she would become a rich lady. Everyone else being stoned, her words were assumed to be fantasy, but Sawyer knew that Barbara was odd and brainy, so he listened. What she said began to make a rather devious sense.

While working at Jan's, Barbara said, she had met a man who was incredibly naive and inexperienced and who had become entranced by her charms. She cultivated his infatuation. They dated for a few months, and she vowed to leave the massage parlor if he'd marry her, lending her stability and the prospect of a secure future. When she suggested they invest in an insurance policy to provide a financial foundation to his estate, he agreed. She insured him for close to a million bucks, with herself as the beneficiary. The setup demanded delicate maneuvering, she explained to Sawyer, but the rest of the plan was simple.

Because of her extensive background in biochemistry, she was familiar with toxic substances and knew how to culture botulinum toxin in her apartment. A laboratory was not necessary. The chemical supplies were readily available. When the botulinum toxin was prepared, she would wed her lover with the huge insurance policy, honeymoon in Mexico, and feed him her homegrown concoction. Botulinum toxin, of course, was a lethal agent in food poisoning, and a fatal case of food poisoning in Mexico, though tragic, was not uncommon. It would not be treated with suspicion by the authorities. The body would be returned to Madison and cremated, and Barbara would tearfully collect the insurance bonanza.

No way she could miss, Barbara had insisted. Already a marriage date had been scheduled, and her fiancé had received a passport for travel abroad. In a mere six or eight months, maybe less, she would be wealthy.

Sawyer was astonished. It couldn't succeed; it sounded too easy. His head was spinning, and Barbara was on a frenzied rap, and every objection he posed she dismissed with a coherent elaboration.

The next day Sawyer told Curtis of the bizarre conversation. Curtis spoke to a friend who practiced law, discussed the plot, and chose to talk with Barbara directly, partly to confirm that the crazy plan was not an invention of Sawyer's drug-ravaged mind, partly because he was intrigued, partly because he was aghast that Barbara had revealed her scheme to a roomful of strangers during an orgy of sex and drugs. Was she completely out of control? Was she so silly as to believe she could pull it off?

But Barbara seemed reticent to expound on Sawyer's report. It was a private matter, she said, and what did he care anyway?

He didn't care, Curtis replied; he just didn't want to see her do something dumb. Besides, he cautioned, people rarely fuck with insurance companies and win, especially when the prize is nearly a million dollars in cash.

Sawyer must have been fucked up, Barbara said. He must have been hallucinating. But as she denied the story, Curtis noticed a chalkboard posted on the refrigerator. The slate contained a list of what might have been chores, except that two items riveted his gaze—marriage license, passport—and both were checked off. Barbara spotted the direction of Curtis's stare and discreetly attempted to block his view. He left, and when he came back two days later the chalkboard had been erased.

On the second visit Curtis told her bluntly that what she planned was murder and that she wouldn't get away with it. The scheme was preposterous. If she had blurted

the tale to Sawyer, who else knew? Who else had she
bragged to about her imminent riches?

The questions upset her, because she was aware that
she had a tendency to forget what she had said or done
when zonked out on 'ludes and wine.

Too many people knew, Curtis repeated, and the secret would never remain secret for long, certainly not long
enough for her to collect the insurance money.

It was then that Barbara dropped the facade. She
planned to murder a shipping clerk at the university for a
huge insurance payoff—$750,000—and she detailed the
operation, as if wanting to convince herself that it was
feasible and not doomed, as Curtis had argued.

Curtis reiterated that, although she had exploited men
in the past, sexual manipulation and petty blackmail were
amateur games compared to murder. Barbara did not
reply. He thought no more about the matter until Berge's
death.

Urso had poured down two refills of coffee. Lulling
had listened and sucked his pipe. Curtis stared out the
window.

"That's about it," Curtis declared, then paused. "I
asked her where she got the idea—you know, where did
she learn so fucking much about insurance and how it
pays? She said one of her regular tricks from Jan's was an
insurance executive. They'd go sailing in the summer on
Lake Mendota. She'd fuck him like crazy and pump him
for info. Then, when she got tired of him, she threatened
to tell his wife about how those late-night fishing trips
weren't fishing trips, unless he cosigned a loan for her. Of
course he did, and of course she defaulted, sticking him
with a bill for a couple thousand dollars, and thanks for
the good time. She was shrewd, Barbie was. Do we got a
deal here, gentlemen?"

Lulling and Urso nodded. Curtis insisted on shaking
hands. He paid for the food and the coffee, left the waitress a five-dollar tip, and roared out East Washington in
his Lincoln Continental.

—— 29 ——

The conversation with Ken Curtis at the Embers Restaurant boosted Lulling's spirits. He set about verifying what he had learned.

Unless Larry Sawyer was coaxed or coerced into making a statement to police, what Curtis had been told concerning the party and Barbara Hoffman's insurance scam was inadmissible as evidence because it was hearsay. Besides, Sawyer's altered state of consciousness due to the drugs he had consumed might invalidate his word. Anything Hoffman had said directly to Curtis in the proceeding days was surely crucial and could be admitted as evidence in a court of law. Lulling worried about Curtis's veracity.

The motivation to manufacture a bogus story to sell to a DA under pressure to prosecute and convict was real and apparent. Curtis was bold enough to attempt the deception.

Lulling sent a query to the county clerk's office to discover whether Barbara Hoffman or Linda Millar or Jerry Davies had applied for a marriage license anytime during 1977. Within hours the detective was handed a photostat of the application.

On April 15, 1977, an Application for Marriage License was completed by Gerald Davies and Barbara Hoffman. The documents were signed, a fee was paid, and a time was reserved for April 22nd. Judge William Buenzli would perform the civil ceremony. It was explained that two witnesses were necessary. However, the couple did not appear on the assigned date, nor did they contact the clerk's office to reschedule.

Information regarding a passport was also sought. Lulling was forwarded a photocopy of an application filed by Jerry Davies on May 19, 1977, with notice it had been approved and a passport issued on May 31, 1977.

It seemed Ken Curtis might be trading with truth. Lulling pored through the materials they'd collected on Barbara's alias, Linda Millar. According to Curtis, Barbara had confessed her plan to Sawyer and then to himself sometime in the spring—late March or early April. A study of the dates on the library card, savings passbook, post office box, and change of beneficiary forms demonstrated that Linda Millar did not come into existence until May 1977. Consequently Lulling surmised that Barbara was aware of her blunder. Since she had told Sawyer and Curtis of her plan, and since she did not want to scrap the money and time invested in her plot to murder Jerry Davies, Barbara decided to change names and hope she could succeed with an alias. Seven hundred fifty thousand dollars was too much to let go.

Other parts of Curtis's tale were corroborated. Through a series of legal wranglings resulting in a court order, bank records were opened and Barbara's banking transactions were scrutinized. In 1975 and 1976 Barbara had obtained a series of loans from the University of Wisconsin Credit Union and other local financial institutions for amounts varying from $500 to $3,000. The loans were cosigned, each by a different gentleman, all considered excellent credit risks. It was a simple pattern. After making the initial two or three payments, Barbara defaulted on the loan, leaving the cosigner to repay the outstanding balance.

While Curtis had hinted at a "small-time" blackmail practice, he didn't elaborate and clearly wasn't aware of the scope of Barbara's activities. Lulling had the names of Barbara's "benefactors," as he referred to them, and he set about the delicate task of interviewing. The list demonstrated Barbara's talent at identifying gentlemen with special qualities: money, a family, social status they could not afford to have rocked by scandal. They were men who would pay to keep their infidelity secret. College professors, business executives, lawyers were included, and contact with each individual was made discreetly.

Some cooperated with the investigation; some refused. Usually the promise of anonymity or the threat of a subpoena encouraged them to submit to an interview. Most of the men expressed embarrassment at having allowed themselves to be maneuvered into such a compromising position. An insurance executive remarked that Barbara had pumped him for information about life insurance policies, casually lulling him into talking about business and then questioning him about different coverages, about how and when companies paid off.

A college professor who had become acquainted with Barbara at Jan's and had taken her to the theater as well as to various motels around the city felt after the blackmail scheme that she had sized him up, weighed him, and decided precisely how much she could bilk him for without provoking a violent reaction or a report to the police. He had lent her money, which was never repaid, as well as cosigned a loan through the U.W. Credit Union. When at first he balked about her obvious scam, she called him at home, during the dinner hour, and threatened to continue the calls until he paid off the loan.

The tales were desperate, and the fact that no one had considered reporting this to the authorities Lulling found incredible. Barbara must have been a very busy woman during those years, he concluded, and she must have squandered a hell of a lot of money, because as carefully as he could trace she had less than $100 in the bank at the time of her arrest.

This new evidence was crucial to the prosecution's case. It confirmed Ken Curtis's story and convinced Lulling that leniency for Cerro in exchange for Curtis's testimony was not only a worthwhile trade; it was the only chance they held for gaining a conviction. None of the information would convict her by itself; however, it bolstered the reams of circumstantial materials already accumulated and added a cohesion to the case that had been lacking. The circumstances were complex and bizarre, but now Barbara's actions could be viewed and presented as elements in an avaricious scheme that included a double murder.

Doyle bitched and moaned when Lulling told him of the conversation that he and Urso had had with Curtis at the Embers Restaurant. But when the senior detective explained what he had learned, the DA smiled. A plea bargain would have to be arranged.

— 30 —

With a modicum of fanfare and newspaper coverage Chuck Lulling retired from the MPD on April 27th, the eve of his fifty-fifth birthday.

Lulling joined the department in 1949, after a short tour in the air force. Many people viewed him as the last of the cops from the old school, cops who had survived on intimidation, cops who dispersed justice with the butt of a nightstick. The early street training and experience had influenced his entire career. Almost every young cop on the force had been thrashed for lack of thoroughness or poor police method or a deficiency of common sense by Lulling's gruff tongue. He had bullied criminals and clashed with the bureaucracy. Few were sad to see him depart.

Nonetheless, Lulling had compiled a sterling record. He was the first police officer in the state to collect an audiovisual confession from a suspected murderer. Since 1960 he had solved more than twenty murders in which he had acted as the principal investigator. His reputation as tough, cocky, bellicose was justified.

Chuck Lulling was not given to maudlin sentimentality. His police career was over. On Monday he and Marian would drive to Arizona and waste a couple weeks gawking at the Grand Canyon, admiring the native Indian leather and stone craft, rubbing lotion on their sunburned shoulders. When they returned, Chuck planned to start a private investigator's trade, which, ironically, would pit him with the lawyers who had tried to pry apart his work and testimony during his thirty years as a cop and which undoubtedly would earn him oodles more than his detective salary. It would be an adjustment.

But the future was three days away.

It was 6:00 P.M., and except for Russ Kurth, who

logged overtime on a drug case, the office was deserted. Gray metal desks, their edges nudged together in the cramped quarters, each with the nameplate of its absent resident, were cluttered with paperwork and telephone hookups, ashtrays stuffed with cigarette butts, calendars jammed with court dates and hearings and interviews. Lulling stared at the cards and presents on his desk, but his thoughts centered on a gullible, shy, awkward kid who had grown into a gullible, shy, awkward adult named Jerry Davies, or, rather, he ruminated on the memory of Davies—the nervous tics, the unruly sideburns, the jeans riding down the hips, the wan complexion, the flannel shirts from K mart, the wire-rimmed glasses that never fit right. From what Lulling had ascertained, not even Davies considered his life anything other than mundane and dull, a continuous loop of film canisters, sporting events, car rides to Spring Green, Pizza Hut pizzas. Barbara Hoffman had been the catalyst for surprise and variation. She was the mercurial element that raised his life to the extraordinary. Desperate for her charms, Davies became oblivious to her dangers. In February Lulling had knocked on Davies's apartment door and warned the shipping clerk that his life was in serious peril because of his association with Barbara Hoffman.

"Well, I ain't dead yet," Davies had replied.

The logic was irrefutable.

Exactly one month had passed since Davies's body was discovered in the bathtub. When everyone opined suicide, Lulling knew it was the coldest, most cunning murder he had ever investigated. Without a major miracle, without Curtis's testimony and a mountain of circumstantial evidence, they would never convict Barbara Hoffman.

Earlier in the week Ruth Davies had phoned him. The insurance company had informed her that Barbara Hoffman had filed claim for the money from the policies her son had originally left to his mother but had changed over to Barbara as beneficiary prior to his death. Due to the extenuating circumstances payment was being delayed, but unless Hoffman was charged with a crime she would

be regarded as proper beneficiary. Ruth Davies was outraged. She had consulted a lawyer. Why was she being
deprived of the money from Jerry's life insurance policies,
and why wasn't Barbara being charged with a crime?

Lulling had tried to explain the intricacies, but she
had no patience for the complexities of the matter. It was
unfair that her son was dead, and it was unfair that she
would not receive the money he had intended for his
mother, whom he had always loved and looked after, and
she repeated the theme until she had herself so confused
and upset that she had to hang up. Lulling entrusted her
with his home phone number, which was unlisted, and
said she could call again and that Barbara Hoffman, sometime soon, would be charged with killing her son.

His desk had been cleaned out. The paraphernalia and
accumulations of eighteen years as a detective—the coffee
mug, the manila folders of newspaper clippings, the photographs of his family, the collection of pipes and packs of
pipe cleaners and empty tobacco pouches—were dumped
into a brown box and tucked under his arm. He remembered that his wife had arranged for a dinner party with
family and a couple of friends at Smokey's of University
Avenue. He was late. Perhaps the prime rib would put him
in a mood to celebrate.

—— 31 ——

At a hearing on May 10th before Judge P. Charles Jones,
Don Eisenberg asked that the allegations that his client
had murdered Harry Berge be dismissed. Eisenberg
charged that "massive prejudicial publicity has created a
tremendous bias in violation of the defendant's Fifth
Amendment right to due process of the law."

The prosecution countered that the defense attorney
himself was the source of much of the media coverage
surrounding the case, making inflammatory statements to
the press and TV medias.

In the next several weeks Eisenberg filed seven separate motions for dismissal of the charges. A medical problem delayed matters. Judge Jones was scheduled for ear surgery, and the motions hearing was postponed until July.

All motions were finally taken under advisement on July 21st. It was Jones's intention to render a decision by mid-August.

—— 32 ——

The avuncular tone was absent from Sam Cerro's voice. He recited the morning baseball odds monotonously, as if reading a weather report, and omitted the usual quips and advice he dispersed to his betting customers.

Sam Cerro had other thoughts to occupy his mind, like the fifteen years he faced for the cocaine bust. A probation officer was preparing a presentence report and recommendation, and Cerro feared he'd get slapped with the maximum penalty. He didn't want to serve hard time, not at his age.

Admittedly Cerro had no one to blame but himself. Trying to purchase coke from a couple of federal agents was stupid. He thought he could beat the charges by claiming the government had induced the crime. But Don Eisenberg, his attorney, pleaded him guilty. What mercy would the courts allow? His life was a roster of illegal conduct—little scams like fraud, gambling, selling stolen merchandise, drug manufacture and distribution, tax evasion, loan sharking.

A month ago Sam had called Jim Doyle and suggested that a mutually beneficial exchange could be arranged. The DA said he could discuss matters only with Cerro's attorney. Therefore he would write to Eisenberg and propose they confer. Eisenberg denied any contact from the DA's office. Cerro again called Doyle, who insisted it was Eisenberg and not the DA who was stalling.

Sam next discussed the matter with Ken Curtis. His partner noted that Eisenberg represented Hoffman and that a deal that included Curtis's testimony would seriously injure Hoffman's chances for acquittal. He suggested that Sam fire Eisenberg, who was obviously caught between two clients, and hire someone to negotiate with Doyle. Cerro resisted the idea. A large retainer had been paid to Eisenberg to handle Cerro's legal problems. Eisenberg had kept Sam out of jail before. The man owned a reputation as the best.

"And he refuses to bargain with Doyle, who's hungry for a deal," Curtis had rebutted.

Sam was left confused.

As the date of his sentencing neared, he felt a panic in his chest, and every day it enlarged, like a rock that grew bigger. Fifteen years! Soon the rock would be so big he wouldn't be able to swallow.

After booking the day's baseball action Sam Cerro dialed the DA. Doyle repeated the dilemma: without the cooperation of Cerro's lawyer nothing could be arranged, and despite Doyle's efforts Eisenberg had not responded.

Cerro said he understood. He hung up and called a lawyer named Al Corzinski. By noon, after a flurry of phone calls, Cerro had dismissed Eisenberg as his lawyer and hired Corzinski.

Eisenberg was irate. Doyle knew he'd have a deal.

And Sam Cerro relaxed a little. Fifteen years in the joint would be fatal, he surmised. But he could ride out six months. He could hide in the shadows and endure.

— 33 —

The district attorney's arrangement with Sam Cerro was consolidated in a few hours. It proved to be the same deal Chuck Lulling had offered three months earlier.

During negotiations Cerro made it clear that he could not promise Larry Sawyer's cooperation. He guessed Sawyer would leave the state to avoid being hit with a subpoena. He did guarantee a full disclosure from Ken Curtis in exchange for a term of six months, plus two years' probation.

Doyle anticipated criticism for bargaining with Cerro. In a statement to the press he elaborated the rationale for his decision. Murder one was treated as the more serious charge. It was the ultimate breech of the social contract among citizens. The prosecution of this act had to be the foremost priority. Therefore, while drug traffickers deserved the strictest treatment, unique circumstances had forced him to compromise. Cerro would still serve time in jail, Doyle was quick to mention.

What the deal with Cerro implied, and what Doyle evaded in his press conference, was that the state had reached a dead end in its case against Barbara Hoffman. It had been four months since Jerry Davies had died from an overdose of cyanide, and no charges had been filed. The police seemed content to let the death pass as suicide, which could be interpreted as a sign of their inability to dig up any evidence implicating Hoffman. The charges concerning Berge rested on Davies's testimony, and Davies was gone. The edifice of circumstantial evidence stood hollow without Davies to anchor it.

The plea bargain with Cerro was criticized in newspaper and television editorials. The lack of progress in the Berge case was attacked, and questions were raised concerning Davies's mysterious suicide. The DA, normally sensitive to adverse publicity, shrugged his shoulders and sloughed it off. The case was far too complex for him to be worrying about media opinion.

At a John Doe hearing held in early August 1978, before circuit court judge Angela Bartell, Ken Curtis took the witness stand. Over Eisenberg's vehement objections Curtis told of Barbara Hoffman's plans to murder someone—an unnamed shipping clerk at the U.W.—for an enormous insurance payoff. He spoke of confronting Barbara with his knowledge and warning her that she would never succeed. He told of what he had seen written on the blackboard in her apartment. He related that she had confessed the plot to him, including the marriage plans and

honeymoon in Mexico and botulism, and that he had
assumed she had abandoned her plans until he'd read
about her alleged connection to Harry Berge's death. It
was essentially the same story he'd told to Lulling that
night at the Embers Restaurant. Now the prosecution had
a new anchor to center its case.

— 34 —

It was the attitude in those days, Liza said. We were
young, and there weren't any rules, and it was fun to
experiment. The waitress brought her more hot water for
her herbal tea. Liza sat in the Ovens of Brittany Cafe and
watched the pedestrian traffic on State Street.

Those days to which she referred were the early seventies, when she had moved to Madison from Viroqua, a
small rural community in the Kickapoo River valley. It
was like traveling to a different planet. Liza had enrolled as
a freshman, class of 1971, with the vague desire to become a veterinarian. Two years later she had dropped out.
Madison held too many distractions. There was the an-
tiwar movement and the women's movement and the com-
mittee against racism. The 4-H Club in Viroqua had not
prepared her for this whirlwind. There were handsome
boys with scraggly hair and beards, and drugs and sex,
and no thought about the consequences of their actions.
Nothing mattered much beyond the immediate moment.
There was a carelessness and a nonchalance about things
that should have been important. It was easy to lose one-
self.

Liza drifted, through boyfriends and political ideals
and into the parlors. The money was good; the drugs were
good. It was an insulated little universe. The women were
young runaways, or coeds like her, and almost everyone
had a favorite anesthetic to help her slide through the
hours at the parlor. Barbara Hoffman liked 'ludes. Liza
chose marijuana. Others opted for speed or booze, but

rare was the woman who did a shift straight. The parlor was a gloomy world, not without humor but mostly dull and oppressive. Drugs made it bearable, made it go fast, made it seem as if it were happening to someone else.

Liza stirred honey into her tea. She wanted to talk to someone about those years in the parlor. Although it was in the past, her work as a masseuse still affected her. Normal relations with men were impossible. But what was normal? The men who frequented the parlors seemed normal. Old definitions had lost their meaning. She wondered if she would ever trust a man again, if she would ever look and not try to guess his secret pleasure or his private perversion. After a time Liza could read which men wanted to be caressed, which men wanted all the extras, which men merely wanted thirty-five minutes of companionship, and which men wanted to be serviced and done. For some the times at the parlors were the only moments of intimacy in a lonely existence. For others a visit was strictly mechanical, like getting the oil in the car changed. Liza had pretended this didn't affect her. But she never held a boyfriend for more than two months.

How did she get out? Liza remembered the day exactly. While shopping for groceries at Kohl's on Park Street, she saw one of her regular customers. He was pushing a shopping cart, picking up milk and butter, and he walked directly past, within a foot of her, without uttering a word, without so much as a glance or a nod. She was invisible. At first she wanted to say hello. Then she just smiled, and when he ignored her Liza wanted to scream. But she didn't scream. Instead she cried. In Kohl's on Park Street, in the dairy department next to the bins of cheddar cheese, Liza sobbed because she was invisible. A week later she quit the parlors.

Liza finished her tea. The hot water was now cold.

It was the attitude in those days. The drugs and sex had addled her head. Boyfriends came and vanished. Rarely did a relationship last more than a couple of weeks before she invented an excuse to break it off. But Liza was changing. She had a day job. She glanced at her wrist-

watch and realized she had to hurry. She had signed up
for a yoga class, and the first session began in fifteen
minutes. Liza didn't want to be late. She thought the yoga
might help her sort things out, put those days and her life
into some kind of perspective.

— 35 —

The court's ruling on dismissal motions, originally scheduled for August 1978, was not issued until September
21st. On that date Judge P. Charles Jones rendered his
decision, rejecting all defense motions that the charges
against Barbara Hoffman for the murder of Harry Berge
be dropped. However, Jones did order a new preliminary
hearing, which would be "limited" to considering only the
cyanide evidence and Davies's alleged suicide notes.

The hearing on this matter was set for October but
was delayed because defense attorney Eisenberg had to
argue a fraud case in California and would not have
proper time to prepare. Thus the hearing was rescheduled
for November 16th.

— 36 —

Barbara Hoffman crawled out the passenger door of her
attorney's ivory Jaguar XJ6 and fixed an implacable expression on her face. From the sidewalk she peered at the
whitecaps that clapped on Lake Monona's waters. Birch
trees shivered on Turville Point. The city beaches—B. B.
Clarke, Olbrich, Olin—were sandy and deserted and
looked like strips of bald skin. Don Eisenberg tugged at
her elbow, and together they entered the courthouse
building.

It was the afternoon of November 16th. Ten months
had elapsed since Hoffman's arrest for the murder of

Harry Berge. The hearings and motions and court dates seemed infinite. Eisenberg insisted that every delay, every postponement, worked to their benefit.

Her case had been sent back to Judge William Byrne by Judge Jones, who had ordered a "limited" preliminary be conducted because of the discovery of new evidence: the thirty-seven times the lethal dose of cyanide that had been found in Berge's body and the letters from Davies exonerating Barbara and implying that he was culpable for the crime. Eisenberg had vigorously protested this change of court but to no avail.

As previously, Barbara Hoffman's appearance prompted an intense excitement in the courthouse. Secretaries stood in the hallway and whispered. Desk clerks pointed fingers from behind glass enclosures as Barbara and Eisenberg waited for an elevator. Television and radio crews labored, wading in a sea of black cable and electrical tape, arranging their equipment for the best vantage from which to record the legal proceedings. Because of a recent Wisconsin Supreme Court ruling, television cameras were permitted, with restrictions, in the courtroom. The court gallery was packed with media people and curious onlookers abuzz with anticipation for the next chapter in the sad, sensational saga, eager for a glimpse of the accused, petite in slacks and sweater, her mouth rigid, her eyes cold and distant behind the tortoiseshell glasses.

Barbara's gaze didn't vary from straight ahead. It didn't scan the crowd for friends or supporters. If she had any supporters, they were not in attendance. Spectators who couldn't squeeze into the aisles listened from the hall. Even Judge Byrne was stunned by the attention. This was a prelim hearing, not a trial, and his courtroom was jammed. The monocular lenses of the TV cameras swiveled from the bench to Barbara Hoffman and back to the bench. Microphones, felt-covered and bulbous, picked up the judge's cough, the rustle of papers, the stenographer's sneeze.

Eisenberg was first to address the court, and he assumed the offense. The defense counsel proclaimed that the case ought to be argued before Judge Jones, that the defense refused to recognize the jurisdiction of Byrne's court and would not introduce any motions until this matter was rectified satisfactorily. Moreover, if a change was not forthcoming, the defense would be forced to appeal.

Byrne and Eisenberg bickered.

Assistant DA Chris Spencer interjected. The prosecution wished to introduce a motion that might render the conflict moot, said Spencer. The prosecution wished to dismiss the charges against the defendant.

Byrne blinked. Spectators clamored. TV cameras pivoted madly from Spencer to the bench to the defense table and caught Barbara Hoffman slumped in her chair. Her face had not cracked its icy composure, but her eyes had widened in disbelief. Had she heard correctly, or was this a wild, spinning fantasy?

Her lawyer clasped her hand. Things progressed swiftly. The judge asked if the defense objected to the motion for dismissal.

Suspicious, his mind racing to detect a trap, perhaps flirting with the egotistical notion that Burr and Spencer were afraid to challenge him on purely circumstantial evidence, Eisenberg replied, unable to conceal the jubilation in his voice. The defense had no problems with the motion, he said, showing the flicker of a victorious smile.

Byrne commanded the gallery to order. He pronounced that the murder charge lodged against Ms. Hoffman was dismissed. The court adjourned.

The merry defense lawyer hugged his client, who had yet to comprehend that the ordeal was over and they had won.

Reporters hustled from the gallery to phone their stations and papers with the dramatic news, but the rest of the crowd lingered, stunned, still waiting for something to happen. Anita Clark approached Barbara for a comment on the startling development. Eisenberg interceded. He helped Barbara into her wool coat and slipped into his leather jacket. They exited without remark to the press, spectators following, flashbulbs popping in gasps of blue, Eisenberg happily accepting congratulations.

The assemblage in the corridor jostled for a view. The scene got noisy, almost boisterous, with a cacophony of bailiffs calling for order, with questions, and curiosity, and the rampant gurgle of speculation. Despite the din and congestion Barbara's first step outside the courtroom, free of the charge of willfully and knowingly causing the death of Harry Berge, seemed light, effortless.

On the second step she was ambushed by two Madison cops.

George Croal and Kathy Frisch pushed to the front of the tumult and intercepted her. They shoved a criminal complaint in Barbara's face, accusing her of the first-degree murders of both Harry Berge and Jerry Davies. Amid the commotion Croal shouted that she was under arrest.

A momentary panic seized Barbara Hoffman. She grabbed desperately for her lawyer. Eisenberg's triumphant grin disintegrated. He turned and beckoned for Judge Byrne, hollered for the bench's intervention. Byrne was gone. Croal latched onto Barbara's arm and steered her across the hall to the courtroom of the Judicial Court Commissioner George Northrup. Eisenberg fumed. His victory was collapsing into chaos.

"Get your hands off her!" he bellowed at the cop. "This is an illegal arrest."

Croal scowled and ignored the warning. Eisenberg charged forward and blocked the path. The hallway reverberated with invective and threat. The two men postured and challenged with clenched fists, behaving like feisty schoolboys begging for a brawl, each egging the other to throw the first punch. Before blows were hurled, bailiffs separated the combatants. Eisenberg, pugnacious, irate, had to be restrained from obstructing the arrest.

Although amused by the theatrics in the hallway, drama was not the reason Burr and Spencer had dropped the original murder charge. The new complaint against

Barbara Hoffman based on the cyanide discovery represented a critical tactical maneuver for the prosecution. According to Wisconsin state law a criminal charge can be refiled if new evidence is found. By dismissing the original complaint the prosecution avoided an appeal issue. Most importantly, however, the new complaint conjoined the two murders so that both cases could be tried at the same time and before the same jury. The burden of separating the murder charges and arguing that they should be contested in different courtrooms, at different times, with different juries, now rested with the defense.

A surprised Judge Northrup was hearing traffic violations when his court was invaded. The pandemonium in the corridor spilled through the double oak doors and into the stale arguments about radar guns and parking fines. Eisenberg escorted Hoffman to the front row, where they huddled in private and studied the complaint she had been served. They were pursued by the procession from Byrne's court—reporters and spectators scrambling for seating space, TV and radio crews lugging their bulky equipment, clumsily barging about, testing the lighting, unraveling cable.

Northrup demanded quiet, but the traffic court had been hopelessly disrupted. He finished the schedule promptly and, without hesitation, began Hoffman's bail hearing.

The new complaint alleged that Hoffman had murdered Berge and Davies with cyanide. The disposal of Berge's body as recounted by Jerry Davies was outlined, as was a brief history of Davies's and Hoffman's relationship and their quest and procurement of a $750,000 insurance policy on Davies's life. The dispersement of Berge's estate, including property and insurance benefits, to Hoffman, a.k.a. Linda Millar, was stated. Davies's subsequent death and the discovery of cyanide by the state crime lab was described. An investigation of the U.W. chemistry laboratories was detailed, including a report of cyanide missing and presumed stolen from Dr. Bruce Selman's lab, of building personnel identifying the defendant as being present in the chemistry facility during this time, of professors stating that the lethal toxicity of cyanide had been discussed in classes Barbara had attended. Furthermore, Ken Curtis's testimony at a John Doe hearing in August, where Barbara's plot to kill Davies had been sketched, was cited. Also mentioned was that Charles Geisen, Eisenberg's law partner, had contacted the DA in early January and offered Curtis's information for consideration of leniency for a client facing criminal charges.

The bail hearing commenced with the defense waiving a reading of the complaint. The prosecution team requested that a cash bail of $30,000 be established, which was twice the original amount. Eisenberg ridiculed the sum as outrageous. The defendant had not missed a court appointment, had exhibited no indication of flight, and posed no danger to the community. Burr emphasized the severity of a double murder charge.

"I don't care if it's one murder or fifty murders, or deaths, as I prefer to call them," cried Eisenberg. "I want a signature bond."

Northrup set bail at $20,000 cash. It meant $5,000 would have to be added to the $15,000 already posted before Barbara could be released.

"You're going to make her sit in the Dane County Jail?" Eisenberg asked, amazed and angry.

"We're dealing with two counts of first-degree murder," said Northrup.

The defense lawyer harangued. He castigated the conduct of the police, the deception of the prosecution, the decision of the court.

"Let me say I'm very disappointed in this court and with you personally," he stormed at Northrup.

"You can hold your press conference in the hall, Mr. Eisenberg," snapped the judge. He announced that the preliminary hearing would be heard before Judge Angela Bartell on November 27th, and court was adjourned.

The media arranged a press conference area in the corridor. Burr and Spencer disappointed reporters when they declined comment and skipped out the stairway.

While the prosecution took refuge in beer and pop-
corn at the Pinckney Street Hideaway, their loquacious
adversary appeared to relish the attention. Eisenberg pontificated, joking with reporters, chatting as if it were cocktail hour at the Nakoma Country Club. He played furious
that the prelim was assigned to Bartell, the same judge
who had presided over the John Doe hearing that
prompted the Davies charge. He acted appalled that Northrup had raised the bail and remanded Barbara to custody until he could gather the extra cash.

A question was put forth about the marriage and
murder plot Barbara Hoffman had contrived for Davies.
Eisenberg cautioned that Curtis was an unreliable personality who may have misconstrued or completely fabricated
the bizarre story of the plot. He predicted Charles Geisen
would testify at a prelim hearing that specific elements in
the complaint regarding the Davies plot were undeniably
false. He stated uncategorically that his law partner had
never mentioned any of the strange tale to him, nor had
Geisen informed him of any efforts for negotiation with
the DA. His legal strategy, Eisenberg elaborated, was to
demand a separate hearing and trial on each of the murder
accusations.

Eisenberg ambled to the elevator, no doubt noting
that a TV camera captured his every gesture for the evening news. In an hour he returned with $5,000 and ob-
tained Barbara's release.

— 37 —

In the weeks following the November 16th debacle defense attorney Eisenberg plotted strategy. He filed numerous motions with the court, including one asking that
Angela Bartell remove herself. Bartell consented and
withdrew. The case was shuffled to Moria Kruegar. However, she'd been involved in the first John Doe investigation in early January 1978. She also withdrew. The case
was placed before circuit court judge James Boll.

On April 16, 1979, Boll commenced a hearing to determine whether the charges of double murder against Barbara Hoffman were sufficient to merit a trial.

The prosecution's allegations as stated in the criminal complaint were sketched, and witnesses were brought forth to verify selected details. The insurance information was solicited.

Ken Curtis outlined Barbara's insidious plans to marry and murder Jerry Davies.

"I told her that I was aware of a plot for her to kill somebody, and that my attorney was also aware of it, and I showed her some insurance laws that I had my attorney Xerox." Two days later, Curtis testified, Barbara had confessed to her plot. That conversation had occurred in early spring of 1977.

Curtis's intervention, according to the prosecution, caused Barbara to amend her scheme. The marriage to Davies was postponed. Barbara established a new identity, complete with social security number, bank account, library card, and post office box. Thus Linda Millar was born.

In October 1977 Harry Berge decided to change his life insurance policy and designate Linda Millar as the beneficiary. Less than three weeks later he instructed his lawyer to alter the deed on his house and list Linda Millar as joint tenant, for "one dollar and other due and valuable considerations."

Berge had become acquainted with Barbara Hoffman at Jan's Health Spa some two to three years prior. With the third premium soon due on Davies's policy, and in desperate need of cash, Barbara had invited Harry Berge to her apartment on December 22, 1977, murdered him with cyanide, and enlisted Davies to help her hide the corpse. The $750,000 insurance policy on Davies remained in effect. In January 1978 Barbara Hoffman was arrested for Harry Berge's murder.

Bail was posted, and in February 1978 Barbara Hoffman mailed a check for the third premium to Transport Life but issued a stop payment a few days later. Davies then changed other life insurance policies he held to name Barbara Hoffman, rather than his mother, as beneficiary. Two weeks later, on Easter weekend in March, Davies was discovered dead in his bathtub, killed by a lethal ingestion of cyanide.

The prosecutor's version portrayed a complex and sinister web of circumstances that revolved around sex, love, and money, a web that had snared a pair of gullible, lonely men, a web spun by Barbara Hoffman.

Eisenberg attacked the state's reconstruction of events. Davies never accused Barbara of having any connection with Berge's death, only with finding the body in her apartment. Moreover, Davies had declared openly that Barbara was innocent of the charges against her. Certainly Davies didn't consider Barbara Hoffman a threat to his own well-being. He'd dated her until his death. The $750,000 insurance policy on Davies had expired in March, which eliminated any motive for killing Davies. Eisenberg also emphasized that the state's contention that Barbara Hoffman had concocted a plan to marry someone, kill him with botulism, and collect the insurance money relied on a witness who had not come forward until seven months after the fact and then only after a plea bargain arrangement had been made to entice his testimony.

During the three-day hearing before Boll the defense offered its own interpretation of the killings. Davies was depicted as a spurned lover. In a fit of jealousy and rage he had murdered Berge, the rival for Barbara's affections, and had implicated Barbara as a sort of punishment for her infidelity. When police acted on his statements, Davies realized the gravity of the insinuation against Barbara. He maintained her innocence, but his entreaties were ignored and his beloved was charged with murder. He saw a doctor for anxiety and was given a prescription for Valium. Upset, depressed, trapped in a situation of his own device that had leapt out of control, Davies wrote four copies of a letter that would clarify the circumstances and exonerate Barbara. He'd swallowed a prescribed dosage of Valium to calm his jitters and then committed suicide by the most

readily available method—the cyanide he had administered to Harry Berge.

The credibility of the scenario was buttressed by the
letters Davies had posted to Anita Clark, Eisenberg, the
DA, and the police on the weekend he had died.

Eisenberg and John Burr sparred over the admissibility of the letters as evidence. The defense lawyer argued
that the letters were a kind of suicide note. Eisenberg cited
court statutes that state that dying declarations are admissible in cases of homicide where the death of the declarant is the subject of the charge. Burr countered that
there was no indication when the letters had been written.
They were not dated. Unless it could be proved Davies
wrote the letters the day he died, they could not be considered suicide notes.

"The statement tending to expose the declarant to
criminal liability and offered to exculpate the accused is
not admissible unless it's corroborated," the prosecutor
argued.

In a victory for the defense Boll accepted the letters as
evidence.

After three days of hearings the court issued its conclusions. The Transport Life policy for $750,000 had been
terminated prior to Davies's death, yet there was no evidence that the defendant was cognizant of the fact of its
expiration, Boll ruled. The decisive witness at the prelim,
the judge recognized, was Ken Curtis. Boll acknowledged
that Curtis's testimony was tainted by his plea bargain
agreement with the DA's office relating to Sam Cerro and
by his relationship with the defendant. These considerations, however, did not negate his testimony. A final com-
plication was Jerry Davies. Boll read a statement made by
Davies at a John Doe hearing:

> I would like to say that I believe she is innocent and
> just panicked. I know myself that I didn't do the right
> thing, and she must have been under a lot more stress
> than I was when she found that body.

Which Davies, the court asked, was to be believed?

The Jerry Davies of the original prelim, whose testimony implicated the defendant? The Jerry Davies of the John Doe, who seemed equivocal concerning the defendant's role? Or the Jerry Davies who'd penned those last letters, apologizing for his blundering and absolving the defendant of any part in the murder? It must be for a jury to decide, said the judge.

The prosecution had established probable cause, Boll ruled. Barbara would stand trial for the murders of Harry Berge and Jerry Davies.

—— 38 ——

On August 21, 1979, Don Eisenberg filed numerous motions on behalf of the defendant.

He requested a change of venue, presented a motion to dismiss charges due to insufficient evidence, sought to have the complaint dismissed because it contained "deliberately false material, reckless material misstatements, negligent material, misstatements of fact, and/or intentional lies." He filed a motion to dismiss because of improper John Doe proceedings. He asked that the murder charges be severed, arguing that if a defendant may be prejudiced as a result of the joinder then the court may order severance. Furthermore Eisenberg contended that "the acts alleged lack any connection in time, place, or design."

The court took all motions under advisement, and all motions were eventually dismissed.

—— 39 ——

Various postponements and delays forced the trial to be rescheduled, from November 1979 to February 1980 and again, to May 1980. Almost a half dozen Dane County judges had participated in some aspect of the case, and the trial was finally assigned to Michael Torphy, a judge who had had no previous involvement in the case's legal machinations.

The selection of Torphy to preside pleased both the prosecution and the defense. The jurist had earned a reputation as tough yet fair. He was extremely well versed in evidentiary law. He refrained from interjecting his personality and dominating a courtroom, preferring to allow the lawyers a broad latitude to develop and argue their case. In a trial that threatened to be as long and tedious as the Berge-Davies murder case—courthouse veterans anticipated three weeks of testimony—Torphy's quiet approach would be a big asset. The trial would move as smoothly and expeditiously as possible. Also, the judge's poise and restraint would act as a counterbalance to the volatile and vitriolic Eisenberg. Torphy would keep the courtroom skirmish focused on the charges and their merits.

On May 9, 1980, after studying defense briefs arguing that the allegations of murder against Barbara Hoffman be severed and conducted independently and in separate trials, Torphy announced that he had rejected the motion. The Berge and Davies charges would be heard together, by the same jury, which would render a verdict on each charge.

"The court concludes that the charges are properly joined and need not be severed. A great bulk of the evidence introducible in the 'Berge' case is arguably introducible in the 'Davies' case to show motive, intent, and/or plan (i.e., the beneficiary of insurance evidence, complications in body moving, Davies prelim, cause of death)."

The ruling was a severe setback for the defense, and Eisenberg was bitterly disappointed. Yet he still felt confident that he could win an acquittal for Hoffman on both charges.

A trial date was set for mid-June.

— 40 —

Despite the two-and-a-half years they'd had to assemble their attack, Doyle and Burr and Spencer were less than confident. Their key witness had been Davies, and he was dead. They had no substantial piece of evidence to intractably link Barbara Hoffman to his murder, nothing tangible such as a fingerprint, such as a neighbor seeing her enter or depart from Davies's apartment on the fatal Easter weekend. They had an incriminating morass of circumstantial evidence, but their pivotal witness now was Ken Curtis, a massage parlor owner, a thug whose testimony had been elicited through a plea bargain deal. And even Curtis had never claimed that Barbara Hoffman had intended to kill anyone with cyanide. Botulism was what she was going to use, Curtis said, but there were no indications of botulism anywhere else in the case. Consequently the prosecution team continued to dig, probing the evidence already collected. Had something been missed or overlooked?

Material from Berge's home in Stoughton and from Davies's apartment in Madison had been gathered and stored in the basement of the City-County Building. Burr and Spencer dug through a carton of Davies's personal papers that had been confiscated but not considered applicable as evidence. They knew that Jerry Davies, like Harry Berge, was a creature of compulsive habit. Chris Spencer fingered through Davies's checkbook, and the pattern that emerged was as routine as his life.

The entries were identical from month to month— payments for rent, utilities, telephone, car loan, newspaper delivery. Six to ten checks had been written each month, with miscellaneous checks to Pizza Hut or Kohl's or for Badger hockey tickets. The regularity astonished Spencer, and he wondered if his own existence would appear so mundane if viewed through his monthly bank withdrawals. At last a name repeated that was unfamiliar—Laabs. No further explanation or description.

Laabs—March 1977, $71.32. Laabs—again in March, then twice in April, for varying amounts. May showed other entries for Laabs. There was one entry for June, and then the name didn't appear again in Davies's checkbook. What was the flurry of payments for? Was it money to a friend? But who lends a friend $26.66?

"Ever hear of a place called Laabs?" Spencer asked John Burr.

The senior prosecutor shook his head and studied the anomaly in Davies's checking account. It was like a splatter of blips on an empty radar screen. The two lawyers scrambled upstairs and searched a Madison telephone directory. No listing in the white or the yellow pages. A secretary fetched a Milwaukee County phone book. Spencer volunteered to trot over to the public library, where phone directories for Wisconsin and most major U.S. cities were kept current. However, Milwaukee held an answer.

Laabs was listed. It was a chemical supply and equipment company.

Spencer immediately dialed the number and asked if it was possible to check on an order that was a couple years old. He was told to call back, for it would take time to retrieve the old orders and invoices, but yes, the records were still available and the company would cooperate. When Spencer called back at ten minutes to five that afternoon, nothing had been found.

Neither Burr, Spencer, nor Doyle rested well that night. Chances were that the Laabs thing was a fluke and another blind alley. Jury selection commenced in less than two weeks. Their case was a patchwork of circumstantial evidence, and it was easier to discern threads that frayed and unraveled than the weave that stitched the pattern together.

The next morning Spencer took a call from Milwaukee.

A large order had been placed with Laabs late in February 1977. It included beakers, test tubes, syringes, and watch glasses, among many other things. Part of the order was delivered to apartment 306, 638 State Street, in three separate shipments. The remaining items, which had been back-ordered, were sent to apartment 7, 2305 South Park Street, in four separate shipments. All items were sent COD, paid for by check by Gerald T. Davies, and posted through United Parcel Service—except for one special shipment.

Small quantities of sodium cyanide and potassium cyanide had been ordered. Since these chemicals were poisons—the UPS did not handle what were considered Class B poisons—the cyanides were sent by a commercial trucker, Motor Transport Company, delivered to apartment 7, 2305 South Park Street, and were signed and paid for by Jerry Davies.

The salesman who took the original order told Spencer that the order had been placed by a woman over the telephone and that she'd called back only once, and that was to change the shipping address.

Spencer could not contain his excitement. He and Burr conferred with Doyle. A list of the materials ordered was being sent from Laabs the same afternoon. UPS and Motor Transport would be contacted, and their receipt forms would be confiscated for evidence. Eisenberg would have to be notified under the state's disclosure laws.

Instead of the inference that Barbara Hoffman could have pilfered cyanide from the university, they now had solid evidence that she had had the murder weapon delivered to Madison. The irony was that Jerry Davies had signed and paid for the poison that had killed him.

PART III
A Judgment of Sorts

— 1 —

For the two-and-a-half years since the initial charge of murder had been lodged against her, Barbara Hoffman had been free on bail. Her residence remained 638 State Street, apartment 306. She inhabited the same white-washed rooms where Ken Curtis had used her infatuation to gain sexual favors on an idle summer afternoon, where Jerry Davies had slept, dreaming of a future filled with love and marital bliss, where Harry Berge had asphyxiated and died due to cyanide poisoning. For the past two years Barbara had been employed by the state of Wisconsin as a limited-term clerical worker. She had audited psychology courses at the university. The fact that she was only one semester shy of a bachelor of science degree in biochemistry apparently had little relevance for her.

On June 15, 1980, the day before jury selection for her trial was to begin, Barbara celebrated her twenty-eighth birthday.

— 2 —

On June 16, 1980, jury selection for the Barbara Hoffman murder trial began. Defense attorney Eisenberg was buoyed by the extensive delay in bringing the case to court.

"Do you realize there are people in Madison who don't even know who Barbara Hoffman is?" he commented gleefully to a reporter.

Judge Michael Torphy informed the jury pool that those selected would confront an enormous task. The court expected over a hundred witnesses, perhaps two hundred exhibits of evidence, and a trial that might last three weeks, during which time they would be sequestered.

The prosecution did not have a rigid concept of the perfect juror. Burr believed an adept lawyer's intuition was the best guide to jury selection. Because of the morass of circumstantial evidence that represented the bulk of their case, Burr and Spencer wanted people with common sense, people who seemed to have the capacity and intelligence to endure a lengthy trial and remember the knots of evidence and how they were connected. Each potential juror was considered individually. People with an active religious affiliation were preferred.

On the matter of Barbara's background, would a juror view a woman who worked in a massage parlor as a whore, or as a little girl corrupted and led astray, or as a mixed-up college kid who needed money? It was a volatile issue, and rather than guess at a juror's reaction Burr and Spencer decided to base their decision on other factors. They wished for an older jury, though they didn't want anyone with a child Barbara's age, fearing a sympathetic response to Barbara's parents, who were scheduled to testify. They also didn't want a person whose opinion had been affected by the barrage of pretrial publicity.

"When was the last time you read or heard anything about this case?" was Burr's constant refrain.

If the prosecution approached jury selection in a miscellaneous manner, the defense used stricter guidelines in ascertaining who was acceptable.

"I want a smart, sophisticated, liberal juror," Eisenberg told reporters at the end of the first day's proceedings. "One who realizes that massage parlors are a fact of life yet is sensitive enough to know that people can still form real relationships in that atmosphere."

He wanted people whose opinion would not be swayed by the testimony of authority figures. Eisenberg asked potential jurors whether they would place more credence on a police officer's word than on the testimony of any other witness. Did they understand the law's presumption of innocence? Did they understand that an allegation was not a verdict of guilty issued by the police? Would they be offended by strong language used in the heat and fury of a court battle?

Eisenberg had assembled a composite of the ideal juror. He employed the individual voir dire extensively, probing religious habits, television preferences, and political inclinations in an effort to discover who matched his model. He asked what social functions people attended, what newspapers or magazines they subscribed to, what hobbies they enjoyed. He was curious as to which of the following people—President Eisenhower, President Kennedy, Martin Luther King, Jr., or Ralph Nader—potential jurors admired the most. Eisenberg wanted a juror with progressive leanings. Eisenhower people would be too conservative to understand Barbara Hoffman. People who chose Kennedy would be more open-minded, more liberal about social and sexual mores. King and Nader admirers, he figured, might be more willing to question authority and would not be awed by the testimony of cops and state experts that the prosecution would present.

Unlike the prosecution, Eisenberg examined people's attitude toward massage parlors. "Do you believe a person who works in a massage parlor is either a whore or a prostitute?" he posed. Should massage parlors be shut down? Should consenting adults be left alone to do what they wished?

Appearance and occupation were important indicators to the defense. Eisenberg wanted Barbara Hoffman judged by hip sophisticates, minority people, blue-collar workers, young adults with an orientation toward the drug culture. But in a city with a black population of less than 3 percent, where the work force is predominantly clerical and service-related, dominated by the university and the state government, such a mix would have been difficult to concoct.

Consequently Eisenberg relied on experience and savvy to determine the type of juror he desired. No sociological surveys were undertaken, nor were psychologists hired to scrutinize the potential jurors. Such tools were expensive and often wasteful, and like Burr, Eisenberg felt a good attorney should follow his instincts.

The selection process was completed in two-and-a-half days, and on the early afternoon of June 18th a jury was seated. It consisted of seven men and five women, the oldest fifty-seven, the youngest eighteen, with a mean age of thirty-four years. All jurors claimed to be regular churchgoers, though none belonged to any fundamentalist group. Barbara Hoffman's guilt or innocence before the law would be decided by a student, a maintenance man, an engineer, a manager of a local Farm and Fleet store, a secretary, a security guard, an art teacher, a typist, a postal clerk, a road crewman, a nursery gardener, and a housewife.

Both prosecution and defense claimed to be satisfied with whom they had chosen.

— 3 —

The day before jury selection commenced, Burr and Spencer moved into a motel near the capitol square in order to devote their full energies to the trial and avoid the inevitable distractions of home. This created a strain on both families.

Already the lawyers had been working long days in preparation, and the small irritations—the late dinners, the early departures, the absence when a kid was sick or when the kitchen sink didn't drain—were having a cumulative effect. Spencer had two youngsters, and his active participation in their upbringing allowed his wife a reprieve from constant child-care duties. Now that time was forfeited.

The Burr home had welcomed its third child just

three months previously. The responsibilities of parent-hood were dumped on his wife and his mother because of Burr's intense commitment to the case. Procuring grocer-ies, changing diapers, getting the eldest to soccer practice became a test of fortitude and nerves. For another three weeks to a month, for however long it took, Judy Burr had to maintain the kids, the household, and her sanity in lieu of her husband's appearance.

Both lawyers spoke to their families each night on the telephone, and yet they felt exiled and suffered pangs of separation despite their absorption with the prosecution of Barbara Hoffman.

Whatever the hardships, Burr considered the semi-isolation a necessity. The case against Barbara Hoffman was sprawling, complex, intricate. It required an intense attention to detail and a prolonged concentration on a multiplicity of minor elements. Hoffman had been daring and ingenious.

She had not left a trail of fingerprints. No one had witnessed either victim alive and in her company on the day of his death. The method of killing, cyanide, had been discovered, but no traces of the chemical had been found in her possession or at her residence. There was no solid proof that she had ever purchased or pilfered the lethal dosage. Hard evidence against her was severely lacking. What the prosecution had gathered was an overwhelming quantity of fragments, scattered pieces that when re-arranged and properly reassembled could portray nothing other than her obvious guilt.

Nevertheless the coordination and presentation of ev-idence and testimony and the soldering of these fragments into a solid case were not the sole pressures on Spencer and Burr. The drama contained sundry dimensions.

The DA's office had withstood an avalanche of criti-cism for the plea bargain of Sam Cerro. Doyle had publicly explained his rationale, yet the feeling persisted that a drug dealer and acknowledged gambling kingpin had been treated softly in exchange for a dubious guarantee of tes-timony by a thug who earned a livelihood promoting vice.

Because of the delay in bringing Hoffman to trial, Cerro had already served his six months and was out on probation. There was now no leverage with Ken Curtis that could assure his testimony would be as powerful as in the John Doe and prelim hearings of over a year ago.

The DA had no recourse if Curtis's memory should suddenly become fuzzy. Furthermore, Curtis's character was anything but unimpeachable. How could the DA protect him from Eisenberg's ferocious cross-examination? And if the main witness was assailed, did the rest of the case totter? And if Hoffman was acquitted, how was justice served?

The television cameras provided an added pressure. The presence of video was a precedent. The Hoffman case was the first televised murder trial in Wisconsin history. Clips of the proceedings would highlight nightly newscasts. A cable TV company was broadcasting the trial in its entirety. The public would see a true courtroom soap opera as the revelations about love and sex and insurance money were aired.

Reputations would be earned or tarnished. Errors in judgment or strategy would occur in plain view. Neither a stenographer's transcript nor a newspaper article showed a lawyer stuttering over a question, or stalling for time as he tried to think how best to interrogate a hostile witness, or tediously debating an esoteric technicality of evidentiary law and having his motion rejected by the court. Burr must have fretted over the camera's unflinching eye. Court records and newspapers did not show pockmarks, the frayed collar of a pin-striped suit, or a face etched with cynicism and overwork.

Perhaps the most profound pressure put on the senior assistant DA was exerted by his own ego. John Burr had never lost a homicide trial. He had an almost perfect record in major cases of all kinds. He was tough, and he obtained convictions. He respected the framework of the judicial system and believed it delivered justice to individuals and to the society it purported to serve. The system was not without flaws, but the system was not rigged. Burr played the game hard and fair. He respected his opponents and was respected in return.

Don Eisenberg, however, was beyond the limits of Burr's tolerance. The veteran prosecutor would never admit his disdain for Eisenberg, for that would be granting Eisenberg a satisfaction he didn't wish him to have, but Burr despised the defense attorney.

To Burr, Eisenberg argued his cases in the papers, challenged judges, humiliated witnesses, was uncooperative in pretrial negotiations. Burr thought Eisenberg worried more about posture and publicity than about what was best for his client. In Burr's opinion, acclaim, not acquittal, was Eisenberg's priority.

Burr resented the defense attorney's conspicuous style and was irked by the defense attorney's renown, which he considered the result of unabashed self-promotion and media hype. There were better defense attorneys in town, and they didn't charge $120 an hour.

Yet Eisenberg was a formidable force in a courtroom. Clever and quick, he could transform a trial into a street brawl. He intimidated witnesses, and he was capable of stupefying a jury with his smooth, extemporaneous talk.

John Burr had a difficult case and a dangerous foe. He couldn't tolerate losing, especially not to Don Eisenberg.

Wednesday evening faded as the prosecution team discussed strategy in Burr's office. The vestiges of dinner—pizza crusts and Pepsi cans—littered a desk. Burr puffed a cigarette and stared out the window. A pink lacquer glossed Lake Monona's surface as the sun dropped quickly in the west. A water-skier in a wet suit skimmed over the water, waves curling from his skis like swirls of filigree.

Chris Spencer tuned in a Milwaukee Brewers game for distraction. Diagrams of the Davies and Hoffman apartments were taped to the wall. Propped on a file cabinet was a chart of the first day's probable witnesses. Photographs—color prints of the snowbank on Tomahawk

Ridge where Berge's body was discovered and the snow-bank behind 638 State Street where blood matching Berge's type was found two-and-one-half inches above the pavement in January, on the third examination—were balanced precariously on an empty Styrofoam coffee cup. Photocopies of Barbara Hoffman's phone records for the dates surrounding the days of Berge's and Davies's deaths, which had been subpoenaed from Wisconsin Bell, were thumbtacked to a bulletin board. On an index card Spencer had penciled APPARENTLY EXTRANEOUS BUT POSSIBLY IMPORTANT ITEMS OF INTEREST and stuck the label onto the board, which became a hodgepodge of miscellaneous information.

After reviewing the list of exhibits and prospective witnesses for the opening day, Burr and Spencer considered their opposing attorney. They decided to refrain from sparring with Eisenberg.

It was John Burr's strong belief that juries permitted defense lawyers to posture loudly and gesticulatively but that they were suspicious of flamboyant prosecutors. Society had elevated defense lawyers to the status of legendary folk heroes, whereas prosecutors quietly and efficiently amassed evidence and performed their duties. His own style fit the stereotype well.

Burr was sincere and persuasive. He dressed and spoke simply and with decorum. His image contrasted sharply with that of the brash Eisenberg. The prosecutors decided to emphasize this difference and hopefully to exploit it to their advantage.

They also decided to allow the defense attorney all the opportunity to harangue that he might want. Burr felt that Eisenberg often talked himself into trouble. He became entranced with the power of his own words and had difficulty shutting himself off. He might get nasty with a witness the jury perceived sympathetically. He might challenge a judge for the domain of the courtroom and alienate a jury. Rather than fight to contain Eisenberg's tirades, they would let him pursue them.

—— 4 ——

On June 19th the trial commenced.

As Burr addressed the court, Eisenberg was a frenzy of tiny and perpetual motions—scribbling points of rebuttal, paging through a ponderous notebook, rummaging about in his briefcase, pursing his lips, drumming his fingertips together as if supplying percussion for the prosecutor's drone. Rings ornamented Eisenberg's fingers and reflected the court lights, slivering the wattage into magnificent prisms.

Torphy's courtroom was jammed to overflowing. Fire marshals cleared out people who lined the walls, content to stand. Except for the camera and audio crew, everyone had to have a seat. Television monitors were hooked up in the hallway so that spectators too late to cram inside, as well as secretaries, office clerks, and lawyers on coffee breaks, could watch the drama. Bailiffs controlled the traffic in and out. Ordinarily gallery space would have been reserved for friends and family of the defendant, but strangely, Barbara Hoffman had no one in attendance to lend support or encouragement. Save for her attorney, she was alone.

A front aisle was designated for representatives of the press, but the majority of the media camped in a conference room across the hallway where special monitors had been arranged and where they could smoke or gossip when the proceedings got tedious.

Eisenberg's pronouncement to the contrary notwithstanding, two years of hearings, motions, and postponements had not dispelled public fascination with Barbara Hoffman's tawdry saga. The legal delays in bringing the former massage parlor masseuse to trial merely fueled the conjecture and mystery surrounding her character and the nature of Berge's and Davies's deaths.

Every preliminary hearing, it seemed, had revealed new developments or uncovered a startling discovery that demanded a reevaluation of the circumstances and a realignment of the players. Shadowy figures lurked on the periphery. The insurance agent who had sold Davies and Hoffman the $750,000 policy and then skipped to Mexico had successfully eluded police interrogation, yet he granted a telephone interview to a local newspaper in which he denied any wrongdoing. The friend who had originally told Curtis of Barbara's botulism plot remained nameless and had left the state to avoid a subpoena. Anonymous sources familiar with the police investigation whispered about chagrined college professors and business executives who had cosigned bank loans or written Barbara personal checks for thousands of dollars and now feared that their sexual liaisons with the notorious Barbie would be aired from the witness stand.

Rumor and embellishment were rampant. Women who had worked in the parlors, who knew Ken Curtis and his ruthless manner, wondered if Barbara Hoffman was simply a pawn in some grand conspiracy or if this was Curtis's twisted form of revenge for Barbara's brash defiance in leaving the parlor scene. Others speculated that the marriage-Mexico-botulism plot was an elaborate concoction by Ken Curtis to acquire a lenient sentence for his nefarious friend, Sam Cerro. Police and prosecutors put little faith in such gossip.

A few people intimate with Madison's prosperous sex business guessed that Curtis might have had an ulterior motive, that he feared Hoffman as a potential rival in the parlor trade and used his information not only to aid Cerro but to eliminate her threat. It was a fascinating speculation.

On her 1975 income tax return Barbara Hoffman, student and female counselor, claimed $22,112.50 in total wages, with Jan's Health Spa as the employer. This was two-and-a-half times the amount Jerry Davies had earned as a shipping clerk for the U.W. with almost ten years' experience. Reliable estimates placed Barbara's real earnings at probably twice the total reported, if tips, outside work, and unrecorded hours were included. After four years as an impoverished college student the massage parlors had been a windfall. And if a windfall for the lowly counselors, the business had to be extremely lucrative for the ownership.

Despite a loose management style—some nights Curtis neglected to pick up the day's receipts, leaving a nervous receptionist to hustle home with $4,000 or $5,000 in her purse—the parlors flourished. On Friday and Saturday nights customers couldn't get in the door to pay their cash and shoot their sperm fast enough. Madison supported a dozen massage spas and escort services, several bars that featured topless or nude dancing, a smattering of adult bookstores. Sex was a thriving commerce.

Perhaps Barbara Hoffman wanted a larger share of the prosperity than what was apportioned to a masseuse. It was no secret that when not dizzied by drugs and sex Barbara possessed a facile intellect, and it was no secret that she did not foresee performing sexual acts as a permanent livelihood.

Using a lawyer friend to front for her, she had attempted to buy a silent interest in Visions, one of Curtis's burlesque bars. Before the deal was consummated, Curtis learned of Barbara's involvement and squashed the sale. He resented her ambition, resented her defiance in luring clients outside the confines of the parlor, where he couldn't extract his hefty cut. He vowed revenge. Because his influence in the skin trade was extensive, other maneuvers by Barbara to quietly gain control of a massage parlor operation were stifled. No one was willing to risk Curtis's animosity. Barbara was effectively excluded from the domain.

Some observers of the drama attached a deep psychological significance to this defeat and frustration. Spurned by Curtis as a lover, stymied by him from entering the sex business, Barbara had internalized her rage and rechanneled it. Berge and Davies were chosen as her road to riches.

In the two years between the crimes and the trial Barbara Hoffman went from newsworthy to notorious. She became an article of fascination, regarded more with

curiosity than with suspicion. She was a brilliant school-
girl led astray, a drugged-out dolly, a cold, conniving
vixen, a victim of male exploitation and abuse. Perhaps
each portrait contained a bit of the truth.

In the courtroom the TV camera panned from the
prosecutor—in a dark suit, his tempered, reasoned voice
speaking harsh accusations—to the defendant. Barbara
wore a softly tailored mauve suit, pumps, and a blouse
with frills. Her appearance behind the oak defense table
was serene. The tortoiseshell glasses obscured any hint of
fear and added a detached, scholarly aura to her face. She
could have been a graduate student politely listening to a
guest lecturer. Her composure seemed like a second skin.
The flashbulbs, the reporters' questions, the throng of
spectators had not frazzled her when she'd entered the
courthouse. Her slender frame had knifed through the
maddening ensemble as if encased in ice. Not an ounce of
her cool had melted under the judge's gavel or the TV
camera's hot glare.

John Burr's opening volley contained no surprises.
"Miss Hoffman is charged with first-degree murder. First-
degree murder, there are two elements. First, that Miss
Hoffman intended to kill Mr. Berge and Mr. Davies. Second, that she caused the death of each."

The prosecutor's tone was subdued as he outlined the
state's case. "We're going to take you back to Christmas
Day 1977. The first witness you'll meet, Detective John
Cloutier, who had been unlucky enough to draw Christmas duty, was downstairs, in this building, the Madison
Police Department. At that time he came into contact with
a—with, the evidence will show, a thirty-one-year-old
$10,000-a-year U.W. Department of Audio-Visual In-
struction employee. . . . Mr. Davies took him out to Blackhawk Ski Jump, pointed to a mound of snow. In that
mound of snow Detective Cloutier pointed to the nude
body of a white male. . . . The evidence will further show,
ladies and gentlemen, that late 1976, early 1977, application was made for a six-figure insurance policy for G.
Davies. . . . A $750,000 policy was issued to Mr. Davies in

March 1977. The beneficiary, his estate. A short time later the ownership in and beneficiary of that policy was transferred to Barbara Hoffman. . . . A Mr. Ken Curtis will be testifying that he told Miss Hoffman he was aware of a plot for her to kill a person. . . . Miss Hoffman confirmed that she did in fact plan to kill someone with botulism after first marrying him and taking him to Mexico. She told him she had planned to kill this person for $750,000 in life insurance."

But Burr's opening remarks seemed to anticipate the problems of a case built on circumstantial evidence. "Please listen to all the testimony in this case, direct and cross-examination, every exhibit, each and every witness. Look at them as they're testifying. These chairs are not comfortable. The acoustics in here are terrible. . . . It will likely get very hot, so it may be uncomfortable. So please, please listen to the evidence very, very carefully."

The words sounded like a plea.

The defense, Eisenberg said, would withhold opening remarks until the state had presented its case. The defense attorney grabbed for the underdog role, a position he preferred. He talked to the jury briefly, asking their help and goodwill in his fight against the court-prosecutor conspiracy.

The first witnesses called were Madison police officers who described Davies's visit to precinct headquarters on Christmas morning 1977, and the uncovering of a body, later identified as Harry Berge, in a snowbank on Tomahawk Ridge. The initial search of Barbara Hoffman's apartment at 4:55 P.M. that day was detailed, including the finding of envelopes, a library card, and a bank book belonging to Linda Millar.

Kenneth Couture stated that he saw books on autopsies and death investigations on a bookshelf in the living room but that the volumes were not confiscated. He also noted that both the bathroom fan and the air conditioner fan in the living room had been left on.

John Cloutier had investigated Berge's home in Stoughton the following day and noticed Barbara Hoffman's phone number scribbled on the cover of the telephone book. Furthermore, receipts dating back to December 21, 1974, issued from various Madison massage parlors, were discovered in Berge's closet. Some of the credit card receipts were initialed by B.H.

Besides police officers, co-workers of Berge at the UniRoyal plant also testified. William Stelling, from the personnel department at UniRoyal, testified that on October 13, 1977, Berge had transferred his 34,500-dollar life insurance policy to Linda Millar. He seemed under no pressure or duress when he did this.

Dane County's register of deeds, Carol Mahnke, was called to the stand. She related that on October 28, 1977, Berge had changed the deed of his home, making Barbara Hoffman a joint tenant. Berge's attorney, Kenneth Buhrow, remembered outlining the various methods of ownership to Berge, then altering the deed according to his client's instructions. Berge was relaxed and comfortable throughout their meeting and seemed under no external pressure.

A representative of Wisconsin Bell gave testimony that Barbara Hoffman's phone number had been changed frequently, as often as five times a year. A record of the long-distance calls made from apartment 306, 638 State Street, from October, 1977, to April, 1978, was entered as evidence.

At the time, these long-distance records seemed of marginal importance, just another small piece in the vast collage of circumstantial evidence. Burr wasn't even certain of their relevance. But there was no objection, so they were put into the court record in hopes that later they might prove useful. The long-distance calls would sit unnoticed for a week. But the next time they were mentioned, they would stun the courtroom.

The prosecution moved methodically, using its interrogation like rocks in accumulating a mountain of testimony against Barbara Hoffman. The evidence was stacked chunk by chunk. It was dull, painstaking, and difficult to refute. The irascible Eisenberg chipped away where he could.

Couture was grilled for not obtaining another search warrant to seize the autopsy books he claimed to have seen. The search of the apartment was criticized. The door had been yanked off the hinges to gain entrance. Eisenberg attacked the officers' slovenly methods of investigation. He used the cross-examination of Stelling and Buhrow to emphasize Berge's calm demeanor when transferring insurance and property, with the implication that Berge had acted independently of any pressure, especially from Barbara Hoffman.

Yet as the first day of the trial closed it was clear that Eisenberg's flamboyance had been muted by the prosecution's assiduous presentation of detail and fact.

—— 5 ——

Friday, June 20th, and the second day of the trial opened with Chuck Lulling on the witness stand.

Two years away from the MPD had not quelled Lulling's fascination with the deeds that other people do. He worked as a private detective and was happy to be outside the constraints of the city bureaucracy. He considered it an irony and a compliment that a majority of his clients were defense attorneys who had challenged his investigative methods when he'd been a cop.

Retirement had not affected Lulling's swaggering posture or brash confidence. His shoulder stiffened with bursitis. However, the ivory hair and mustache, the sanguine complexion remained unchanged. He wore a suit jacket and tie and cowboy boots and an ego too big to hide. A moment before being summoned Lulling stood in the hallway, swapping the scuttlebutt with old courthouse acquaintances, the bowl of his pipe casting a thick fog of smoke.

Because of the animosity between Lulling and Burr, Chris Spencer conducted the direct questioning. The scope of the testimony was limited when Torphy ruled that the former detective supervisor could not relate conversations that had occurred between him and Davies without corroboration. This eliminated exploring Davies's relationship with Hoffman in the months after Berge's death.

The interrogation of Davies on December 25th was recalled. Lulling spoke of Davies's extreme upset and state of turmoil. But it didn't take long for Eisenberg to challenge the witness.

"Can you give us a description of what Mr. Davies looked like at the time?" asked Chris Spencer.

"Are you speaking of his physical condition?"

"That's correct."

"Extremely nervous," answered Lulling.

"Could you elaborate on that?"

"Well, at one point in the questioning I was of the opinion . . ."

"Objection to what his opinion was," shouted Eisenberg.

"You may state what you saw, what you observed," Torphy instructed the witness. Lulling began again.

"It looked as though . . ."

Again Eisenberg was on his feet.

"Objection as to what it looked like, though he can state as to what he saw."

"That's correct," said Torphy.

"What did you see?"

"I saw that one more question was probably going to produce a faint."

"Did his nervousness continue throughout the interview?"

"Yes, sir."

Lulling recounted his part in the search of Hoffman's apartment and the gathering of evidence. Berge's movements, from work to the tavern to home and to Madison, were reconstructed, with Lulling's computations regarding the timing involved. He also remarked that blood had been discovered in a snowbank behind 638 State Street on January 19, 1978, and that he personally had transported the specimen vials to the state crime lab for typing.

As many in the courtroom had anticipated, Eisenberg's cross-examination of Lulling was combative. The two men had a history of angry confrontations and bitter exchanges, both in and out of court. On past occasions Eisenberg had accused the detective of bullying tactics during interrogation, of soliciting false confessions, of subverting Miranda rights, of fabricating evidence and failing to file proper reports in an effort to hide information from the defense. As soon as Spencer finished, the defense lawyer glared at Lulling and attacked.

"What's your reputation for truth and veracity?" Eisenberg fired.

Burr objected that it was an improper question and was sustained. Eisenberg rephrased it.

"Mr. Lulling, do you lie?"

"I think everyone has," Lulling quipped.

"Do you lie under oath?" Eisenberg asked fiercely.

"No, sir."

"Have you ever falsified any police report?"

"No, sir."

"Ever planted evidence?"

"No, sir."

"Mr. Davies was extremely nervous, and one more question might have produced a faint, is that correct?"

"Yes, sir."

"Just like a man who had committed a murder?"

"I don't agree with that description," replied Lulling.

"Have you ever seen people who have just committed murder, and have they come in to you being extremely nervous?"

"I don't recall anyone who has just committed murder ever coming to me."

"You always go out and get them?" Eisenberg asked facetiously.

"I try to," answered Lulling, but Eisenberg grinned.

Every question seemed an effort to impugn the former detective's character.

Eisenberg ranted about the blood in the snowbank behind 638 State Street. Why was it recovered three weeks after the alleged homicide? Why had it gone undetected on prior searches?

Lulling attributed the delay to severe weather conditions—a forty-one-below-zero windchill on Christmas Day, the date of the first search—and to shoddy police work. The explanation did not satisfy Eisenberg. He strolled the courtroom and pumped volleys at Lulling, strongly insinuating that the blood could have been planted by an overzealous investigator.

Lulling did not squirm under the heat of the lawyer's innuendo.

"Mr. Lulling, when was the first time that you executed an affidavit or applied for a search warrant of Barbara Hoffman's apartment at 638 State Street?"

"I don't recall."

"When was the first time you were in her apartment at 638 State Street?"

"I can't give you a date on that, counsel."

Eisenberg handed him a copy of the complaint for search warrant dated December 27, 1977.

"Does it say that Charles Lulling is the one who applied for that search warrant?"

"Yes, sir."

"And I take it that you were looking for evidence of a homicide?"

"Yes, sir."

"Did you find any blood when you went to that premises on December 27, 1977?"

"Not that I recall."

"You looked for it, didn't you?" shouted Eisenberg. His questions were quick, banging like reports from point-blank range.

"I certainly did," replied Lulling, unabashed.

"You again searched Barbara's apartment on another occasion, didn't you?"

"I believe so; yes, sir."

"That could have been January 6, 1978 . . . is that correct?"

"Yes, sir."

". . . again you were looking for evidence of a homicide?"

"Yes, sir."

"And you didn't find any blood at that time, did you?"

"Not that I recall."

"Were you present when the apartment was searched on that date, and were ultraviolet lights used?"

"I believe that . . ."

"Just were you present on that date?" fired Eisenberg.

"Well, my recollection is that I did see Deputy Oasen with a light."

"And you used Hemastix that particular day, didn't you?"

"I never used them."

"Persons under your supervision?" Eisenberg shot, obviously tired of Lulling's insolence.

"On the 6th?"

"On the 6th, on the 27th—yeah, or didn't you know?"

"I didn't," said the former detective. His voice was modulated and calm. "My recollection of persons using sticks in this thing are confined to Jo Wegner of the state crime lab."

"And that would have been on the 6th?"

"I don't believe that was the date. I'm not sure."

"You're not sure?" bellowed Eisenberg.

"That's right."

"If the previous testimony by Mr. Oasen said it was January 6th, would you think I was mistaken?" demanded Eisenberg. He was at the witness stand now, confronting this uncooperative ex-cop.

Lulling sighed and shifted in the chair. It seemed he was tired of this game.

"I wouldn't agree. The dates—it's so long ago, so much water over the dam, that the dates escape me. But I'm aware of some activity."

"In any event, no blood was found . . . and on January

19th, the day after Barbara Hoffman's arrest, you ordered Officers Gartner and others to look for blood behind Barbara's apartment?"

"That's correct."

"You refused to accompany them to the scene, is that right?"

"I ordered them and certain equipment taken there and certain procedures followed to search for blood, yes."

"But you were busy doing other things?"

"I don't recall what I was doing."

"In any event, on January 19th, they found blood."

"Yes, sir."

"And Miss Hoffman was arrested the 18th, right?"

"Yes, sir."

"And Miss Hoffman had to know, don't you believe, for the last three weeks before her arrest, that she was a suspect in Mr. Berge's death. Correct?"

"Yes, sir."

"And there would have been nothing to prevent her from going behind her apartment and destroying evidence that might have been there," Eisenberg concluded. "Nothing. There was nothing to prevent her from doing that, was there?" His insinuation was clear. If there *had* been incriminating evidence lying in the snow for three weeks, Barbara could have easily disposed of it. "You never saw Barbara Hoffman go to the rear of her apartment where the blood was eventually found to try to destroy it, did you?"

"No, sir."

If Lulling's testimony had been marked by rancor and hostility, the next witness evoked quite a different effect. Burr called Jerry Davies to the stand.

In a scenario approved by Judge Torphy, law student Matt Franke, who was assisting the prosecution, read Jerry Davies's verbatim testimony as given before Judge William Byrne at a prelim hearing on February 16, 1978. This testimony was confined to the events of December 23, 1977, and the disposal of the body found in Barbara's apartment.

Although informed of the unusual procedure, Eisenberg strenuously objected to Davies's statements being recited aloud to the jury. He opposed such a format as prejudicial. Furthermore, he argued, it usurped his powers of cross-examination. Regardless of the fact that he had cross-examined Davies during the prelim, the severity and power and direction of his questioning would have been different had he known the significance of the day's testimony. The arrangement, while not unprecedented, was unfair and placed the defense at a distinct disadvantage.

Torphy had heard the arguments previously, and he ruled against the defense.

Franke ambled to the witness chair. He and Chris Spencer reenacted the script.

Davies's words, as read by Franke, and perhaps because they were articulated by someone other than the timid shipping clerk, transfixed the courtroom. The episode was haunting, almost theatrical. The starkness of the words, the desperation that clung to the edges, the poverty of the relationship echoed.

Barbara Hoffman called after work and asked if he wanted to come over. "I said, certainly."

Davies picked her up at 8:30 P.M. or so, and they drove to his apartment, stayed for a half hour, and drank some wine. They drove back to her apartment, drank vodka and orange juice, and watched TV—"Johnny Carson's monologue, whatever was on"—until midnight, when Barbara dozed off. Davies dozed off too.

They slept on the couch, then Barbara awoke and told Davies "that after work on Wednesday she had found a dead body."

"Where?" Spencer asked, but his voice barely made an impression. His questions faded. It was Davies's words that stumbled on, sad, revelatory.

"In her apartment. In the bathroom . . . it looked terrible, she said, kind of beaten."

Barbara told him she didn't know how the body had got into her apartment.

At 4:00 A.M. Davies went and retrieved his car from

the Lake Street parking ramp and drove to the rear of the building. Barbara went to a snowbank in the corner and dragged out a body wrapped in a sheet. He helped her wedge it into the backseat.

They drove across campus, up Observatory Drive, with Barbara in the backseat with the body, and she suggested they go out to the country, so he headed through Shorewood Hills, then west, out Mineral Point Road. They ended up near the ski jump on Tomahawk Ridge, and she told him to pull over.

They dragged the body to a grove of trees. Barbara removed the sheets, tossed them into a garbage bag, and threw enough snow over the body to cover it. Davies steered the car back onto the road, and Barbara obscured their tire tracks with the branch of a pine tree. They drove back to her apartment. If there was any conversation, Davies didn't recall it.

Barbara told him to clean his clothing, polish his shoes, and vacuum the car. She mentioned it would be better if he forgot about what he had seen.

"I didn't think it was really relevant who it was. It wouldn't have meant anything to me."

He got home and followed her commands about cleaning. That day he went to Spring Green to see his mother, and he returned to Madison the next morning to tell the police what had happened.

The testimony lingered, candid, remorseless, almost devoid of introspection.

A disgruntled Eisenberg called on Jack Priester, a partner in his law firm, to recite Davies's part in the cross-examination. The reading was flat. Eisenberg, on February 16, 1978, had not charged at Davies with the ferocity he had exhibited minutes earlier when Lulling was on the stand. Obviously he had been saving the toughest questions for a more significant occasion. He'd been merely probing Davies. It was a reconnaissance mission, not the war. Eisenberg was certain he could unravel Davies's testimony, shred it into tiny pieces in front of a jury, but that opportunity had been lost.

Thus Davies bore witness against Barbara Hoffman without having to confront a rigorous scrutiny. Under the defense attorney's cross-examination from that day the shipping clerk noted that Barbara had been nervous and upset when she'd told him she had found a body in her apartment. Eisenberg had also asked: "Miss Hoffman told you that she did not kill him, correct?"

"Correct," Davies had answered.

The brief exchange was a reflection of a reflection, a reading of testimony that was a recollection of a conversation. Yet it was the closest the jury would come to hearing Barbara Hoffman declare her innocence.

The rest of the morning and most of the afternoon session proceeded without incident. There were minor squabbles over minor points. Exhibits were entered into the record. The slow compilation of circumstantial evidence continued.

Jo Wegner testified that the blood sample from the snowbank behind 638 State Street matched the blood type for Harry Berge.

Next the jury learned that John Hunt had resided at 638 State Street, apartment 305. John Hunt was twenty-two years of age, employed at Forest Products Laboratories. In dress and demeanor Hunt appeared conservative and sincere. He approached his Bible studies and his life seriously.

On the morning of December 23rd John Hunt awoke between 5:15 and 5:30 A.M. and sat on the sofa to do his Bible readings. He heard a noise, peered out the window and into the small lot below.

"What, if anything, did you see when you looked out the window?" John Burr asked.

"I saw a car parked."

"What kind of car?"

"A black car with a white roof."

"Did you see anyone around the car?"

"Yes, sir, I did."

"Who?"

"Barbara Hoffman."

"How long did you watch Miss Hoffman?"

"Two to three minutes."

"What caused you to look out the window in the first place?"

"The slamming of a door, or a trunk."

After watching Hoffman walk around from the rear of the car, Hunt turned back to his Bible. He heard the squeaks of the building door, the jingle of keys, and Barbara entering her apartment. Shortly she exited again. Hunt heard the outside door and saw the car back toward the green Dumpster.

About an hour later Hunt, who had worked as the building janitor, was completing his cleaning chores. Barbara passed him on the stairs. They didn't speak.

"What, if anything, was she carrying?"

"A clothes basket."

"Could you tell what was in the clothes basket?"

"No, I could not."

Hunt identified Harry Berge's car, a white-over-black Oldsmobile Cutlass, as the vehicle he had seen. He was certain it was not Davies's car behind the building, for Davies picked Barbara Hoffman up every morning at around 8:00 A.M. and drove her to work. Davies's car was white with a black roof, the opposite of what had been parked in the back.

Hunt's testimony was crucial. It provided independent corroboration of Berge's presence at 638 State Street, bolstered Davies's credibility, and rendered another incident of Barbara's suspicious and inexplicable behavior.

To discredit Hunt the defense attacked his identification of the Berge vehicle. Barbara Hoffman had scratched notations on her legal pad, and Eisenberg was also aware of the discrepancies. Harry Berge drove an Oldsmobile Cutlass, a black car with a white roof. Jerry Davies owned a late-model Chevrolet, which had a white body and a maroon top. Hunt had incorrectly identified Davies's car, referring to it as black over white. It wasn't a major blunder, but if the doubt could be exploited, Hunt's credibility might collapse.

The parameters of what the witness saw were established by Burr. Eisenberg attacked the witness's vision.

"How did you know it was Berge's car behind 638 State Street?" asked Eisenberg.

He didn't know, Hunt said, until he was later shown photographs of the car by police and told it belonged to Berge.

"What color is Gerald Davies's car?" Eisenberg inquired.

"White with a black top."

"What color is Harold Berge's car?"

"Black with a white top."

"So this car here was Gerald Davies's car, is that correct?" Eisenberg asked. He was holding up exhibit 97, a photograph of Harry Berge's car.

"No, sir," Hunt replied.

"Black with a white top was Berge's . . . Let's start over. What color was Berge's car?"

"Berge's car, I have been told . . ."

"What do you *know*?" Eisenberg interrupted him. "I want to know what it was, not what you were told."

"This is the car I have seen," Hunt said, slightly flustered and pointing to the photo.

"It was a black car with a white top?"

"Yes, sir."

"What color was Gerald Davies's car?"

"Gerald Davies's car is a white car with a black roof."

"How often have you seen Gerald Davies's car?"

"Oh, twenty times."

"And Gerald Davies's car, the top of his car was black?"

"That is true, sir."

"Who told you that?"

"I can see it."

"Who told you Gerald Davies's car was black-topped?" Eisenberg pressed.

"I saw it."

"Twenty times?"

"Yes, sir."

"Are you certain?" Eisenberg was pushing hard. Hunt seemed annoyed.

"Yes, sir."

"Are you color-blind?"

"No, sir."

"You know the difference between black and green, don't you?"

"Certainly hope so."

"You know the difference between red and white, don't you?"

"Yes, sir."

"Do you know the difference between red and black?"

"Yes, sir."

"Showing you exhibit 31"—a photo of Jerry Davies's car—"what color is the roof of that car?"

"I would say it's reddish or maroon," Hunt admitted.

"What car is it? Is it Gerald Davies's car?"

"Yes, sir." But his voice lacked confidence.

"But it can't be Gerald Davies's car, because Davies's car has a black top. That's what you testified to."

"According to my testimony, yes."

"You told Detective Reuter that a white-over-black, late-model car picked up Miss Hoffman regularly, yes?"

"Yes, sir."

"You told the jury that Davies's car was white with a black top, right?"

"Yes, sir."

"White with a black top isn't black with a white top, is it?"

"No, sir."

The witness was confused. The rapid pace of the questioning, the hostile voice, the disparaging tone and the glare of intimidation, the relentless transposition of colors had knocked Hunt's confidence. If Eisenberg had halted his attack, Hunt's efficacy as a witness would have been blunted and the jury could not have helped harboring doubt about what Hunt had seen.

However, Eisenberg did not cease. He appeared to be dissatisfied with simply discrediting Hunt's vision. Wounding Hunt's credibility, which was all that was necessary, was insufficient. During his cross-examination of Hunt, Eisenberg seemed to sneer while referring to Hunt's Bible devotions, a gesture that could do nothing but alienate the jury.

The cross-examination strayed into other areas but soon returned to the car and its colors.

"What was it you saw, white over black or black over white?" Eisenberg pressed. "Are you sure it wasn't Berge's car you spotted in the mornings? The police report states you saw a white-over-black vehicle on the morning of December 23rd. Couldn't that have been Davies's car?"

The lawyer badgered Hunt about his recollections of color, about the darkness at 5:00 A.M., about his description and memory and eyesight. He flailed at the witness who was not color-blind, who had misidentified the color of a car roof he claimed to have seen over twenty times, who had claimed to recognize Berge's car after viewing it for a couple minutes in the light of a seventy-five-watt bulb at 5:30 in the morning. Yet Eisenberg had underestimated John Hunt.

The incessant forays about the car were a severe mistake. In the midst of the acrimonious cross-examination Hunt collected his poise. Instead of crumbling, he solidified. The perpetual questioning lasted for over a half hour and allowed the witness to restate his observations.

He had seen a black car with a white roof behind 638 State Street on the morning of the 23rd of December; he was certain. He was unfamiliar with the automobile. When police showed him a photo, he correctly identified it, and it was Berge's car. Hunt never corrected himself, nor did he apologize for his earlier confusion. He spoke confidently of what he had seen. Whatever the police report said, he knew what he saw. Whatever terminology was used by the officer, it didn't alter what he had noticed.

The reiteration after the interminable struggle was what made a lasting impression. Hunt was sure of what he'd seen, and he wouldn't be shaken a second time. Eisenberg had let the witness get away.

—— 6 ——

Saturday morning brought Madison blue skies, a sun as fat as a state fair honeydew, and the farmers' market, where local growers displayed an assortment of treats beneath the maple and oak canopies that shade the capitol square. Bushel baskets brimmed with fresh produce—ruby leaf lettuce, sugar snap peas, spinach, and radishes. Willie sold his Forgotten Valley Cheese. Ollie Mhyre, whose denim overalls had more patches than an old tire tube, offered white and purple onions—take your pick—at 27¢ a pound. One block south of the vegetable stalls and coffee vendors Judge Torphy conducted a rare Saturday session. It was June 21st.

The prosecution had switched its focus from Berge to Davies. The tactics did not vary. Slowly and methodically, the state plodded on with its presentation of evidence. Insurance policies and bank materials were subpoenaed and entered into the court record.

On February 24, 1978, Metropolitan National listed Barbara Hoffman's checking account as holding a balance of $14.58. Yet that same day Transport Life received a premium payment drawn on the account for $6,618.30. Three days later Barbara Hoffman placed a stop-payment order on the check.

Through Burr's prodding Pat O'Donohue detailed for the jury the original request, in November 1976, for $3 million of life insurance and the months of negotiation and struggle before Transport Life agreed to underwrite the policy.

Change of beneficiary forms were taken as evidence. On the three small life insurance policies, totaling $20,000, Barbara Hoffman had been made the beneficiary, replacing Ruth Davies. These changes had occurred a mere three weeks before Davies's sudden death and listed Barbara as fiancée/wife.

Eisenberg began his cross-examination of every insurance person who testified—O'Donohue, Phil Sprecher,

David Wallace—with the same question: "If you were going to kill someone, would you buy term or ordinary life?" Each time, Burr objected and the objection was upheld.

In questioning O'Donohue the defense lawyer was able to point out that because the policy was term life rather than whole it had no cash value. Furthermore, false statements by Davies regarding his income, specifically that from massage parlors, would have invalidated the policy. It was also mentioned that the policy held a suicide clause. Should the insured commit suicide within two years of the effective date of the policy, whether sane or insane at the time of the act, the insurance company's liability was limited to the amount of premiums already paid.

In addition to the insurance complexities the discovery of Davies's body was recounted. Residents of the apartment building, its manager, and its maintenance man testified. Again a parade of police officers were called to the stand to reconstruct the scenario and their consequent investigation.

The condition of the body, the water level of the bathtub, the noise of the bathroom fan were explained to the jury. Eisenberg emphasized that not a hair or a fingerprint or any other piece of evidence relating to Barbara Hoffman was found in the apartment. No one had seen her leave or enter Davies's home that tragic Easter weekend or ever.

The letters signed by Davies and mailed that fatal weekend were read to the jury and entered into the record.

Day three of the trial moved quickly. The prosecution proceeded at a faster pace than anticipated, and Torphy was pleased with the progress.

For the jury the avalanche of words and exhibits produced strain. The circumstantial nature of the state's presentation demanded concentration on detail, and quickly the assignment seemed an ordeal. The notoriety of the case, the glare of the TV cameras—silent yet always visible—the excitement of the packed courtroom, the gravity of the charges intensified the pressure and the communal isolation.

The jury was strictly sequestered. Television and radio were forbidden the jurors. Mail, laundry, telephone calls— any contact with the outside world—were carefully screened. One of the jurors could not abide by the regulations, and on Saturday night the foreman spoke to a bailiff about the problem.

David Butterfield, twenty-three years old, a maintenance man by trade, had a penchant for beer. Two drinks were permitted with the evening meal, no more, and a couple of beers barely wetted Butterfield's parched throat. He asked that a case of beer be delivered to his motel room. When told that the request could not be honored, he got angry. What could a few beers harm? he protested. As it became clear he wouldn't get his wish, Butterfield turned nasty. He denounced the rules, cursed the situation, and insinuated that if his desire for a case of beer wasn't satisfied he'd retaliate by causing a hung jury.

Judge Torphy was informed of the threat. Burr and Eisenberg were alerted to the development, and with both lawyers present Torphy questioned Butterfield concerning the incident. The maintenance man admitted that he may have muttered a vague threat. Judge Torphy severely reprimanded him and dismissed him from jury duty. The selected alternate was a woman. A brief announcement was issued informing the press of the change.

— 7 —

It was Saturday, the third day of the trial. Liza slumped into the cushions of an old easy chair, crunching granola and watching the TV from over the tips of her toes. A fly cruised the kitchen.

There was a rap on the door, and the fellow who rented the upstairs apartment entered. Two cans of beer dangled from a plastic holder. He offered one to Liza, yawned, took a seat on the wooden vegetable crate she used as a hassock. His reluctant hostess accepted the beer without prying her eyes from the television set. He inquired about the attraction. Liza shushed him.

"It's the Barbara Hoffman trial," she said finally.

"Trash for the masses," he commented. The spray from his pop top tickled Liza's toes.

His name was Tim, and he claimed to be a Marxist-Leninist historian who couldn't secure a teaching position because of his radical politics. All that Liza knew for certain was that he drove a cab on the night shift, which was why his eyes were bleary at 9:00 A.M., and that he drank an excess of beer. He was tall, lean, but with a belly, and his scruffy beard yearned for a trim.

On the tube Don Eisenberg was cross-examining an insurance agent. The agent squirmed.

"Why are you interested in this bullshit?" Tim asked.

"Because I am," said Liza.

"An elucidating answer. Of course it is the best soap opera in town. My riders are voting three to one Eisenberg'll get her off. They all agree she did it, and they think she'll walk because he's so clever. What's your vote?"

"I abstain," Liza said.

Her visitor shrugged.

"I took a guy from out of town to a massage parlor last night," Tim said. "He got in the cab and said, 'Where can I get a blowjob in this town?' so I took him to the Rising Sun. He gave me this." He held up a ten-dollar bill.

"And some lucky girl got to suck his cock, huh? You're aiding the oppression of the masses, Timothy."

"Ouch, you are a little sensitive this morning. I'm a humble cabdriver, a tool of the establishment, a lackey for the moneyed classes. My conscience does bother me for that shit."

"Quiet," Liza ordered and picked at an oat that had wedged in her teeth.

"You've been watching this drama every day?"

"Before work, yeah. At night they run highlights

from the day's testimony, so I catch what I missed when I get home."

They watched in silence for a while. The camera followed Eisenberg, who paced the courtroom as he challenged a witness. Occasionally it flashed a picture of Barbara Hoffman, visible only in profile, alone at the defense table, jotting notes on a legal pad or listening intently to the proceedings.

Barbara appeared a different person on the screen, Liza thought. So rigid and self-contained. Barbara had always been introverted, almost withdrawn, except when zonked on Quaaludes. Then her personality flipped and her characteristics were reversed. She was transformed from self-enclosed to supremely uninhibited. Liza recalled several notorious photography sessions at a studio on East Johnson Street.

At 817 East Johnson was the Whole Earth Co-op. Mandalas and crystals and cast-iron frying pans shared the window display. Inside, people wearing Birkenstok sandals and tie-dyed T-shirts sold organic vegetables, incense, whole grains, books on psychic healing, tofu, mineral water. An alleyway next to the co-op led to a guitar repair shop. A stairway turned up, and on the second floor were huge looms and the Weaving Workshop. Their neighbor had a blue door with a sign that notified the public that only persons eighteen years or older were permitted entrance. Inside the blue door was a dark hallway and rooms where men snapped pictures of women, often young girls who had run away from home. The girls would dance, wrestle, make love—whatever was the fantasy.

Barbara had participated in these photography sessions. She liked to show Liza pictures and describe the entire lurid show. She'd tell what she did and with whom and for how long and how much the exhibition earned. It was like listening to a little girl retell a playground adventure.

Liza shivered. She didn't want to go back to those days anymore, not even in her head.

"What's the problem? Beer and granola a lousy mix?"

"It's nothing," said Liza.

"You're very secretive today."

"I didn't sleep well, I guess. Too humid."

"Maybe you should take a nap before work."

Liza didn't appreciate Tim's suggestive tone. On the tube Burr and Eisenberg were bickering about the admissibility of certain evidence.

"Let's me and you go to bed," Tim said directly.

"It's too hot."

"So what? It's going to be hot for two months."

"Then I'll be celibate for two months."

"We don't have to make a big production of it."

It never has been a big production, Liza thought. The Marxist-Leninist might be able to spout a fervent ideology, but he rarely lasted more than a few passionate minutes in bed before expending his energies and drifting off to sleep. Polemicists are crummy lovers, she had concluded after affairs with a couple of leftists in town.

She really didn't know why she bothered with Tim. Maybe because his tirades against the capitalist system amused her, reinforced her notion of victimization.

"A little nap, a little love," he said.

"I'm watching the trial," she replied. "And let's not mistake what we do for love."

"Enough. I can see that I hold no emotional or even utilitarian value for you."

"Not at the moment."

Tim tossed his beer can into the garbage bag in the kitchen. Dirty plates and an empty pizza box were stacked on the counter, to the delight of a yellow jacket that buzzed in through a screenless window.

An hour later Liza had completely forgotten her visitor and wondered how the warm, half-full can of beer had come to sit next to her chair. She heard the tinkling of bicycle bells as children pedaled down the sidewalk.

Barbara's hair had been cut short and curled. She wore a blouse with frills. When she turned and glanced at the camera, it was the image of a little girl, fragile and innocent, that Liza saw.

— 8 —

On Monday, June 23rd, the jury learned about cyanide.

Kenneth Kempfert of the state crime lab testified that he was given blood, urine, brain, liver, kidney, and stomach samples from the Davies autopsy to examine. The materials were tested for "every possible drug and poison I could think of," he recalled. One week later he rechecked for cyanide and the mystery of Davies's death was solved.

Davies's body contained two micrograms, or twice the lethal dose of cyanide. One microgram per milliliter constituted a lethal dosage. This was an extremely small quantity. "A microgram is perhaps equivalent in weight to a small segment of a piece of hair, or less," Kempfert said. Small traces of Valium, not exceeding a therapeutic dose, were also found in Davies's bloodstream.

Stomach contents taken from Berge were retrieved and subjected to infrared spectrophotometry. Cyanide again showed its destructive hand. Berge's body contained over thirty-seven times the lethal dose.

Dr. William J. Bauman, the pathologist who did the autopsies and signed the death certificates for Berge and Davies, provided expert medical testimony. He educated the jury about cyanide: ". . . it is a popular conception that you take cyanide and you immediately drop dead, and that isn't true in most cases."

The chemical was extremely deadly because it inhibited the oxidation processes in the body's cells. A victim of cyanide poisoning suffocated, suffering pulmonary aspiration and hemorrhaging in the lungs. Death was neither pleasant nor instantaneous. Heart palpitations and giddiness were the first indications of trouble, followed by a headache and convulsions as the victim struggled for breath. Vomiting often occurred, then expiration as the body was robbed of its ability to get oxygen. These symptoms could extend from two to seven minutes, and if there was food in the stomach a full twenty minutes could pass before the body began its fatal dance. It was an ugly and painful way to die.

Cyanide had a distinctive taste and smell, both of which could be masked from the victim by combining it with food. At an autopsy the pathologist had to check specifically for the chemical to discern its presence. However, there could be hints of its existence. Cyanide could smell like burnt or bitter almonds, and most pathologists would detect the odor when they examined the stomach. "You could kill yourself doing the autopsy if you smelled too much of it," Bauman said. But one-quarter of the population did not register the smell of burnt almonds, and Bauman coincidentally fit that category, and hence the smell eluded him twice.

Furthermore, if there was no food in the stomach, cyanide would leave a cherry color in the stomach contents; when food was present, the coloration did not appear. Thus it was not an accident that Berge and Davies died after eating large meals.

Harry Berge and Jerry Davies were the first two cases of homicide due to cyanide poisoning ever recorded in Wisconsin.

Bauman was at Tomahawk Ridge when Berge's body was uncovered. He described for the jury its frozen condition and the obvious indications of severe trauma to the head and genitals. These blunt-force injuries were inflicted before death. When the corpse had thawed sufficiently to examine, an assortment of minor lacerations was noted—scratches and bruises to the limbs and torso—and these were classified as postmortem inflictions. The abrasions suffered after death were consistent with the banging a body might incur from being dragged down stairs.

The eerie scene in Davies's bathroom was recounted.

Bauman remembered his bafflement at the apparent lack of any external or internal injury. The deterioration of Davies's body—the lips were desiccated, the eyes were drying out, the palm beneath the water was shriveled—made it difficult to estimate accurately a time of death. But the pathologist felt confident that 5:00 to 7:00 P.M. Saturday was a reasonable approximation.

In cross-examination Eisenberg asked questions about size and leverage. Both bodies had been moved some distance after their deaths, and neither body exhibited any rope burns or any other signs that an artificial device had been used to help transport them, so what accounted for their movement? Berge was 5'9" and weighed 155 pounds. Davies was 5'10" and weighed 170 pounds. Yet Barbara Hoffman was only 5'6" and weighed 110 pounds. How could she have moved them?

Burr objected, but Bauman was instructed to answer. It would have been very difficult, he conceded.

Under Eisenberg's persistent questioning Bauman admitted that though Davies's death had the look and feel of a murder it could have been a suicide. The defense lawyer grinned.

Eisenberg's smile, however, did not survive the day. In the afternoon Ken Curtis took the witness stand.

In a case comprised of innumerable and tiny bits and pieces, a case of incriminating circumstances and impossible coincidences, a case where the murder weapon was an insidious intellect and a chemical that dissolved in the bloodstream—elements irretrievable and unavailable for the jury's inspection—in a case devoid of fingerprints and eyewitness accounts, in a case fragile, elusive, and circumspect, Ken Curtis's testimony was crucial to the prosecution. He was the state's main witness, and his singular importance was a cause of dire consternation to Burr and Spencer.

They had no reason to trust Curtis. Would he equivocate on the stand? Would his memory cloud and fade now that he had gotten the deal for Cerro?

Eisenberg, the prosecution feared, was the perfect foil

for Curtis. His firm had represented Curtis over the years. Eisenberg's acerbic tongue would lash and bait and infuriate Curtis, who didn't possess the intellect to fight back. Eisenberg would reveal the sordid details of his relationship with Hoffman, accuse him of retaliation for Barbara's insubordination, accuse him of attempting to frighten and intimidate a potential business rival.

It could get vicious and brutal. Curtis's rumored violence toward women might have a peripheral relevance. Would he protect these intimate details and let his memory go fuzzy? Would he conceal his character and lose his credibility? The prosecution had plenty of trepidation and no choice. Curtis was summoned to the stand.

Burr chose not to hide Curtis's background. The plea bargain arrangement and the ownership of Jan's Health Spa were discussed openly and succinctly. The questioning moved immediately to a conversation Curtis had had with Barbara Hoffman in late March or early April 1977, in which he'd mentioned to her that "I was aware of a plot to kill a young man for $750,000 in life insurance." He also noticed a chalkboard, on which the words *passport* and *marriage license* were written and checked off.

Two days later, in another conversation at her apartment, "Miss Hoffman admitted to me that she was going to kill a man." And she told him of the plot of marriage and Mexico and botulism. She never did tell Curtis the identity of her intended victim, except that he worked at the U.W. and that she'd met him at Jan's Health Spa.

When Don Eisenberg rose to cross-examine, Ken Curtis didn't flinch.

Was it true, boomed Eisenberg, that Curtis made his living from vice, corruption, gambling, massage parlors, and using people?

Curtis denied it.

Eisenberg acted incredulous. What was Curtis's connection to Jan's Health Spa? And the Rising Sun? And Cheri's? And the Geisha House?

Curtis acknowledged that he had an interest in three or four massage parlors, which provided the primary source of his income. He smiled, almost slyly, and leaned back in his chair. "Yes, I guess it could be called vice," he said.

Eisenberg explored the history of Curtis's partnership and friendship with Sam Cerro. His questions were swift and incisive. He challenged the deal with the district attorney, criticizing its ethicality, criticizing Curtis's motives.

Why hadn't he reported what he knew to police when he'd first learned of Berge's death? Curtis said he was not immediately aware of the connections between Berge and Davies and Hoffman. Why did three weeks pass before his lawyer phoned the DA? It took time, Curtis replied, to understand the significance of what he knew.

In a courtroom where the air-conditioning faltered under the assault of a ninety-degree day, where spectators fanned themselves and perspiration drops blotched press corps notebooks, where witnesses fidgeted uncomfortably, their underarms dark with sweat, where pebbles of sweat rimmed the shore of Judge Torphy's broad, receding forehead and the heat seemed to wilt his mustache, Eisenberg clamored and growled like an overheated boiler furnace. His silk suit rippled with dampness as he gesticulated. His words were charged, his demeanor pugnacious. A white cotton handkerchief sopped the wetness from his brow.

Eisenberg fumed about Curtis's story, attacked it as a fabrication. Again he emphasized the long delay, almost eight months, before Curtis had informed authorities of what he claimed to know, and then only after a mutually beneficial exchange had been agreed on between the DA's office and Cerro. He was not fulfilling a civic responsibility by testifying against Miss Hoffman; he was completing his part of a sleazy bargain, behaving opportunistically by exploiting a tragic circumstance for his own advantage. What did Curtis's testimony buy for his friend, who had been convicted of attempting to purchase two kilos of cocaine?

Cerro had received a six-month sentence and probation, Curtis replied.

"What was the maximum penalty?" asked Eisenberg. Curtis shrugged.

"Wasn't the maximum penalty fifteen years in prison and $45,000 in fines?"

The witness shrugged again. He looked bored.

Eisenberg raged at Curtis's silence. "What was Sam Cerro's maximum possible sentence?" he demanded.

Curtis squinted, as if taking aim. "You should know; you were his attorney."

The boiler blew a gasket. Eisenberg disavowed any knowledge of the plea bargain, stating emphatically that he had dropped Cerro as a client.

"No," Ken Curtis corrected him. "You were fired."

No groan was audible, but the breath had been knocked out of Eisenberg. Flustered, he grabbed a Wisconsin statute book and searched for the sentence Cerro might have served had it not been for Curtis's deal with the DA. He howled as he paged through the tome.

Nobody fired Don Eisenberg, and nobody embarrassed him in court. He read from the statute book, barking out numbers, totaling up the maximum penalty, but his howling was like a whine, like a shrill stream of hot air escaping through a leak in its cauldron.

Eisenberg reeled. The cross-examination suddenly had lost its force. The lawyer barked in an effort to recover, but his questions lacked sting. His pacing and pattern had been disrupted.

Eisenberg resorted to another assault on the witness's character. "Haven't you been charged with reckless use of a weapon and battery? Whom did you batter?" Eisenberg bellowed, bringing the prosecution's immediate objection, which was sustained.

The next tactic was to discredit the mystery witness. A friend of Curtis had told him of Hoffman's alleged plot, which had prompted Curtis to intervene. Where was this mystery person now? Why had he not come forward? What did he fear?

The man had fled the state to avoid being called as a

witness, Curtis replied. And Curtis had no idea why, except that he'd wanted to elude the entanglement.

On redirect John Burr defused the issue. He asked Curtis if he knew what lawyer represented the mystery witness.

"Don Eisenberg," Curtis said.

Curtis stepped down and strode through the heat and tension that surrounded him. It had been a gritty performance. His character had been scratched, but his testimony had not been tarnished. He'd absorbed the force of Eisenberg's rage and kicked it back at him. He appeared delighted in his public admission that he made his livelihood from vice. His insolence had protected him from deeper scrutiny and had protected his testimony against Barbara Hoffman.

The next witnesses corroborated that the items Curtis had seen written on the chalkboard were, indeed, obtained. A copy of Davies's passport application, dated May 19, 1977, was entered into the record. An appointment calendar, which reserved a marriage date of April 22, 1977, for Barbara Hoffman and Gerald Davies, was also placed in exhibit.

— 9 —

What became clear as the trial progressed was the depth of isolation that enveloped Barbara Hoffman. She rarely murmured a "good morning" to anyone other than her lawyer. A specimen, a curiosity, a beauteous mystery to the throngs of spectators, she was utterly alone. No sympathetic smiles, no words of encouragement from anyone. If she had friends, they were not in attendance, nor was her family. Neither her parents, who lived a three-hour drive away in Park Ridge, nor her sisters bothered to share her burden and ease the torment. Whether due to her wishes or due to abandonment, Barbara endured the tedium and trauma of the trial with only Don Eisenberg to lend her consolation.

Each noon recess Barbara retreated to the coffee shop in the basement of the courthouse for her lunch, which she ate amid the glances and whispers of the other patrons, some of whom were detectives that had worked on her case; or she paced to the capitol square, chose an empty bench, and ate a meal she had prepared at home and lugged in her shoulder bag. It created a haunting picture: Barbara perched like a bird on a stone bench, hoping to become invisible among the state capitol's endless pedestrian traffic, nibbling on rice cakes or fruit, sipping tea, marigolds and begonias in resonant bloom about her.

Barbara grew thinner as the trial wore on. Her 110 pounds seemed to shrink on her 5'6" frame, and slender looked skinny. She used a minimum of cosmetics, and soon her face was narrow and gaunt.

Though she looked anorexic, Barbara was extremely self-possessed. If any of the testimony had pricked a painful memory, she had not expressed it. Her demeanor was alert, cool, stoic. She made copious notes during particular testimony, or she sat passive and detached, as if lulled into a trance by a boring television program.

What emerged was a strange serenity that accompanied her loneliness, a strange composure that centered her isolation.

— 10 —

Tuesday, June 24th, was long and mundane and ended in a feisty confrontation between Eisenberg and Chris Spencer.

The discovery of the laboratory equipment and chemicals purchased from Laabs, Inc., of Milwaukee was presented. Tom Volkman, the salesperson who had taken the original order, told the jury that the materials had been ordered by phone by a female voice. "It was a large order, which was unusual," and delivery was spread out over a half dozen or more shipments because items had to be back-ordered and shipped as they became available.

The receipts were signed by "J. Davies" or "Jerry Davies" and paid for COD by a check drawn on Jerry Davies's account. The UPS receipt books and bills of lading and canceled checks were entered as evidence.

The turmoil erupted in the afternoon.

Barbara Hoffman's academic career was examined. She was termed an excellent student, one who rarely asked questions, "because she knew all the answers." She had chosen biochemistry as her major field of study, with an ultimate goal of medical school. Her work in the sciences, especially biochemistry, was strong, and she earned an unblemished record of As.

Professor David Nelson testified that she had been a student in a biochemistry course he'd taught in 1974 in which cyanide was discussed. Professor Robert Deibl, who was a specialist in food microbiology, particularly food poisoning, stated that Barbara was a student in a class he taught that included a section on food poisoning. Eisenberg strenuously objected to the relevancy of the testimony. Neither professor had proof that Miss Hoffman had been in attendance on the days cyanide was discussed, and if she had been, so what? Torphy overruled and allowed Spencer to proceed with the questioning.

Spencer and Eisenberg had battled in court previously, with the defense lawyer victorious. Spencer was young, a couple years out of law school, and not entirely comfortable with the bang and tussle of criminal law. Eisenberg sensed this hesitation. He pounced on any flicker of weakness in an opponent and exploited it.

The list of compounds and equipment ordered from Laabs was discussed by Professor Deibl under Spencer's direction. The academician stated that a number of the compounds could be used to grow anaerobic organisms such as botulin, and Eisenberg immediately protested.

The compounds could be used to grow something other than botulin, Eisenberg said. Deibl's conclusion was sheer speculation and should be stricken from the record.

Spencer rephrased the line of questioning, but again the defense lawyer attacked. This line of inquiry was irrelevant, he barked.

Spencer altered his approach once more, stumbled, and was stymied by Eisenberg's vehement interruptions. Torphy allowed the scuffle to continue. Spencer blustered, hopelessly entangled, and the defense lawyer pressured him relentlessly. Eisenberg wanted Deibl's testimony tossed out. It was misleading, irrelevant, and improper, and Spencer muttered a feeble defense for what he wished to prove.

Finally Judge Torphy agreed with Eisenberg. He ruled that Professor Deibl's entire testimony be erased from the record, and the jury was instructed to disregard everything Deibl had said.

The rage with Deibl wasn't over. That night the prosecution contacted him and asked if he'd be willing to testify again, with Burr conducting the examination. Deibl responded that he felt his judgment regarding the Laabs stuff was relevant and important. The prosecution agreed. Their case was close to the end, and they wanted Deibl's opinion on the record.

The next day the prosecution reintroduced the microbiology professor as a witness. Eisenberg was furious in his objection. Burr argued that the information Deibl had was related to the statements of a previous witness—Ken Curtis—that Barbara Hoffman had plotted to kill someone with botulism.

Torphy ruled for the prosecution. The testimony was admissible evidence to demonstrate Hoffman's state of mind and intent.

Deibl described the Laabs order to the jury: pipettes, rubber tubing, mouthpiece, calcium carbonate, one-quarter pound of peptone, beakers, a thermometer, pH paper, test tubes, clamps, support rings, a graduated cylinder, yeast extract, dextrose, glassine paper, watch glasses, cyanide, and twenty-five syringes. Essentially the materials constituted a mini-laboratory. All the ingredients necessary to grow botulin were present in the Laabs deliveries, and Deibl recited step by step precisely how it could be done. Only two of the items ordered had no use in the process: cyanide and syringes.

Eisenberg constantly interrupted the testimony, harassing Burr and Deibl, but his irate outbursts were without effect except to draw reprimands from the bench.

Cross-examination was futile. The defense hammered away at the fact that the Laabs items could be used to grow things other than botulism.

Yes, Deibl conceded, other bacteria.

"And isn't it further true," pushed Eisenberg, "that some of the items on those invoices before you would not be used to culture botulism or any other kind of bacteria? Isn't that true?"

"No, I can't say that," Deibl rebutted.

When asked by Burr what other uses these compounds may have had, besides growing bacteria and possibly botulism, Deibl answered with authority, "I don't know of any."

The defense was unable to shake Deibl's firm assertion, and with the completion of Deibl's testimony the prosecution rested its case.

Eisenberg argued that the state had failed in its duty to present adequate evidence and that the charges against Miss Hoffman should be dropped. Torphy took the motion under advisement and recessed court until the afternoon.

— 11 —

Barbara Hoffman's defense began on the afternoon of June 25th, with a brief opening statement in which Eisenberg guaranteed a refutation of the prosecution's outrageous charges and fabrications. The defense planned to offer an alternate explanation to the scenario the state had proposed. A clear and unbiased look at the facts showed a radically different view of what had happened. Barbara Hoffman had been trapped by an upset boyfriend and an overzealous prosecutor. Fueled by jealousy and rage, Jerry Davies had murdered Harry Berge and then, in desperation, had taken his own life several months later, depressed by the trouble he had wrought.

Scheduled witnesses for the defense included Robert and Vi Hoffman, Barbara's parents. Eisenberg boasted that jurors would be "flabbergasted" by their testimony. Also promised was a "big surprise" witness who would devastate Professor Deibl's prejudicial remarks and judgment. The controversy over Deibl—having his testimony scratched, then permitting him to retestify—had rankled Eisenberg. He referred to the microbiology professor as a prostitute who had sold his professional opinion to the state. The defense would present an eminently qualified expert to rebut Deibl's interpretation regarding the items purchased from Laabs.

The first three witnesses called on by the defense, however, contained neither revelation nor surprise. Their connection to Barbara was limited to her work at EDS Federal and as an interim clerk for the state of Wisconsin, Department of Health. They vouched for her intelligence and punctuality. They provided character references designed to demonstrate that Barbara was not the monster some people had assumed and that the prosecution had depicted.

Dr. Paul Slavik reported that he had examined Jerry Davies on January 19, 1977, and had issued a prescription for Valium. Davies had appeared anxious and agitated and said he was having trouble sleeping. The patient went on to mention that his girlfriend had been charged with murdering someone and that she was "innocent." On cross-examination Dr. Slavik admitted that although Davies had been upset he had not seemed depressed or suicidal.

In an effort to discredit Chuck Lulling's conduct and testimony Eisenberg called Assistant DA Donald Antoine to the stand. The young prosecutor admitted that he disliked handling cases that Lulling had investigated because he did not trust the detective's methods of gathering evidence. He said that he had once called Lulling a liar regarding another case, and he characterized Lulling as "less than honest." Asked to expound on what he meant, Antoine acknowledged that he believed Lulling did not always tell the truth.

After Antoine's testimony the court recessed for the day. The five witnesses summoned by the defense had done little to counterbalance a week and a half of incriminating testimony from dozens of witnesses and the ton of circumstantial evidence and exhibits accumulated by the prosecution.

"But tomorrow their story gets destroyed," Eisenberg quipped to reporters as he exited.

—— 12 ——

By 8:00 A.M. a crowd had assembled in the hall outside the double oak doors of Judge Torphy's courtroom. It was already eighty degrees, and heat clotted the courthouse. Spectators shared sweat and sections of the morning paper. Law students debated strategy. Retirees and taxi drivers and lawyers with a couple hours to kill discussed love and money and intrigue.

Every time the elevator door whooshed open, heads swiveled in anticipation. A reporter meandered through the crowd, seeking opinion, jotting the comments in her notepad. A chubby woman with varicose veins and Bermuda shorts hugged her husband and explained that they were visiting their daughter, who was a student at the U.W., and they'd decided to pass the morning attending the trial.

"Even over in Kenosha we heard of Don Eisenberg." She smiled. The husband fingered the brim of his AMC cap and smiled too.

The scuttlebutt was that Barbara's parents would testify, and because no one had noticed a friend or relative of the defendant in attendance thus far, the rumor evoked fascination as well as speculation as to why the Hoffman family had been so conspicuously absent.

The law students discussed the merits of putting Barbara on the witness stand. An old man in a T-shirt and cardigan snoozed on a bench. The dab of shaving cream lodged behind his ear looked like a larva's thick webbing.

The regulars toted lunch bags and jugs of iced tea so they could sit through the lunch recess and not risk forfeiting their seats.

When requesting a change of venue many months previously, the defense had claimed the trial would degenerate into a carnival atmosphere due to extensive media coverage and the morbid curiosity of the community. Such fears were not borne out. People were shocked and fascinated and titillated by the allegations of cunning and subterfuge, by the lurid exposures regarding Madison's unsavory and prosperous blue world, by the aura of mystery that enveloped the drama's central character, Barbara Hoffman. People flocked for a glimpse of the notorious celebrity, whom many had already presumed was guilty of double murder. Yet as people exercised this perverse expression, they retained a sense of their midwestern dignity. They did not charge the elevator door when Barbara Hoffman arrived. They did not pursue her autograph or hound her during recesses. Her rights to space and movement and privacy were respected.

The people who flocked to the trial observed and listened. What was being investigated was the darkest chambers of human deeds, and many simply wanted to watch, mesmerized by the grappling and the struggle.

The newspapers played to the sensationalism. "Barbara Hoffman: Still a Mystery After 30 Months" ran a headline in the *Capital Times*. Reporter Jackie Mitchard wrote that Barbara had a "galvanized self-possession, a grace and coolness that mystified some and made others uneasy." Another headline read "Jury's Choice: 'Cold-Blooded' or 'Little Girl.'" The paper quoted a college classmate: "She wasn't easy to know. Hell, she wasn't even easy to describe."

The television cameras and the photographers' lenses exhibited much less restraint than the galleries that gathered every day. The media encroached, the media confronted, whereas the regulars were content to see the process played out and maybe catch a shred of insight into the mystery of Barbara Hoffman.

A bailiff tossed open the doors and admitted the gallery. People searched for their favorite seats. Some had occupied the same spot for all seven days. The banter was light, punctuated with laughter. They could have been waiting for the Wisconsin Chamber Orchestra to perform a pops concert out on the capitol square. Someone lauded Eisenberg, compared him to a symphony conductor playing to the jury, and someone else frowned in disbelief. Torphy's courtroom was poorly air-conditioned, and the heat oppressed and stifled any prolonged outbursts of vitality.

The first witness of the morning was a cherubic woman with an open, oval face. Her mouth, softly highlighted by red lipstick, trembled at the edges. Hair spray held her coiffure in place, and courage held her composure. Vi Hoffman described her family as close and loving, clichés that sounded genuine only because she believed them. Her eldest daughter was a social worker in Boston, and the youngest girl studied at Indiana University. Barbara was a middle child who always "had a special love for flowers and plants." Violet Hoffman toiled as a secretary, having returned to work when her children no longer needed constant attention at home. She was quick to mention that the job did not preclude her fulfilling her motherly duties and quick to mention again that her daughters were capable of fending for themselves. It was a normal household, and Vi Hoffman's sincerity did not induce one to question her definition of normal.

When asked to expound on Barbara's background, Vi Hoffman recited the accomplishments with a tone of pride yet without surprise, as if Barbara's academic achievements were expected, like payments delivered on a promise. Barbara had been an AFS exchange student and a national merit scholar. She was fluent in three languages, competent on the French horn, and the recipient of a scholarship to Butler University, where she'd earned the Dean's List each semester. That standard had not changed when she'd transferred to the U.W.–Madison. Her record of straight As continued, despite the challenge of her science courses. Barbara was happy. Her life appeared in order.

In August 1976 Vi Hoffman learned that things were not as they seemed with her daughter. During a late-night phone conversation Barbara confessed to her mother that she was working in a massage parlor. Vi was stunned. Disbelief, dismay, then despair overwhelmed Vi Hoffman as her daughter explained the tragic situation. Through an ad in the student newspaper Barbara had interviewed for a receptionist position in what was presented as a health spa. Because the pay was good, she remained when she discovered what truly went on. Her intention was to work for a semester and quit. When she saw the easy money to be earned as a masseuse, the temptation swayed her. She was working part-time.

Recollections of the agonizing phone conversation eroded Vi Hoffman's composure. She wept as she repeated her daughter's confession.

"She said she had made a terrible mistake and that she was going to quit. She said she didn't know what she was getting into at the time and she was sorry." Vi Hoffman remembered Barbara as "quiet and withdrawn during that period." A couple weeks later Barbara called to let her know that she had quit the parlors. But she followed the good news with another stunning announcement.

"She thought maybe it would be necessary to change her name so that her massage parlor—that short time wouldn't follow her, so she could more easily get into—get back into her normal lifestyle."

The Hoffmans suggested their daughter move back home; however, Barbara declined the offer. She thought it important to overcome what had happened rather than run away. Besides, she liked Madison. She would stay.

The parents accepted her judgment. In spring 1977 Barbara began working full-time at EDS Federal, starting out as a data entry clerk, and was soon promoted to assistant supervisor. The error of Barbara's past had been eclipsed.

As Vi Hoffman reconstructed that sorrowful episode

in her family's life, her pudgy shoulders trembled and her face was streaked with tears. She wept at the awful memories. The hurt had cut deep, for parent and child.

Vi Hoffman's suffering seemed almost palpable. The courtroom was hushed throughout her entire testimony, and some spectators sobbed quietly with her. Eisenberg's questions had been delicate and direct and paced with enough hesitation to allow the jury to feel a mother's pain. Then he guided his witness further along.

Barbara had spoken to her parents of Harry Berge sometime in late 1976. He sent her cards and gifts. It appeared Berge loved her, but the emotion was not reciprocated.

"She considered him—he was a friend," the mother said, and from her intonation it was obvious she believed friendship was the extent of Barbara's relationship with Berge.

Barbara had also told her parents about Jerry Davies, that she dated him, that he drove her to work every day. While Barbara enjoyed Davies's company and kindness, she was not serious about him and had never mentioned any plans for marriage.

Several times a year since Barbara had moved to Madison in 1973 the Hoffmans had visited their daughter. Rather than stay in a motel they bedded at Barbara's apartment. For Christmas 1977 Vi Hoffman's husband drove up to Madison, accompanied by Boomer, their dog.

Her husband left on December 22nd, and he and Barbara returned home midday on Christmas Eve, laden with colorfully wrapped gifts. Christmas Day followed routine. All three daughters were at home. They attended early services, ate a late brunch, exchanged presents. Late that night the wonderful holiday was interrupted by the Park Ridge police. Barbara was taken to the station and returned within the hour, distraught by the mysterious death of her friend Harry Berge.

The next morning the Hoffmans drove their daughter back to Madison. Her apartment was sealed. They went to Rennebohms, had coffee, and called the police, who arrived to open the premises. The apartment "looked like it had been ransacked." Barbara was visibly disturbed. Her father suggested she retain an attorney. Barbara went to a phone book and called someone whom they went to see the same afternoon, which was Sunday. Whatever reason the police had to search the apartment was never explained to them by the police, Vi Hoffman said.

The Hoffmans went back to Park Ridge the next day, as Barbara was confident she was in no trouble with the authorities. On January 18th they were informed that their daughter had been arrested and charged with first-degree murder. Stunned by the incomprehensible news, numb with astonishment, they extracted their life insurance savings, secured a second mortgage on their home, and raised bail money for Barbara, who seemed perplexed, withdrawn, and frightened. Her lawyer said the case was beyond his expertise and recommended they hire Don Eisenberg. The Hoffmans did as he advised.

Months passed with no explanation from the police as to why they were suspicious of Barbara. What little information the newspapers carried seemed stocked with rumor. On Easter weekend Vi Hoffman and her husband again visited Barbara. They arrived Saturday, around noon, went out for dinner, and retired early—no later than 10:00 P.M.—sleeping on the sofa as usual. They rose early, went to church services, and enjoyed the holiday with their daughter. At 6:00 P.M. Sunday evening they returned to Park Ridge. Within the week they found out about Davies's death. Barbara was "shocked and upset."

Asked by Eisenberg if her daughter had ever talked about Ken Curtis, Vi Hoffman, after almost two grueling hours of testimony, replied yes, the name had been mentioned. "Barbara seemed to be afraid of him."

The court recessed for 15 minutes to allow Vi Hoffman to regain her composure for the cross-examination. Her face was puffy from her crying. Her voice was racked with sorrow.

Vi Hoffman's testimony was not only emotional and dramatic; it directly refuted the state's version of events. It offered an alibi that exonerated her daughter: Barbara could not have been guilty of these heinous crimes, for one or both of her parents had been with their daughter on or about the time these murders were committed. Robert Hoffman was sleeping on the sofa in his daughter's apartment the night the prosecution alleged she was driving around the countryside burying a body in a snowbank. The Hoffmans were spending a quiet Easter weekend with their daughter when the authorities contended she was feeding cyanide to Jerry Davies and sliding his body into a bathtub. The contradiction was stark and undeniable. If Vi Hoffman was credible, the jury would have to find Barbara not guilty.

The prosecution did not grill Vi Hoffman on every detail of her exhausting and doleful testimony. John Burr read, correctly, that the gallery, the press, and perhaps the jury had been deeply touched by the woman's pain and confusion at events that had spiraled far beyond her control. The natural response was sympathy. Burr's cross-examination was short and courteous.

The first question was obvious: why hadn't she divulged this story to the police?

Vi Hoffman answered that Barbara had an attorney who had been told the information, and she trusted it would be handled as he saw best. Besides, police never once contacted the Hoffmans until June 2, 1980. They were never interviewed, never called, until two weeks before the trial.

The admission was a small surprise and a large embarrassment for the Madison cops who had handled the investigation.

Burr trod gently. What he seemed most concerned about were Mrs. Hoffman's sleeping habits. Was she a light sleeper? Did anything disturb her the Easter weekend she slept in her daughter's apartment? Was there any movement or commotion that night? Any telephone calls? Any telephone conversations? The odd questions were supplied with swift answers.

Yes, Vi Hoffman claimed that she was a very light sleeper and easily disturbed. Nothing had bothered her that night. There were no phone calls, no one shuffling around. The family went to sleep early, without any disturbance during the night.

Burr thanked her. He had no further questions.

Spectators and press were quizzical about the curious method of inquiry the prosecution had chosen. Vi Hoffman's testimony remained unchallenged and untainted.

Robert Hoffman followed his wife to the witness stand. He was fifty-eight years of age, a mechanical design engineer. He had a soft, reluctant manner. Whereas Barbara's mother impressed as gutsy and emotional, her father appeared introspective and detached. He described his middle daughter as "spontaneous with her affection," a trait that was probably alien to her dad. He stated that Barbara had been financially self-sufficient since her twenty-first birthday, and his intonation indicated his approval. Though his daughter studied biochemistry at the U.W., she was not a chemist, and he had never noticed any chemicals or lab equipment in her apartment.

As he did with Vi Hoffman, Eisenberg brought up the topic of the massage parlors. Barbara's involvement was discussed and dissected, but the father's analysis lacked the power and drama of the mother's wrenching, tearful remarks. "She wanted to wipe out that period of her life. It was nothing but bad memories, that she was afraid that some mark or stigma had been put on her that would follow her for however long—I don't know, maybe for the rest of her life."

"What, if anything, did she say about Ken Curtis?" asked Eisenberg.

"She said he was a terrible man. She said she feared him."

Robert Hoffman then enumerated the frequency of his visits to Madison. He related where he usually parked, what time he went to bed, and what time he awakened. He testified that the night Berge had died he was in his daughter's apartment and nothing unusual had occurred.

What about the automobile John Hunt had observed at 5:30 A.M.?

The Hoffmans' car was a late-model Plymouth, black with a bronze top, and Barbara must have been moving it so that it wouldn't be in the way in the morning was Robert Hoffman's simple explanation.

Barbara's father stayed at her apartment the next night, December 23rd, and again nothing extraordinary happened.

This statement was in direct conflict to the testimony given by Jerry Davies at a prelim hearing in February 1978, which had been read to the jury on the second day of the trial. At the time Jerry Davies claimed that he and Barbara were drinking vodka and orange juice and watching the "Tonight" show, Robert Hoffman insisted that he was snoozing on the sofa after a busy day of Christmas shopping with his daughter.

Mr. Hoffman's remembrance of the Easter weekend when Davies had died coincided precisely with the account given by his wife.

"Why didn't you tell the police of your being with Barbara?" was John Burr's first query of the witness.

"I told Mr. Eisenberg," the father replied.

The prosecutor gave Mr. Hoffman an incredulous glance, which he shared with the jury.

"Did you ever inquire of your daughter, subsequent to her being charged with the first death, anything to the effect of 'What basis are they charging you?' "

"I'm sure I asked that question, and she said she had nothing to do with it and she didn't know."

"In your own knowledge, did you ever try and find out on what basis she was charged?"

"No, sir. I relied upon Mr. Eisenberg."

"When were you first asked to remember in detail the events of that weekend before Christmas, when you came up to get your daughter?"

"When I read the first page of the complaint and read that Gerald Davies was pointing his finger at Barbara."

"And of course you went right to the police station and told the police these things?"

Eisenberg spoke up for the witness. "The police wouldn't have listened if he did."

"There is a question before the witness," said a stern Judge Torphy.

"Did you go to the police with this?" Burr repeated.

"No, sir."

Burr let the answer hang in the air for all to contemplate. Unlike his questioning of Vi Hoffman, where he had been careful to filter any judgment or emotion, Burr sighed in disbelief. Then his tune turned cynical.

"When did you realize you had been with your daughter at the time Mr. Davies died?"

"I knew we were with her on Easter."

"Did you tell the police anything about that?"

"No, sir."

"Did you tell anybody in the district attorney's office anything about that?"

"No, sir."

Robert Hoffman had learned of Davies's death when he'd read an article in a small local paper that ran a reprint from the *Wisconsin State Journal*. He never phoned his daughter and discussed what he had read, because he knew the accusations were not true.

On December 22nd and 23rd and on March 25th, Mr. Hoffman acknowledged, he had slept on the sofa in the living room of Barbara's apartment. The phone was on a table nearby. Under Burr's persistent questioning, he admitted that he was a very light sleeper, that there were no disturbances, no late-night phone calls, no commotion on any of the nights. If there had been any, he would have awakened immediately, he said.

A strange, befuddling sensation lingered in the courtroom when Robert Hoffman had completed his testimony. Ostensibly the parents had provided an alibi for the daughter that the prosecution only peripherally had challenged. Their statements were in solid contradiction to the state's interpretation of events, and if a jury believed the

Hoffmans' recollections it had to vote for acquittal.

Vi Hoffman's testimony was imbued with a powerful emotional appeal that transcended any judgment concerning her veracity. The hurt was plain and visible, and whether her tale was truth or mendacity her pain was undeniable. Robert Hoffman's testimony did not detract from the sympathy generated by his wife, but it sobered things.

What became clear was that the parents were not offering a different perspective on the evidence and circumstances; they were presenting an alibi. It was not a mixture of what the prosecution had argued and what the prosecution may have overlooked or ignored; it was an alibi that implied that Davies had lied, that John Hunt had lied, that Berge's blood in the snowbank was a lie or a frame-up. Nothing of what the parents had said addressed the insurance policies or the marriage license or the chemicals from Laabs or Ken Curtis's decisive testimony. None of these things were explained away by what the Hoffmans suggested to be true.

Perhaps more profound than any abstraction was how Barbara's parents sounded. Often the same words, the same phrases were repeated, as though they'd been reading from a script. While it was not unusual for two people married for over thirty-one years to seem similar in their choice of words, they sometimes responded to the same question from Eisenberg with identical phrases, parroting each other, as if the answer had been discussed and rehearsed. Robert Hoffman, particularly, was stiff and devoid of spontaneity. It seemed he had weighed what he wanted to say and said it.

The reaction of a listener to Vi Hoffman's testimony was to accept it without question. But when Robert Hoffman had stepped down from the stand, the reaction was to wonder about collusion. The alibi was too neat. It seemed tailored to cover as broad an area as possible. It contained too many coincidences.

The surprise expert witness, whom Eisenberg had bragged would soundly repudiate Professor Deibl's testimony, was called next. Joseph Robinson was a professor of pharmacy at a Canadian university. His effect was less than devastating. He reviewed the Laabs items and Deibl's testimony and disagreed with a single, minor aspect of what the prosecution witness had said. The compounds and equipment ordered from Laabs indicated the growth of an anaerobic organism, such as botulin, was intended. Nonetheless, other bacteria could have been cultivated. This was merely a restatement of what the microbiology professor had contended, with slightly different emphasis.

On cross-examination Robinson admitted that he could not and would not refute Deibl's opinion. Hence the surprise witness surprised no one, except perhaps the defense.

With Robinson the defense rested its case.

The prosecution had presented nearly seventy witnesses and two hundred exhibits in documenting its charges against Barbara Hoffman. Eisenberg had called fewer than a dozen witnesses in rebuttal.

Court adjourned at 2:00 P.M. Thursday afternoon. Closing arguments were scheduled for the next morning.

— 13 —

Each afternoon when court had adjourned, John Burr poured down a couple of draft beers at the Pinckney Street Hideaway, then sauntered up to his office for a few minutes alone, where he could consolidate his thoughts and peruse the mail and the day's messages and memos.

Throughout the trial the DA's switchboard had been deluged with calls regarding the Hoffman affair. People who followed the drama on TV phoned in to commend or criticize or question Burr, and the frumpy prosecutor took immense delight in reading the viewers' comments. It wasn't unusual to receive forty or fifty calls a day from the fascinated public. Most citizens suspected that Barbara was guilty, and most predicted she'd win acquittal, either

due to lack of evidence to prove her guilty beyond reasonable doubt or because of Eisenberg's guile. Often the caller
proffered suggestions or advice.

A woman from nearby Waunakee who had watched
every minute of the proceedings developed a theory concerning the cyanide deaths. She hypothesized that Barbara
had attempted to disguise the chemical element to the
killings, which was why the bathroom fans were left running and the air conditioner fans were switched on in the
middle of winter. Cyanide can have an odor, and the
circulation would disperse it. The temperature in both the
Hoffman and Davies apartments was extremely high, almost ten degrees above what could be considered normal,
and the humid environment would aid the body's deterioration and make the toxin harder to detect. Traces of
cyanide would disperse more quickly in a warmer setting.
The police had already surmised this fact, but the woman
from Waunakee had a slant on the Davies murder that
none of the investigators had fathomed. Maybe it hadn't
been bath water that Davies's corpse had been placed in,
but dry ice. Police found the body forty-eight hours after
expiration, yet the water in the tub was lukewarm. Dry ice
would melt slowly, stay relatively warm, and allow the
body to remain warm, thus hastening the absorption of
cyanide and making its discovery more difficult.

The ingenuity of the woman's theory intrigued Burr.
The practicality of proving it and introducing it into court
was another matter.

Not every caller was this clever; however, the majority of calls indicated that folks watched and listened closely.
On Thursday afternoon another armchair detective who
had been loyally tuned in to the trial noticed a curious
omission in Vi Hoffman's testimony. Both Vi Hoffman
and her husband had claimed they drove from Madison to
Chicago on Easter Sunday, March 26, 1978, at about 6:00
P.M. The trip would have been virtually impossible, the
caller noted, because of adverse weather conditions.

That Easter Sunday the area was battered by a tremendous ice storm. O'Hare Airport closed for days, and

Interstate 90, which connected Madison and Chicago, was also closed as a result of the severe weather. Anyone in Madison would never have tried such a drive. Gas stations closed. Hardly anyone ventured out. Yet the Hoffmans neglected to mention what should have been the most remarkable aspect of the weekend—the drive home.

If a TV viewer recalled the storm, why hadn't anyone in authority investigated the possibility? Burr cussed Lulling. The detective had retired before the Davies homicide investigation was under way, and although Burr personally despised the man, the weather was one of those tiny details that others overlook and that Lulling, in his tedious, compulsive, irritating manner, would have examined.

On Thursday, when the defense rested without summoning Barbara Hoffman to the witness stand, the noise heard from the prosecution team was a surprising sigh of relief. Surprising, quipped a reporter, because they seemed grateful that she hadn't been called to testify.

Prior to the trial and again before the defense presented its case, Burr and Spencer had debated Eisenberg's possible strategies and made the assumption that he would not place Barbara Hoffman on the stand. Consequently the prosecution had spent no effort readying a cross-examination, devoting its time instead to the myriad details and complexities that seem endless in a trial of such duration and magnitude. If Eisenberg had called her as a witness, the prosecution team would have been embarrassed by its lack of preparation, ineffectual in its rebuttal, and outmaneuvered by the wily defense lawyer.

Soliciting testimony from Barbara Hoffman would have been a precarious task, fraught with perilous ramifications. Eisenberg had faced a nasty dilemma. Obviously there was an avalanche of questions Barbara would have had to endure if she were exposed to a strenuous cross-examination. The wrong answers or the wrong appearance might bury her deeper than the prosecution's six days of circumstantial evidence. But often a jury wants the chance to hear the defendant tell her own story, deny the charges, and assert her innocence. Barbara's unflappable handling of the DA's questions and her firm denial of murdering Berge and Davies might have been the excuse the jury needed to grant an acquittal.

Was Barbara capable of the performance? Her demeanor during the trial was unshaken, the epitome of self-containment and cool. What no one except her lawyer realized, however, was the cost of her detachment, the supreme energy that was invested to deflect the pressure and to create a small, silent space of quietude and safety. No one except Eisenberg comprehended her fragility. His decision to withhold her direct testimony was maybe a greater relief to Barbara Hoffman than it was to John Burr.

The press and the gallery discussed Eisenberg's decision, arguing its wisdom and its folly like bleacher bums second-guessing a baseball manager's choice to stick with a starting pitcher in a bases-loaded jam. Similar to baseball fans, neither the press nor the spectators knew all the variables. Still, it didn't keep them from their opinions.

John Burr burped from two quick draft beers. He plopped the mail he was reading idly onto a stack of memos and called home. He had seen his family only once in the last two weeks, and when one of the kids answered, Burr felt like a stranger. His wife worked at sounding cheerful, but the exasperation in her voice could not be disguised. He told her that Friday was closing arguments and, no matter what happened, tomorrow night he'd be sleeping at home.

— 14 —

Perhaps it was the heat, perhaps it was the pressure; whatever the cause, John Burr's initial closing argument faltered.

It was Friday, June 27th. Judge Torphy allotted the prosecution one and a half hours for its closing. The defense was permitted three hours for final argument, and the prosecution was given one and a half hours for rebuttal. The courtroom seemed more crowded than before. The air-conditioning was inadequate, and the smell of bodies and tension permeated the chambers, oozed into the hallway, and infected those who jammed around the TV monitors for a glimpse of the last day's proceedings.

Burr stumbled badly.

"The purpose of a closing argument," he said, and then he hesitated in mid-sentence, as if uncertain where to go.

"There are a number of closing arguments, if you will. Someone once said that all lawyers are frustrated actors. I'm not persuaded that the purpose of a closing argument is assisted by standing up here and yelling and screaming and crying as some people have done on occasion."

He reviewed the case for the jury, beginning with Davies's appearance at police headquarters on Christmas Day, but his chronology lurched forward and backward like the posture of a punch-drunk boxer. He stood at a podium, stiff and uncertain. He blundered over words and ideas, searching for the appropriate phrase or the precise remark, which persisted in eluding him.

There was an abundance of evidence to sort and coordinate. Testimony from the first two days of the trial seemed light-years distant, and Burr sought to remind the jury of all that it had heard. He scrambled.

". . . some people have said what happens today is like mixing all the facts you got for the last seven or eight days, combine them with the law, and a verdict comes therefrom."

There was so much to cram in. Dates were tossed to the jury with vague reference to their significance. Insurance policies, bank accounts, UPS delivery dates were jumbled. Burr got lost in the summary, got entangled in the mass exhibits and testimony, and was unable to hack a clear path. Time flitted away. He started naming witnesses as if reciting the roster of a baseball team.

"Mr. Lowell was here—he is the gentleman who has control over Mr. Berge's insurance records. Mr. Raymond Petersen brought exhibit fifteen, which is some phone records. . . . Witness number seven, as you know, was William Stelling. . . . Witness number nine on Thursday was Detective Kenneth Couture. The next witness was Jon Sippl, detective—I believe the last witness that morning. Second to last. No, the last witness."

The jury appeared confused.

After an hour and a half Burr sat down, bewildered by his terrible performance. The biggest case of his career, and the lights and the heat and the pressure had unraveled him.

"I blew it," he muttered to Chris Spencer, who couldn't disagree.

If Burr ended in a muddle, Eisenberg began grandiloquently. "I have been tempted in this one to just say, I surrender, I quit, I give up. I mean, after all, you have heard all the facts from Mr. Burr, and obviously what Mr. Burr has told you is correct, and therefore, why should I say anything to you? But maybe I better not surrender.

"I have been practicing law for twenty-four years, protecting citizens. I protect them from overzealous policemen and overanxious district attorneys who charge too fast without sufficient evidence. I cry. I cry for justice."

Using a bell as a metaphor for the presumption of innocence that surrounded his client, Eisenberg explained to the jury burden of proof and reasonable doubt. The bell can be dented and cracked by what the prosecution presents, he said, but according to the law the bell must be shattered completely for the defendant to be judged guilty.

He pontificated on justice, quoting Pope Paul VI and Albert Schweitzer. He boasted that the fate of Barbara Hoffman, "that little girl over there, has been in my hands for over two-and-a-half years."

Then Eisenberg ripped into the state's case. Why was no blood discovered in the apartment or in the bathroom? Why was there no hair?

"Officer Robert Doyle went to the apartment on December 25th. He was looking for, quotes—usable evidence—unquotes. 'I found nothing.' Ted Oasen, a Dane County sheriff, went back on December 27th with another search warrant, and they went back with ultraviolet light and with Hemastix. They found no blood. Everything that they found in that apartment was negative."

There was no indication and no evidence whatsoever that Harry Berge had been in Barbara's apartment on the night he died.

Why was no blood discovered in the snowbank behind the apartment building the first three times the police checked? Was it because Chuck Lulling had planted the blood that was miraculously found in the snowbank on January 19th, the day after Barbara's arrest?

"I don't like Chuck Lulling. I think he's a liar, and I have got evidence of that, and you have got more evidence of that. Is it inconceivable that this overzealous policeman, about to retire, on his last case . . . wants to get his man? And in this case his lady? Is it inconceivable that Mr. Lulling went back there with a little blood and planted it? I'm not saying he did it. But you see how plausible that is."

If it took two officers to haul Berge's body onto a stretcher, how could "that frail little girl over there" have transported him down three flights of stairs? If it took two officers to pull Davies out of the bathtub, how could Barbara have put him there? If she was under surveillance when she returned to Madison on December 26th, how did she move Berge's car around so it wasn't located until a week later? If Barbara had killed Harry Berge, why did she stay in town for a month waiting to be arrested? Why didn't she leave Madison?

Eisenberg stalked the courtroom, leonine, ferocious.

It wasn't Linda Millar who put her name on the deed of Harry Berge's property, he bellowed; it was Berge himself. No one coerced him. Kenneth Buhrow explained the different ways for Berge to leave his property, and Berge chose joint tenancy. No one else was there. Berge was under no pressure. It was a voluntary decision.

He quoted Dr. Slavik's testimony: "Gerald Davies told me his girlfriend had just been charged with first-degree murder and she didn't do it."

Eisenberg acknowledged that he'd known about the Hoffmans' visits to their daughter on the Christmas and Easter weekends when the alleged murders took place, and he acknowledged withholding that information from the police. He claimed to the jury that if the police had been notified they simply would have changed the dates of the deaths and thus nullified the parents' crucial testimony.

Again he blasted Lulling. "Why didn't Lulling, or any other officer, knowing that Barbara Hoffman was in Illinois on Christmas, ever go and see Mr. and Mrs. Hoffman until June 2, 1980, twenty-five days ago? Why didn't Lulling, the great policeman, go and say 'Mama, Daddy, how long has Barbara been staying here?' Is that good police work?"

Next he directed his tirade at John Hunt. Certainly Hunt did not know what he saw the early morning of December 23rd. Berge's car was black over white; the car Robert Hoffman drove was black over bronze. At 5:15 A.M. it was pitch-black outside and the only illumination in the parking lot came from a seventy-five-watt light bulb on a neighboring building. Hunt heard a car door slam and glanced out the window. "What's the significance of a door or a trunk slamming? There is no evidence that Mr. Berge was ever put in a trunk or ever put in his own car. What's the significance?" Hunt was sleepy, Eisenberg insisted; it was dark, and all he saw were shadows.

Furthermore, if Barbara did have some secret to conceal, why would she conduct her mission at 5:00 or 6:00 A.M.? She had resided at 638 State Street for years. She was aware that John Hunt rose early. She knew he did his janitorial duties every day at that time. She knew that if she was up and about it would not be unlikely for her to bump into him as he completed his chores.

The defense lawyer shifted his thrust and slashed at the prosecution's version of Davies's mysterious death.

"Jealousy. Murder. Suicide. All the facts point to it. All the circumstantial evidence." He reminded the jury that Davies's own words, in the letter penned prior to his death, exonerated Barbara. No one had seen Barbara Hoffman enter or leave Davies's residence that weekend. No one had heard any argument or struggle or commotion from apartment 7. The drapes were left open, and the lights were on. Davies's bedroom slippers were next to the tub. "Now, did Miss Hoffman, who the prosecution would want you to believe is a chemist and a real estate person [co-owner of Berge's Stoughton property], is she also an alchemist? Is she also a magician? Is she able to change herself into a phantom, into an invisible person, and drift into that apartment and commit the murder of Gerald Davies? After they contacted the buses, the cabs, the mailmen . . . Nobody ever saw Barbara."

Eisenberg reminded the jury of Ken Curtis's notorious livelihood, and he lambasted the vice king's testimony.

The defense counsel roamed the courtroom, delighted to have one final and unimpeded blast at Curtis's character. He harangued about the plea bargain agreement between Curtis and Cerro and the DA's office and implied that it was a collusion by adversarial parties, each with something to gain, a collusion that made Barbara Hoffman a powerless victim of self-serving men. Why had it been eight months after Berge's death before Curtis had come forward with his information? Had he delayed in order to invent a story that would fit the known facts?

The Laabs materials received a perfunctory mention and dismissal. Professor Deibl's analysis and opinion, however, Eisenberg fiercely criticized. He reminded the jury that the cyanide had not been sent to Barbara Hoffman but to Jerry Davies, who signed for it and paid for it and applied for a passport the day after receiving it.

Was that a mere coincidence? Or was it a clear indication that Davies intended to kill his rival for Barbara's affections and then flee? Davies couldn't bring himself to leave Barbara, and he couldn't resolve the trouble he had wrought. Driven by jealousy and fear, he'd killed Harry

Berge. Repentant and defeated, he'd committed suicide.

"There were no bruises on Mr. Davies, as though he had been dragged. There was one scratch, a shaving scratch. Mr. Davies, unfortunately, died in the bathtub, and all of the evidence, circumstantial and otherwise, leads to only one conclusion, and that is suicide," Eisenberg asserted.

The letters Davies mailed out were his final testament. The letters were not carbon copies. Each was written separately. He wanted the authorities to understand the truth of what had happened, to understand that Barbara's inclusion in this awful tragedy was a nightmarish mistake.

Eisenberg reminded the jury that the enormous life insurance policy the prosecution had emphasized as a motive for so much of Barbara's actions had expired a month prior to Davies's death. It was worthless. The policy was invalid, and Barbara Hoffman could not collect a penny on that policy. A partial payment had been refunded to her; thus she'd been aware of its expiration.

The defense attorney talked about Barbara Hoffman's parents. He expounded on the parents' veracity and integrity and recounted Robert and Vi Hoffman's crucial testimony.

Sweat peeled from Eisenberg's face, rolled down the thick muscles of his neck, and soaked into the starched collar of his shirt. Sweat whipped through the air in droplets as he gesticulated, enraged at the suffering the Hoffmans had endured. He conjured the confusion and horror they must have felt. Their home, their life savings were risked so that Barbara could be free until her court date, until this hideous nightmare could be ended. Vi Hoffman's tears contradicted the prosecution's bogus charges, and Vi Hoffman did not lie.

Eisenberg paced to the jury box and issued a challenge. "Now, if you believe that either of those people is lying," he cried confidently, "then find Barbara Hoffman guilty. How about that!"

The defense had been allotted three hours for its

closing argument, and Eisenberg had devoured every second of that time. The closing address portrayed the lawyer's style exactly, as if this single speech were an embodiment of his persona. Every element of Eisenberg's character was exhibited, at its best and its worst. The magnificent oration mixed fervent passion with eloquent persuasion with rodomontade. His tongue cut surgically and slashed savagely. His words stabbed swiftly and surely or bludgeoned heedlessly, carried on by the weight of their motion. He beseeched the jury for justice yet played the bully. He pleaded for compassion for his client, whose actions had been misconstrued, then arrogantly deprecated a cop's small but embarrassing error as if he harbored a personal vendetta. Rather than discredit, it looked as if Eisenberg tried to destroy.

Some observers felt that amid the hyperbole and the brilliance Eisenberg forgot pertinent details or overlooked small facts. It was said that he parlayed a sharp intellect, a brazen confidence, and a satin tongue into a theory of defense. At moments he appeared a carnival barker with fancy clothes and a law degree.

The repeated reference to Barbara Hoffman as a "frail little girl" proved particularly inane. It ignored so many realities: that Barbara Hoffman was twenty-eight years old and not a girl but a woman; that she had worked for more than two years in Madison's massage parlors; that she had been independent of her family for years; that her intelligence and study could have earned her admission to medical school if she had desired it. Her history, her complexities, had been exposed to the jury, yet Eisenberg resorted to what he perceived was a catchy phrase in the hope that it would gloss over the reality, maybe in the hope that the words would sound powerful enough to distort the reality.

"You can see how different lawyers are," Eisenberg said. "You can see the difference between John Burr and myself. But even with my expertise, mistakes can be made. I don't think I've made any."

He finished his closing with a command to the jury.

"When John Burr gets up to make his final argument, his rebuttal argument, be Barbara's lawyer. Ask 'What would Don Eisenberg say to that?' "

John Burr's initial closing had been listless and meandering. His rebuttal displayed an incredible transformation.

Whether it was the contemplation of justice not served, or the sudden vision of personal and public defeat, or the din of Eisenberg's bombast that sparked the resurgence Burr himself later was unable to explain. His tone was not angry. The words were not a desperate and reckless tirade. Rather than flail wildly as he felt the case slipping away, Burr remembered his dictum that the prosecutor was not supposed to be flamboyant. He assessed his resources, pondered his opponent's fiery closing, and conducted a coherent and strenuous assault on Eisenberg's defense, prying every crack into a hole with wedges of circumstantial evidence.

Burr stood to address the jury, unbuttoned the jacket of his beige summer suit, and launched an unrelenting offensive that did not cease until his hour and a half had expired.

Without delay, without vituperation, Burr challenged the veracity of Robert and Vi Hoffman's testimony. He snatched the long-distance phone records from the exhibit table. The listings pertained to the Easter weekend Davies had died. The Hoffmans had maintained they were visiting their daughter. Burr recalled their steadfast claims that nothing unusual happened the night they spent in Madison.

"Saturday night, when everybody went to bed at ten and nothing happened because they're all light sleepers—" He waved the telephone bill like a battle flag. "March 26, 1978, a one-minute phone call to Capitol Heights, Maryland, at 0:32. Twelve-thirty in the morning. But nobody got up. Nobody talked on the telephone. Nobody did anything. March 26, 1978, a ten-minute call to Chicago at 12:58, almost one o'clock in the morning. March 26, 1978, a one-minute phone call to Capitol Heights, Maryland, at 1:08 A.M."

Three long-distance calls within a span of forty minutes, when everyone was sleeping, when there were no disturbances, when the phone was positioned a few feet from the Hoffmans, who lay on the sofa. "And they wouldn't lie for their daughter. Is that piece of paper from the phone company lying? Mr. Eisenberg told you that if they lied, then she's guilty. Did they lie?"

Introduced as evidence on the first day of the trial, the phone records were a devastating revelation. Burr expressed astonishment that the parents could sit mute for two-and-a-half years, allowing their daughter and the entire family to suffer, when they could have ended the suspicion and torment by coming forward with their story. The rationale that the authorities would amend the times of death if this vital information were announced was preposterous. Even after the arraignments and preliminary hearings, when the times of death were firmly established, neither the Hoffmans nor their attorney mentioned the alibi. Their silence was contrary to how parents would react. Their silence was guarded rigidly because it was a fabrication. But the veteran prosecutor quickly excused the parents. "I think they told you the truth about the Barbara Hoffman they knew, they know and love. And I'll tell you something: in their shoes, I probably would have done the same darn thing. I think the evidence in this case shows another Barbara Hoffman exists. The other side of her. A side the evidence has shown."

Burr corrected the defense's contention that Barbara had lacked a real motive. "Think about motive when you're in there. Think about the elimination of a witness against you in a murder case. Think about a total of $69,500 in insurance money, and a house."

Burr assailed other of Eisenberg's assertions. Lulling couldn't have planted blood in the snowbank behind Barbara's apartment building on January 19th. A check of medical reports showed that Berge's blood type was not known until weeks later. There were no telephone records of Barbara Hoffman phoning Laabs in Milwaukee, not because the calls were not made, as Eisenberg proposed, but because the telephone company destroys its records after six months. Berge died in December. The documents were requested shortly thereafter, but the orders to Laabs had been placed in March and April and were no longer available.

And the suicide letters? "You have your foreman read it out loud," Burr told the jury. "This is a suicide note? Here's a guy who's putting his 'house in order,' and he's gonna leave $35,000 to a woman he loves and leave her charged with two, or one count of murder. Where does it say in there 'I, Jerry Davies, killed Harry Berge, and I'm willing to go to jail for it'? Make sense? Under what circumstances were these letters written? You'll note they're undated. . . . Why are they undated? Someone might want to mail them when someone knows he's dead."

Davies's actions were strange for a person about to commit suicide. "Mr. Davies filled out a Visa application to increase his credit. Ate a large meal. Didn't leave a will for dispersion of his personal property. Wrote a check for April's rent." Then he climbed into a bathtub and put a pill in his mouth and died. It stretched the limits of credibility.

Furthermore, if he had killed Berge, he would have noticed that death by cyanide was anything but pleasant. Why would he then choose the same horrible means of death for himself? If Davies was the murderer, why did he receive the cyanide on May 18th, apply for a passport on May 19th, then procrastinate for seven months? Crimes of passion were spontaneous. Why wait?

"Why did he implicate the one he loved?" Burr asked. "Why go to the police? Why?"

With the barrage of questions echoing in the courtroom, Burr concentrated next on the similarities between the two killings.

"Let's take a look at the facts for a moment. Both of these gentlemen were nude. Both died of a lethal dose of cyanide. Both had eaten a large meal before they died on holiday weekends. Both knew the defendant. Both met her at the same place. Both were single and loners. Both had insurance policies on which she was a beneficiary. More than a superficial coincidence, folks?"

Burr paused.

"The manner in which both these crimes were committed marks them in one distinctive, significant way. If you're a jealous lover, you don't kill with cyanide. Cyanide death requires a theme based on trust and love. You don't kill a rival with cyanide. I don't think there was any force involved in what Gerald Davies and Harry Berge did. They did it out of trust, love, affection. Blind trust and blind love."

During his initial closing argument he had seen members of the jury yawn, close their eyes, almost nod into sleep. They'd looked hot and distracted. Eisenberg had awakened them with the cries and bellows of his volatile closing argument. Now Burr had seized their attention. The jury was alert and listening, and he focused their consideration on Barbara Hoffman's intricate involvement in the lives and deaths of Harry Berge and Jerry Davies. In a placid, assured voice Burr began a methodical recitation of the circumstantial evidence accumulated against Barbara Hoffman.

The recitation was concise and powerful. Burr refrained from embellishment and sentimentality. He stuck every significant shred of evidence in front of the jury's eyes, in an exact and calculated manner that magnified its force. He read a letter from Barbara Hoffman to Transport Life asking for an address change for all correspondence regarding the Davies policy, from her post office box in Madison to another address. Less than two days after the Transport Life policy had expired, Jerry Davies amended the beneficiary of his regular life insurance policies, which totaled $20,000. His mother, Ruth Davies, was excised, and Barbara Hoffman was entered as the new recipient. Less than three weeks later Davies was dead.

Ken Curtis's testimony was reiterated. Burr reviewed Barbara's botulism and Mexico and marriage plot scheme and emphasized how Curtis's confrontation with Barbara in late spring of 1977 had forced her to adjust her plans.

"Curtis tells her, 'You'll never get away with it,' and watch what happens now."

Wedding date: 4/22/77. Wedding is canceled.

Library card application, 4/28/77, and Linda Millar pops up.

5/10/77: Change of beneficiary for $750,000 policy signed by Mr. Davies charging ownership to the defendant.

Exhibit 136, on 5/10/77, Laabs order. Poisons.

5/13/77: More Laabs order. Shipped to 2305 South Park (Davies's address).

5/14/77: Post office box application, Linda Millar.

5/23/77: Laabs order, 2305 South Park, a watch glass.

6/1/77: Last Laabs order.

7/1/77: Miss Hoffman goes to work at EDS Federal.

7/2/77: First Federal passbook, Linda Millar.

7/11/77: Change of beneficiary and ownership forms for $750,000 policy approved.

7/26/77: Second premium is due. Defendant is now the owner and beneficiary.

10/13/77: Mr. Berge has his insurance changed to benefit Linda Millar.

10/25/77: He changes the deed to his house.

12/22/77: Berge is dead by 9:30 P.M.

12/23/77: Mr. Hunt sees defendant around Mr. Berge's vehicle.

12/24/77: Mr. Berge's body is disposed of.

The sequence of circumstantial evidence poured on unabated, pummeling the idea of Barbara's innocence with short, quick jabs. Burr did not have a knockout punch. There was no hard, irrefutable piece of evidence that would demand a guilty verdict, so Burr hurled an array of bruising, stinging jabs, wounding from every angle.

"It all leads to one and only one conclusion," Burr declared. "The defendant, in a cold-blooded manner, poisoned two men to collect insurance money."

At 4:25 Friday afternoon, after Judge Torphy had read his final instructions, the Berge-Davies murder case went to the jury.

— 15 —

The jury deliberated for seven hours on Friday night before retiring. Its task was resumed early Saturday morning. The jurors asked for rereadings of testimony. They wanted to know what time John Hunt had said he'd observed Barbara Hoffman in the predawn hours of December 23rd, and they wanted to hear again Lulling's testimony about blood found in a snowbank behind 638 State Street. The jury also wished to examine certain evidence.

Over Eisenberg's vehement objections Judge Torphy permitted the jury to review the telephone records that Burr had argued proved Mr. and Mrs. Hoffman's perjury. They were also allowed to see a copy of the cashier's check used to pay the initial premium on Davies's Transport Life policy.

At 2:45 in the afternoon, after only fourteen hours of deliberation, the jury foreman notified the bailiff that a decision had been reached.

Jim Doyle and his family had been about to depart Madison for a week's vacation to their cabin in the northern Wisconsin backwoods when he got a phone call that the verdict was due. A verdict reached so soon upon the conclusion of a lengthy and complex trial usually indicated the jury had not been convinced of the prosecution's argument and an acquittal was forthcoming.

Doyle and Burr had feared this scenario. Both were convinced of Barbara Hoffman's guilt. Both recognized the difficulties of proving her guilt beyond a reasonable doubt.

When Doyle heard that deliberations had concluded,

he didn't question the news or wait for the official announcement. He sat at the kitchen table, and while his two boys gathered up fishing bait and basketballs for the week up north he composed a brief statement for Jerry Hancock, a friend and an assistant DA, to read to the press. Doyle praised John Burr's efforts in prosecuting the case and attributed the defeat to a lack of hard evidence. Though he personally did not agree with the verdict, the DA's office respected the fundamental wisdom of the jury system and would abide with the decision.

Doyle folded the statement, dropped it into his mailbox for Hancock to retrieve later, and set off with his family to their north-woods retreat. Hopefully a week on a lake with nothing to do would allow his frustrations to subside and the public flak over losing the case to defuse.

The defense had presumed a similar conclusion. At Rohde's Restaurant, one block from the Eisenberg law offices, cases of champagne were put on ice for the victory celebration. The media would be invited. Perhaps Barbara might consent to be interviewed, and Don Eisenberg could revel in the glory of his triumph.

The courthouse was nearly empty, and the courtroom appeared bleak and cavernous after the fanfare of the previous two weeks. Thirty or so spectators were scattered in the gallery to hear the decision announced. The swirl of a buffing machine resonated through the hallways as a janitor waxed the floors. The footsteps of cameramen echoed.

Barbara Hoffman sat at the defense table as her lawyer chatted with reporters. Eisenberg wore a dark suit and white shirt, somber dress for the flamboyant attorney who everyone thought was about to get the biggest victory of his career. His conversation was not casual and cocky. His mood was quite serious, as if he were trying to suppress his joy that an early decision meant an acquittal or trying to suppress his doubts that it could also imply a hard and fast guilty verdict.

Judge Torphy convened the proceedings. Barbara's

hands were clasped, and she stared straight ahead, peaceful, as though this moment in court was no different from any other during the two-and-a-half years of adjudication.

Barbara's parents, who had expressed their resolute love for their daughter from the witness stand, a love that had not been shaken by this horrendous ordeal, were not present. They had come to Madison to testify on Thursday and had returned to Park Ridge the same evening.

As the bailiff conveyed the verdicts on Berge and Davies to the judge, the camera's eye peered in on the defendant. She was utterly poised. Torphy glanced at the papers and shuffled them in his hands. Burr and Spencer waited.

Throughout the trial Torphy had referred to the case and its victims as Berge and Davies, in the order of their deaths, but now, at the denouement, he switched the order.

On the charges of murdering Jerry Davies, Torphy read placidly, the jury finds the defendant—not guilty.

Before the gallery could finish a collective gasp, as Eisenberg rose from his chair in expectation, as cameras pivoted from the bench to the defendant to capture the elation, as Barbara Hoffman sat silent, her sangfroid unbroken, Torphy read the second verdict. On the charges of murdering Harry Berge, the jury finds the defendant—guilty.

Eisenberg slumped back into his chair as if repelled by the force of that single word. His head dropped to the table, pinned in bitter defeat. He grasped Barbara's hand.

From Barbara there was no reaction. She sat immobile. Her face was not paralyzed, stunned, or catatonic. Barbara merely stared ahead, apparently unfazed by it all.

The jury was polled. Eisenberg asked for bail while Barbara awaited sentencing and appeal. Burr objected, and Judge Torphy denied the request.

Barbara and her lawyer were permitted a few minutes alone in a courtroom office. Then she was handcuffed and led away by the deputy sheriff.

━━ 16 ━━

John Burr and Chris Spencer celebrated the verdict with a couple of beers, then drove to their homes, exhausted from the trial, glad to be done with the case and its tragedies, in dire need of a private retreat.

Jim Doyle interrupted his vacation when he received news of the jury's verdict. At a press conference on Monday morning Doyle thanked the prosecution team for their extraordinary efforts and congratulated them on the conviction. The guilty verdict on Berge and the not-guilty on Davies indicated that the jury was not prejudiced by having the murders tried together and that they'd weighed the evidence carefully and made a thoughtful judgment according to the facts. To Doyle it was an example of how thoroughly and responsibly a jury can conduct itself. He singled out Ken Curtis as a citizen often in trouble with the law who, nevertheless, should be lauded for performing an important civic duty.

Robert and Vi Hoffman would not be prosecuted for what Doyle believed was perjury on the witness stand. Their situation had been extremely difficult. Any parent could understand their trauma, and he did not feel justice would be gained from their prosecution.

The DA's harshest remarks were hurled at Don Eisenberg. Before the trial began, Barbara Hoffman had signed an affidavit stating that she was cognizant that Eisenberg had represented both her and Sam Cerro at one time, and this could be construed as a conflict of interest. The affidavit was a protection demanded by Torphy so that Barbara Hoffman could not appeal at a later date on grounds of inadequate representation. Despite this safeguard, Doyle suggested Eisenberg be investigated by the state bar for conflict of interest, as he considered the defense lawyer's actions unethical and in violation of the state bar's codes.

Eisenberg was in the courthouse at the time of

Doyle's charges. When confronted by reporters with Doyle's remarks, Eisenberg was disgusted. "I think the district attorney should investigate the facts before he flows with oral diarrhea of the mouth," he said angrily.

For Chris Spencer the Hoffman trial had a very pragmatic result. His ineffectiveness at direct examination and the combative nature of the criminal courtroom convinced him to pursue other aspects of law. He was a good lawyer, but not a good criminal lawyer. Within a year he quit the DA's office and took a position with American Family Insurance, whose headquarters were in Madison.

For Burr especially the case had profound implications. The morning after the trial's conclusion Burr and his two sons, ages five and seven, went shopping at a Kohl's supermarket for doughnuts and eggs. The cashier had recognized his face from the newspaper coverage and congratulated him on the conviction; she also complimented him on his fine-looking children. It was a harmless comment, and Burr smiled, but the recognition by a stranger startled him. Because of the extensive media attention, he was a public figure now. For a prosecutor this was disturbing. Regarding the safety of his children, Burr became suddenly paranoid. He had shunned publicity, yet he was being hailed and congratulated whenever he left his house, as other incidents were to prove.

In the weeks that followed, Burr seldom ventured from home except to go to work. He was depressed and extremely protective of his family and his privacy. He realized that after much intense and prolonged effort his emotions had to tumble, but he hadn't anticipated that the drop would be so severe. His other assignments seemed trifling and mundane compared to the drama of the Hoffman case.

At age thirty-eight Burr had argued and won the most publicized murder trial in Wisconsin history. In terms of his professional career it would be the biggest challenge of his life. He doubted any other case could be as intricate and exciting, and he had three decades yet to practice. There seemed nowhere to go but down, and though his reputation as a winner had been sealed by the verdict, the months after were anticlimactic. Burr considered leaving the DA's office and entering private practice. The victory had been bittersweet. For John Burr time and his family carried him through the bouts of depression and disillusionment. He abandoned ideas of a private practice, and by autumn flickers of his old enthusiasm sparked anew.

— 17 —

Sentencing was scheduled for Wednesday, July 2nd, but the ceremony was a formality. Wisconsin law does not provide capital punishment, and conviction of first-degree murder carries an automatic sentence of life in prison, with eligibility for parole in eleven years, four months. The average life sentence served in the state is nineteen years.

Eisenberg again asked the court to set bail, pending the outcome of defense appeals, and Torphy denied the motion. The judge also dismissed five separate defense motions requesting the conviction to be overturned.

Torphy asked Miss Hoffman if she had any statement to make before sentencing was imposed.

Barbara stood. Her words were lucid and direct. "I did not commit the crime of which I was accused and of which I was convicted."

It was the single remark she had uttered regarding the Berge and Davies murders.

Torphy sentenced her to the Taycheedah Correctional Institute for Women in Fond du Lac.

On Thursday, July 3rd, Barbara Hoffman was shackled and transported by sheriff's deputies to the Taycheedah prison facility. She did not speak during the three-hour drive. She appeared completely calm and self-possessed.

— 18 —

In early 1980 Al Mackey left Wisconsin. He moved to southern California, where he had family, but his drinking problem and his financial woes moved with him.

Friends kept him informed of the Barbara Hoffman trial. The verdict neither surprised nor depressed him.

Al Mackey passed the majority of his days on the beach, drinking beers, staring at the ocean as if he had lost something that he expected to resurface in the whitecaps of the next wave. He grew maudlin in sentiment, crusty in appearance. He dreamed of buying a sloop and sailing the Caribbean. His demise seemed inevitable. The odd jobs he took did not suit him. Alcohol seemed to be the single constant in his life. Tired, defeated, he shuffled back to Madison.

The years of abuse caught up with Al Mackey and in one swift moment exacted their toll. Mackey suffered a massive stroke. His body shut down and quit, and for a few precious seconds his brain was deprived of an adequate supply of oxygen. The damage was profound. His basic motor skills and his memory were severely impaired.

There would be no more beers, no more late-night visits to massage parlors. For Al Mackey the future was hospital wards and physical therapy sessions and the distant dream of recovery.

— 19 —

Since Barbara Hoffman had been acquitted of murdering Jerry Davies, and because she was named beneficiary on the insurance policies Davies had obtained through Phil Sprecher and Central Life Assurance, she demanded full payment. The policies had a total value of $20,000.

The claim was disputed by Ruth Davies. She had been beneficiary of the policies until her son made the sudden changes only three weeks before his death. Ruth Davies argued that Hoffman had manipulated her son into amending the policies, then had killed him for pecuniary gain.

When Eisenberg scoffed at the charge, Ruth Davies's lawyer threatened a civil suit. In a bizarre twist it would have been possible to have Hoffman charged with Davies's murder in a civil court action. A jury would have been convened, and Hoffman would have been tried for Davies's murder in order to decide whom should be awarded the insurance money. However, in a civil case the criterion for guilt is not as severe as in a criminal matter. Instead of being convinced of guilt beyond a reasonable doubt, the jury need only be persuaded by a preponderance of the evidence. Fifty-one percent guilty would be enough to render a guilty verdict.

The different standard of judgment caused Eisenberg to propose an out-of-court settlement, which Ruth Davies accepted. Consequently, Barbara Hoffman and Ruth Davies split the $20,000 insurance payment.

— 20 —

To Burr and Doyle the Hoffman conviction presented a peculiar irony.

In a case as elaborate as a puzzle, the pieces never fit exactly. Questions remained unanswered. Barbara Hoffman proved an elusive and enigmatic figure. No one—not lovers or lawyers or cops—caught more than a glimpse of her. Her motivations, her desires, her self were carefully hidden. The case against Hoffman had been won, yet her mystery persisted.

Even as the prosecutors went to trial, they had serious doubts about what actually happened on the night of December 23rd. Why did Hoffman murder Harry Berge? Was $35,000 and a small house in Stoughton her motive?

They had convinced a jury, but privately they were

baffled. Why did she murder Berge for such a paltry sum when Davies had been set up for $750,000? Why not kill Davies? Hoffman had invested time and money—over a year's planning and $13,236 in insurance premiums—in preparing him for the kill. Why ruin such a careful and elaborate scheme?

And why kill Berge in a third-floor apartment in downtown Madison? Disposing of the corpse was beset with problems. If she wanted to murder Berge, why not do it elsewhere—at his home in Stoughton or on any quiet country road between there and Madison? Why kill someone in a place where getting rid of the body was almost impossible without help and where the chances of detection would be greatest?

These questions puzzled Burr and Doyle. It was hard to make sense of what had happened. As they looked closer, the questions multiplied.

The differences in the two deaths were as striking as the similarities. Davies's murder was meticulous and premeditated. It was plotted with attention to the smallest detail. Especially to Burr, whose career was prosecuting these kinds of cases, the murder seemed flawless. The body was clean of any marks or indications of foul play. There was no evidence that anyone other than Davies himself had been involved. Suicide was the perfect cover. However, with Berge it was not so neat. The body had been beaten. There were signs of a struggle—the four-centimeter scratch on the neck, the horribly swollen genitals. Berge had suffered an angry, violent death. Davies's death appeared natural, almost serene.

Both men were killed by cyanide. From her background Barbara should have known precisely how much to administer, but Davies's body contained twice the lethal dose and Berge's body held thirty-seven times the lethal dose. Why the overkill with Berge? Burr and Doyle wondered.

If cyanide was in crystal form, Burr had been told, thirty-seven times the lethal dose would equal about one teaspoonful. Perhaps, Burr surmised, Berge had inadvertently killed himself. As bizarre as this premise sounded, it made a sad and morbid sense. Burr and Doyle developed a theory that resolved their doubts and fit the facts of the case. Only it could never be proven in a court of law.

By early 1977, they speculated, Barbara had Davies ready for the kill. The insurance, the wedding date, the passport, the Laabs materials for growing botulin—everything was in place. Then Barbara did something stupid. She got very high at a party and blurted out her scheme to a friend of Ken Curtis's. Curtis intervened. So Barbara postponed the murder. She knew the botulism idea had to be scrapped, but she was unwilling to abandon what she had worked so hard to arrange. Her plans were amended. Cyanide would be the murder weapon, and on May 27th cyanide was delivered to Davies's apartment. Linda Millar was invented as a cover, and Barbara waited. But Harry Berge interfered. She was done with Berge, having forsaken him for Davies, who was the big prey. Berge tried to win back her affections. He appeared at her apartment two days before Christmas and pleaded his love. It was late. Berge was a coffee drinker, and Barbara fixed him a cup of instant. He went to the cupboard and served himself a teaspoon of sugar.

Only it was not sugar. It was the cyanide that Barbara had bought for Jerry Davies. In crystalline form, cyanide and sugar are indistinguishable. The police had overlooked it when they searched her apartment on Christmas Day. Maybe Barbara was in the bathroom when Berge stirred in the cyanide. Maybe Barbara was so high on Quaaludes she didn't realize what he had done. Maybe she just didn't care.

Berge drank the coffee. Immediately his mouth and throat began to burn. His thoughts spun crazily. He knew Barbara was trying to break off their relationship. He knew he'd recently signed over his house and his insurance policies to her. Berge panicked. Each breath became a struggle. His head throbbed. Barbara had duped him, played him for a fool. In his anger and panic he lunged at her. Barbara kicked him in the groin. Berge went into convulsions, but now his anger had triggered her fury. Barbara grabbed a frying pan—the most handy and effective weapon available—and attacked. She battered Berge into submission. Within minutes it was over. The cyanide had taken its fatal hold.

There was no doubt in Burr's or Doyle's mind that this scene set in motion the events that culminated in Jerry Davies's death. Davies had been murdered in a cool, calculated manner. It was a perfect crime. The jury had rendered the only verdict it could when it had voted acquittal for the Davies murder. Berge seemed the counterpoint. When he arrived at 638 State Street on December 23rd, Harry Berge was not supposed to die. His death was an accident that trapped Barbara Hoffman in her own web of manipulation and deceit. The irony was that she had been convicted of the crime she did not commit. For Burr and Doyle it was a strange sort of justice.

— 21 —

The drive from Madison to Fond du Lac is idyllic. July's sun sets the verdurous countryside aglow. Corn sparkles green and shoulder-high in long, perfect rows. Meadows of alfalfa spread like squares of textured silk. Dairy farmers perform their chores.

The terrain changes as the drive continues north. The earth buckles in hillsides covered with woods. Evergreens are plentiful. The farms appear smaller, less prosperous. A trailer park rests on the edge of a town—long, thin corrugated tin cracker boxes assembled around a small lake—then there are motels with swimming pools and fast-food restaurants, and banks, bars, an IGA food store, then the stretch of road again, the cracked concrete patched with rivulets of tar, and the side roads that disappear into rural nothingness.

The Taycheedah Correctional Institute for Women sits a couple of miles outside Fond du Lac. From the highway the facility evokes a serene and pastoral air, like a private women's college or an exclusive retreat. The appearance is deceiving. It is a prison, and Barbara Hoffman is a full-time resident.

The years have changed her some. According to her attorney, Don Eisenberg, her slender frame has added almost fifteen pounds. Religion has become important, and she claims to have a personal dialogue with Christ. She seems to have lost interest in the legal aspects of her case. Her state court appeals have been denied. She has instructed Eisenberg to discontinue all efforts at overturning her conviction on appeal at the federal level.

Yet the enigma of Barbara Hoffman remains. She has never granted an interview or made remark or comment concerning her case. If she has a desire to be heard or understood, it has never been expressed. Even in prison she is a solitary character, mysterious and reclusive. Perhaps she knows no other way to be.

On a July day the air smells fresh, as if cleansed by the sun's broad beams. The sky above the Wisconsin hills is waxed blue and flawless. Not a single cloud intrudes on the heavenly expanse. The blue seems infinite and perfect.

Epilogue

Ten years later, Barbara Hoffman is not forgotten. Mention her name to a Madison resident and there is a flash of recognition, then a shudder as the sordid circumstances of her notoriety are remembered. The publicity generated by the case was ruinous for the sex business in Wisconsin's capital city. The places where Barbara cast her spell of sexual magic are gone; Cheri's is now a European-style café, Jan's Health Spa is a hair salon. There were over two dozen burlesque bars, massage parlors, and escort services in operation when Barbara Hoffman killed Harry Berge on December 23, 1977. Now there are three.

For everyone involved, the Hoffman case has had a profound effect.

Chris Spencer, who helped prosecute Hoffman, left the DA's office shortly after the case was concluded, the trial and its nasty skirmishes with Don Eisenberg having convinced him he was not cut out to be a courtroom lawyer. He still works for American Family Insurance, where after several promotions he is associate general counsel. Spencer still plays ice hockey on Sunday mornings.

Chuck Lulling retired from the Madison Police Department in 1978. The Berge investigation was his last case, but detective work remains in his blood. Lulling lives in Madison and works as a private investigator. The swagger in his step, the pipe, the walrus mustache, have not changed.

Liza, who worked in the massage parlors and befriended Barbara Hoffman, has reconciled herself with that brief, tawdry piece of her past. She has earned a degree from the University of Wisconsin–Madison, married, and is the happy mother of a young son.

In 1983 Jim Doyle decided not to seek another term as district attorney and went into private practice. His involvement in Democratic party politics and progressive political causes remains strong. As of this writing he is running for election as attorney general for the state of Wisconsin. He still dribbles and shoots a basketball as quickly and as efficiently as he argues a point of law.

Despite offers to go into private practice, John Burr remains an assistant DA. Time has not changed Burr's style—quiet, methodical, thorough. And it hasn't changed the fact that Burr is one of the best at what he does— prosecute major criminal cases. His record of victories is long and impressive; however, the Hoffman case stands out as the most arduous and rewarding of his courtroom convictions.

For Don Eisenberg the relationship with Barbara Hoffman had severe repercussions. It was a difficult and risky task, defending Barbara, and the loss tarnished his reputation. More severe problems followed. In 1984 the Board of Attorneys Professional Responsibility, an adjunct of the Wisconsin Supreme Court that enforces the ethics code for state lawyers, found Eisenberg guilty of conflict of interest in the Hoffman case. His license to practice law was suspended. Eisenberg applied for reinstatement a year later but was denied. In 1988 he again applied for reinstatement. On November 1, 1989, the Wisconsin Supreme Court, citing financial improprieties not connected to the Hoffman case, revoked his license. Although Don Eisenberg now resides in Orlando, Florida, his ties to Madison are strong. His name still provokes controversy. He has bitter enemies and ardent supporters in the legal community. His courtroom antics are legendary.

Barbara Hoffman remains a mystery. The Taycheedah Correctional Institute for Women in Fond du Lac, Wisconsin, is her home, and she has steadfastly refused any and all requests for interviews. Barbara has shown no interest in the technical training or educational programs offered at Taycheedah. She has no work detail, attends no classes, and does not associate with other inmates, choosing instead to isolate herself in her room. Barbara Hoffman is eligible for parole in August 1991.